Popular Culture and Religion in Medieval India

Victor Babu

2005
Kaveri Books
New Delhi - 110 002

First Published in 2005

ISBN 81-7479-051-9

Published by : **Rakesh Goel**
Kaveri Books
4697/5-21 A, Ansari Road,
New Delhi - 110 002 (India).
Tel.: 011-23288140, 23245799
e-mail: kaveribooks@vsnl.com

Laser Typesetting by : Aarti Computers, Delhi - 110 009.

Printed at : Chawla Offset Printers, Delhi - 110 052

PRINTED IN INDIA

FOREWORD

I take it as a great privilege to write a foreword to this book which is meticulously prepared, scholarly as well as informative. This work covers the medieval cultural history of Andhradesa.

Supernatural powers have been considered with reverence and fear ever since the inception of human society. Things like epidemics, natural calamities, sickness and death have been viewed with much interest and enthusiasm. Man tried to explain away these things by way of rituals, customs and propitiatory rites. In India, early Aryans invested divinity to the forces which they could neither control nor understand and these natural forces were personified as male and female Gods and Goddesses. In the course of history, Brahmanism, Jainism and Buddhism and later what is referred to as Bhakti emerged. In medieval Andhra Vaishnavism, Saivism, Sri Vaishnavism and Veera Saivism appeared and became popular. However, along with mainstream sects, people, particularly who belonged to lower castes, had their own worldview, beliefs, presuppositions and practices. Later attempts were made to sanskritize these local Gods and Goddesses. Hence these beliefs and practices, pilgrimage and other rituals and propitiatory rites became common both for upper and lower categories of people. Therefore, popular culture was not only widespread particularly among lower order people, but it also enclosed forms of thought and practices like *Jatara, Kumumari, sigamugadam* and *Sidi Vrelatam*.

In this book the author has succinctly depicted as to how people of both higher and lower orders thought about these supernatural phenomena and tried to manipulate them accordingly to their benefit. I feel this book will fill the gap which exists in the cultural history of medieval Andhradesa.

I hope that scholars, students of History, Anthropologists and Sociologists will welcome this book. Even general readers will find this book interesting. I wish this book a great success.

Hyderabad

Professor R.L. Hangloo
Head & D.S.W
Department of History
University of Hyderabad (Central)
Hyderabad (Andhra Pradesh)

PREFACE

'History from below' as a concept in the recent historiography has made several advances in understanding past societies. The aim of reconstructing 'History from below' has been to bring the marginal, subordinate groups onto the stage, analyse their range of possible actions, seek out their motives and assess their influence. Such an approach is based on the conviction that the groups in question were important by virtue of having influenced historical processes in some significant way not previously understood. Again, any historical process may not be complete without a portrayal of the contributions made by subordinate populations through their work, their suffering, or their distinctive forms of expression. We cannot properly discuss warfare or plague without making clear their impact on the victims, even if the latter were unable to change the conditions under which they were living. Therefore, the study of popular culture is intended to extend and deepen our understanding of people who constituted the subordinate and subjected.

The study of popular culture is also more fruitful when we study the interaction between 'elite' and 'popular' than distinguishing between these two. Connections are established between the popular culture and larger processes. In order to learn about political action, social organization, the operation of gender or the transformation of religion, the evidence of varieties of sociability, forms of violence, complexes of beliefs, types of resistance, systems of rituals and hidden forms of power has to be sought out. A distinction has to be made between 'popular culture' (the forms of thinking and acting of politically or economically subordinate groups) and 'mass culture' (culture disseminated by modern forms of mass media which are not generally controlled by popular groups).

People in Medieval Andhra had their own notion of world-view. They held a variety of beliefs about the world, God and spirit. Some spirits were believed to be responsible for certain epidemics. Some deities were also thought to be both benevolent and malevolent. The wrath of the goddesses was believed to be the cause of many disastrous things, for example, sickens, crop-failure, rain-failure etc. Therefore, the supernatural was manipulated. This took the form of many rituals, customs and traditions, like, *jatara*, human sacrifices, *kanumari*, *kavu ritual*, *noti talalu*, *sigamugadam* and *sidi vrelatam*. For many people who performed these rituals, it was an expression of their deep-seated beliefs about the world in which they lived. These rituals and customs were popular especially among the low and depressed class people, not only because it increased their 'worldly' options and opportunities, but also because it made sense theologically; because it reflected a view of the world which was already inhabited by particular kinds of deities who were believed to control natural forces and who could be pleased or mollified by the 'victims' suffering of self-sacrifice. The rituals in their religious and cultural aspects became a resource—something which, if used effectively to please or manipulate supernatural power, could make a difference between health and sickness, fertility and infertility, rains and drought or life and death. In carrying out this study many owe my debts of gratitude.

I wish to express my profound thanks to my supervisor Dr. R.L. Hangloo for all his help. He is more than a research supervisor to me. I greatly appreciate his kind help in giving his time for my work, particularly for valuable suggestions, corrections and for putting the whole work in right perspective.

I place on record my thanks to the libraries and Institutions where I received help in this work. University of Hyderabad, Osmania University, Archaeological Museum Library, Andhra Pradesh State Archives and State Central Library are duly acknowledged. These institutions helpeo me in a great way to get my research data and material.

Victor Babu

Contents

ABBREVIATIONS

APHC	Andhra Pradesh History Congress
ARE	Annual Reports on South Indian Epigraphy
CI	Cuddapah Inscriptions
CIS	Contributions to Indian Sociology
CSSH	Comparative Studies in Society and History
IAPC	Inscriptions of Andhra Pradesh, Cuddapah
IC	Islamic Culture
IESHR	Indian Economic and Social History Review
IHR	Indian Historical Review
JOAS	Journal of Asian Studies
JOPC	Journal of Popular Culture
MAS	Modern Asian Studies
NDI	Nellore District Inscriptions
PP	Past and Present
SIH	Studies in History
SII	South Indian Inscriptions

INTRODUCTION

Popular culture has become a fascinating and a most promising area of research, not because it is privileged over other concepts but because of the new agenda which is being set out in the recent historiography. Liberal historiography, positivism, Marxism dominated historical narrative until recently. Of late annals historians have provided many insights in understanding past societies.[1] Historiography, which was influenced by Marxist ideas, pre-occupied itself with the base and superstructure, class, economic exploitation and ideology. As a result other aspects of a given society which are also relevant in understanding the social complexes were more or less marginalized. Moreover, dominant narratives are being constantly contested on the ground that a particular discourse does not talk about marginal groups. The most vocal in articulating this alternative discourse is subaltern school. This school is trying to construct alternatives by giving space to hitherto unheard voices and trying to bring marginalized sections, groups of the society to the center-stage of historical narrative.[2]

Even Annals School shifted its focus to the sensibilities of people. As the first and second generations of Annals historians gave primacy to land, labour, structures and time respectively, history of mentalite project gave space to the mentality and ideas of the people.[3] It was increasingly realized that a study of emotions and sensibilities was necessary with a view to understand a society in a more comprehensive way and in its totality. Also, the project of 'history from below' came to mean a gravitational shift in scholarly interest from national to local or regional, from public institutions to domestic life and from the study of state craft to that of popular culture.[4]

The notion of popular culture always represents same sort of attempt at broadening the basis of history, to enlarge its subject matter and scope. It makes use of new raw materials – oral sources, and offers new maps of knowledge. The 'discovery of the people' in late eighteenth century Europe – i.e., the discovery of popular ballads, and the use of folk-life materials to reconstitute the ancient past—was in the first place, as Peter Burke argues, the work of literary scholars and poets seeking in peasant culture an escape from the artificialities of the salons and courts.[5] However, the idea of 'popular culture' was first formulated by German writer, J.G. Herder and emerged as an important area of study in late eighteenth century.[6]

'History' meant essentially Ranke-type history, the political history of the nation-states. There was also cultural history, Burckhardt-type history, which was concerned with attitudes and values and their embodiment in symbolic forms such as paintings and plays.[7] However, both kinds of history were concerned with elites, the political historian studied the doings of kings and statesmen; the cultural historian studied artists and intellectuals. Neither of them was concerned with the attitudes and values of shopkeepers, factory workers, peasants and craftsmen, servants and fishermen, beggars and thieves.[8]

As we have already noted, until recently only political, economic and social factors have been studied. Although there are some works on cultural aspects, they were studied only from above and superficially because these works also gave primacy to economic, social and political aspects. As a result the history of popular culture in Medieval India followed a serious neglect. Besides, no attempts were made to study the dynamics of medieval state, its legitimization process, its ideological apparatuses at all

India level. Therefore, we choose to concentrate on Medieval Andhra region which also suffered this negligence. It is with this in view that we intend to fill up these gaps and understand the phenomenon of popular culture and state in Medieval Andhra, we are here making a modest attempt in this study. Even as our main thrust is on popular culture, an attempt has also been made to relate it to the elite culture. Hence, it precludes the historical description of the origin, growth and spread of a custom, ritual or philosophies of different religions-or sects.

It needs to be made clear at the very outset that this study is concerned with the culture of ordinary people such as – tribal, peasants, artisans, women and lower sections of the society, who were non-literate and whose history and culture hardly found any place in the official records of Medieval Andhra. An attempt has also been made to understand the dynamics of popular culture and the changes it underwent between fourteenth century and seventeenth century under the influence of these dominant groups for whom the Medieval Andhra state existed.

Although a conceptual study cannot be marked out temporally in the same meticulous manner as a traditional history of politics, it is necessary to define chronological and spatial contours of the study. It is simply because we have also stated as our object of study. Political history of the dynasties that ruled over Medieval Andhra does not lie under the scope of the study. However, for the sake of space and time our study begins from fourteenth to seventeenth century. The region we are concerned for the present study is Andhra, comprising all the Telugu-speaking parts of present Andhra Pradesh. These four centuries have been viewed as a single unit representing as medieval period in Andhra history.

The methodology followed in the study is interdisciplinary besides making use of primary and secondary sources which are relevant for the study.[9] This is aimed at an analysis of the mental structure of Medieval Andhra people. An attempt has been made to understand Medieval Andhra culture in its own terms. Since culture is also shown as power by Foucault, it is studied in relation to power relations and other societal structures.

A few questions need to be answered here. How can we find out what the popular culture of past generations was really like? Because the main problem which the popular historian faces is about sources despite the existence of plethora of medieval Telugu literature and inscriptions. Majority classes who constituted popular culture and participated in it were illiterate and were sometimes not found fit by medieval writers as the subjects in their texts, except as passing reference. Therefore, we have to increasingly depend on myths, festivals, attitude, and other aspects which have come down to us through memories from generation to generation down to our own times.

When we do not have direct access to the attitudes and feelings of peasants and artisans through inscriptions, perhaps we can do so through oral tradition. In compensation, we can profit from late-eighteenth century discovery of popular culture and use of notes of the folk-songs and folk-tales collected by scholars like C.P. Brown (1798-1884), a civil servant in East India Company.[10]

Another approach to the study of popular culture is chronologically oblique, it is the regressive method. This term was coined by a French rural historian. He proposed to read history backwards. Historians of popular culture are in a position much like Marc Bloch and Jan Vansina. It was only in the nineteenth century that ballads and stories were systematically collected from oral tradition and the peasant customs and festivals were meticulously described.[11]

We have depended on these scholars for their methodological analytical framework which has given us some significant clues to proceed with this study. The various aspects that this study on popular culture and state in medieval Andhradesa include: a) popular culture in medieval context, b) varieties of popular culture and their appropriation, c) popular religion in perception, d) popular religion in practice, e) power relations within the state structure apart from the introduction and conclusive remarks. Like all other studies it also has its limitation, but these do not overwhelm the significance of this study because of its being the first of its kind particularly in the Andhra Region.

References

1. Please see, Marc Bloch, *The Royal Touch: Sacred Authority and Scrofula in England and France,* London, 1973; Lucien Febvre, 'Sensibility and History: How to Reconstitute the Emotional Life of the Past, in Mukhia & Aymard (eds.), *French Studies in History*, Vol. I, Delhi, 1987. For problems in the history of mentalities see, Andre Burguiere, 'The Fate of the History of Mentalities in the Annales, *C.S.S.H.*, Vol.XXIV, 1982, pp.426-37.
2. For a discussion on 'Subaltern School' see Ranjit Guha (ed) *Subaltern Studies*, O.U.P, Delhi, 1980.
3. Lucien Febvre, 'Sensibility and History: How to Reconstitute the emotional life of the past' in Mukhia & Aymard (ed.), *French Studies in History*, Vol.1.
4. E.J.Hobsbawn, 'History from Below – Some Reflections' in Fredrick, Krantz (ed.) *History from Below: Studies in Popular Protest and Popular Ideology,* Oxford, 1988, pp.13-27.
5. Peter Burke, *Popular Culture in early modern Europe*, London, 1978, p.7
6. For the causes of discovering culture of people, please see Peter Burke, 'The Discovery of Popular Culture, in Raphael Samuel (ed.), *People's History and Socialist Theory,* London, 1981, pp.216-26.
7. Peter Burke, op. cit., 1978, p.68.
8. Peter Burke, 'Oblique approaches to the history of popular culture' in C.W.E Bigsby (eds.) *Approaches to Popular Culture,* London, 1976, p.69.
9. Although this study is based on literary works and inscriptions, to some extent, perceptions of psychoanalysis have also been reflected upon to understand the mental structure of the period.
10. Once again, we have to remember the mediator. Collectors did not always write just what they found. They censored, they polished they improved. They are mediators and not the only ones. Collectors, sometimes, did not do all their collecting themselves,

but relied on their informants and friends. Thus, there is some force in the traditional historians objection that it is impossible to write the history of popular culture because the documents are lacking or untrustworthy. We have to study the oral through the written and the illiterate through the learned. What it does mean is that we can never afford to forget that we are employing indirect or oblique approaches to popular culture.

11. We have depended on these scholars for writing the history of Andhra popular culture backwards and for using nineteenth century as a base, reconstructing the whole popular belief system and then moving back to consider its more fragmentary evidence of earlier period. However, the historian knows that he cannot jump thousands of years in this way, because so many changes might have taken place in that long period, the aim is not to jump millennia but to walk back a century or two by means of regressive method.

1

POPULAR CULTURE IN MEDIEVAL CONTEXT

It is said that the problem of popular culture lies with its definition itself. Because it contains two serious ambiguities. Both 'popular' and 'culture' are problematic terms. Firstly, we must specify who are the people we are talking about?.[1] Secondly there are ambiguities and transformations in the concept of 'popular' itself. If only we could clarify the exact meaning of 'popular' and specify clearly what is meant by the term 'people' , then the problem would disappear, this is precisely because why almost all books or articles on popular culture begin with a list of possible meanings.[2] Dai Smith defines popular culture as "the description and analysis of the popular tasks, customs, folk beliefs, manners and entertainment within any given social order.[3]

Peter Burke, the most famous historian on popular culture, defines popular culture as "the culture of the non-elite, the little as opposed to the great tradition: a system of shared meanings, attitudes and values and the symbolic forms... in which they are expressed: the 'structure of feeling' of the subordinate classes.[4]

In order to gain a basic insight, an initial theoretical hypothesis or useful interpretative tool in this field of enquiry, we need to specify social context and types of society. It is necessary to draw the distinction between 'popular' and 'popularized' i.e., between popular culture and popularized culture. Differences between popular culture and popularized culture are as important as the similarities. While 'popular' indicates an implicit state or condition, more precisely, a phenomenon which is widespread owing to some intrinsic or at least non-specified condition, the popularized presupposes a specific process inside which one could discern a certain degree of autonomy. In other words, the term popular signifies a widespread condition or state of affairs which, even while, exhibiting a certain degree of change or growth, has as its main characteristic the fact that is given. More precisely, while the term 'popularized' connotes the very opposite, namely a type of culture which is both widespread and widespreading as a result of organized social action.[5]

There is on the one hand, an area, indeed, a category of phenomena which belongs to what is commonly called a traditional, mainly rural type of society. There is on the other hand, a not less distinct area belonging to a modern industrial society. Therefore, any study of popular culture has to begin from a phenomenological duality, more simply, the objective existence of two kinds of popular culture separated and differentiated from each other by the process of modernization. This is not to say that they do not share a series of important characteristics. However, even when they co-exist they derive their specific character from the fact that they are genetically related to two types of society or two different stages in the development of one and the same society, traditional and modern.[6]

Peasant culture and primitive culture are also categorized as popular culture or varieties thereof. Sociologically a peasant or primitive culture is not only popular but also universal or communal. It implies that it is shared by all members of a community. Hence, the division between popular culture and high or learned culture collapses in a peasant or primitive culture.[7] Then one can ask whether a common or commonly shared culture can in principle also be a popular culture. It should be useful to make a distinction between common and popular culture.

Apart from relation between popular culture and elite culture, we need to take into account cultural flow and overlap. Peter Burke argues that there is two-way traffic between two cultures. Yet the emphasis should be on uniqueness of the overlap. The elite participated in popular culture (popular culture was everybody's culture). They were bi-cultural, culturally amphibious: the people did not participate in the great tradition; therefore, the crucial difference in medieval Andhra was that between the majority for whom popular culture was the only culture and the minority, who had access to great tradition but participated in the little tradition as a second culture.[8]

There are many spheres of popular culture where the culture divide is weak. There are many areas where both the learned and ordinary people rubbed shoulders together. For example, myths, rituals, traditions, religious practices, fairs, festivals, games, performance of place and dancing etc. are where both come together. There is further evidence of overlap when we move to religious picture – rituals, customs and belief in astronomy, palm-history, magic, to name only a few, we come across various examples of overlap.

Therefore, does all this threaten the usefulness of the term popular culture? It has been argued that it does not do so, when one asks the questions about social space.[9] It is not enough to simply locate 'low' and 'high' in the same place. One has to determine what they were doing in that place, what their respective roles were, whether they participated on equal terms.[10] Issac argues that shared pastimes cut across but did not level social distinctions, and given the right conditions shared pastimes, rituals could reinforce hierarchy. Even if there was a brief spell of knock about humour in some pastimes and hierarchy was suspended in some rituals, it was always clear that it was a temporary matter. The social framework was always plain. In the realm of ideas, too, it is not once again enough merely to locate spheres. One has to ask what beliefs were held by whom within the broad categories. Values at popular level were also not necessarily at one with those proclaimed by religious establishment.[11] Popular attitudes, opinions, expectations were often sharply at variance with those of their social superiors.[12]

There is a whale of difference between traditional popular culture and modern popular culture. The main sociological criteria used in the study of popular culture in modern societies are:

(a) on the relationship between class and culture;

(b) on the relationship between an author and his work;

(c) on the relation between market, as an economically organized institution and cultural production.

However, culture is rooted and runs along the lines of class division according to the first criticism. It also postulates that high or learned culture corresponds to high classes. It assumes that high culture belongs to upper classes and popular culture to lower classes. In other words, the former is the culture of a few, (so the expression elite culture), while the latter is the culture of many people. Bourdiev argues that in contemporary industrial society, there is one culture only, i.e., the culture of the dominant classes and consequently great masses have to define their cultural status by simply opposing or rejecting this, i.e., without possessing a positive alternative.[13] Another scholar Birnbaum opines that in modern societies education has produced a cultural stratification of population.[14]

The relationship between the author and his work becomes the yardstick in distinguishing what Zev Barbu calls highbrow elite and lowbrow popular culture. R. Escarpit argues that popularity of a literary work can and should be assessed in terms of readership, a notion which includes the number of reprints, number of individual readers and number of references in periodicals, newspapers or recorded conversations.[15]

The novel and drama of 18th century England have been described as components of popular culture by Lowenthal. He distinguishes between true art (which roughly corresponds to highbrow culture) and popular culture. He suggests that the drama and novel of the period were popular because to the extent to which. the playwright and novelist projected in their work patterns of behaviour and structures of experiences and fantasies shared by the members of the lower classes which constituted a majority of the population.[16] So what are the differences between the traditional and modern popular literature? In traditional literature the project is essentially extra societal, more precisely it involves the whole community in a utopian world, a world in which the 'fair maid' is the dream of everyone, as the husky witch is the nightmare of everyone. Hence, the highly metamorphic mode of expression of traditional literature.[17]

Presentation of life in popular literature of modern societies is intra-societal in two alternatives or complimentary senses: (a) as a genuine cultural expression of lower classes of society, (b) as an artifact produced by a minority for the consumption of a majority. The idea of popular culture in the modern era is almost inseparable from the idea and practice of instrumental rationality. This manifests itself in a variety of forms but the basic principle is the same, i.e., production or adaptation of culture carried out by a minority on behalf of society as a whole and for the specific aspirations, tasks and standards of a majority.[18] Again, concern with entertainment tends to become dominant and at times unique feature of popular culture in modern period.

Third criterion by which we distinguish popular culture in industrial societies is the role of market in the process of cultural production and consumption. Process of cultural production, in many advanced industrial societies, is to a great extent sensitive to and often determined by the market. In modern industrial societies art has become a commodity. The contemporary pornographic literature and science fiction are also referred to as modern version of popular culture by some authors. What is noticeable in this is gradual reversal of positions with regard to the social framework. What in early stages of modern era was a majority phenomenon has gradually turned into its opposite, a conscious product of a ruling minority. In some modern societies popular culture has got political and ideological character. In such a context concept of popular culture has no specific descriptive function. It is, in fact, a normative and prescriptive concept which signifies what the people, the majority, great masses ought to feel, think and be. Traditional and working class culture is on the decline in modern industrial societies. As a result it has become difficult to talk about the existence of 'alternative' culture in contemporary industrial society.

However, when we look at medieval period, we can see two different, (but one as far as their goal is concerned), trends in the writing of popular culture of medieval Europe. These two trends developed differently in two different countries namely Britain and France. In Britain, historians started studying culture and power in late 1950s and 1960s. They moved towards social history. It can also be identified as 'People's History' and 'History from Below'. Although the concept of 'people's history' was vague in the beginning, all of them wanted to focus on popular culture. They talked of economical, geographical, technological, political and cultural systems only in relation to people and their influence on people.[19] Later on there was shift of focus, when history came to be viewed from people's perspective. They attempted to study how power was perceived and not just how it was exercised. This led to the development of the category of 'experience'. How do people experience change and transition and how these experiences change overtime have also been studied.[20] They did not stop here and moved further to develop the notion of 'people making history'. There arose some significant questions.

(a) How do people constitute, define and shift or transform the world?

(b) How do people constitute, reconstitute structures and live in them? So every day actions became important.[21]

Taking a cue from these insights, modern practitioners of medieval popular culture studied a number of aspects of this subject. Festivals, folk beliefs, theatre, various forms of entertainment, religious sectarianism, riots, cheap printed literature like broadsides, ballads, pamphlets, newspapers, and chapbooks were studied. Sex, marriage, law have also been studied from non-elite perspective.

In France popular culture, as the culture belonging to common people, has been characterized in two ways. It has been identified first, with a set of texts, the small books sold by peddling and known under the generic term of Bibliotheque bleue, and secondly, with a group of beliefs and acts taken as the components of popular religion.[22] In both cases the popular is defined in contrast to something it is not (scholarly and learned literature or the normative Catholicism of the church). Popular culture has been studied under 'History of Mentalities' in what has come to be called Annales school of thought. So, Witchcraft, popular poetry and the resistance to the resolute and controlled imposition from above of the catholic reform have been studied. Attitudes towards life, death, disease and sexuality also became the objects of study.[23]

In the same vein, Emmanuel Le Roy Ladurie, in his doctoral thesis, carnival of Romans, devoted eight pages to this carnival. He argues that the poor danced out their hostility to the rich, crying "Flesh of the Christians, four deniers the pound' and declaring that "the rich men of the town had enriched themselves at the expense of the poor".[24] Another book of his Montaillou is an account of the mental, emotional and sexual life of late 13th century peasants in a remote Pyrenean village. This is considered to be an outstanding work on popular culture. It is basically a reconstruction of mentality of the *Cathars* (heretics) of France.

Carlo Ginzburg, an Italian historian, made an effort to reconstruct the mentality of medieval Italian peasants called *Benandanti* (an Italian heretic sect) in his work, *The Night Battles: Witchcraft & Agrarian Cults in the Sixteenth and Seventeenth Centuries*.[25] An obscure Frivlian Miller becomes hero in his other work, *The Cheese and the Worms*. He analyzes Millers testimony before the inquisition and describes him as an admirable representative of commoners.[26]

Keeping these perceptions of medieval popular culture in view we look at the nature of this phenomenon in medieval Andhra context. Characterization of popular culture in medieval Andhra is an arduous task. First of all, the sources out of which the historian traditionally culls a narrative were hard to locate in Indian society. This problem is more acute for the historian of popular culture.

Because he has to study oral through the written and the non-literate through the learned. Secondly, there is a remarkable difference between medieval European and Indian societies in general and medieval Andhra society in particular in terms of evolution pattern, formation of social systems, social relations and religious life.[27] The institutional structure of medieval Indian society of which medieval Andhra was an integral part was also markedly different from medieval European religious system. For example, Indian religion, Hinduism is basically a loose conglomeration of various sects and schools of thought.[28] This is borne by the fact that there was no Sanskrit or indigenous term, to define a person who held beliefs that were even today held by Hindus. As such this term cannot be applied to medieval India. Brahmanism (the large pool of divergent ideas held by various schools of Brahman priests and philosophers), was a basic fact of Indian religious history. It was distinct from Buddhism and Jainism. But what defined dharma, the rules of conduct, was the caste system and social rituals which in practice engulfed all, the devotees and patrons of the Brahmanas, Buddhists and Jainas alike.[29]

The creation of 'Hinduism' as a single religion was a process which took place in the medieval centuries.[30] Therefore, when the system itself was in the process of assimilation and acculturation, it becomes difficult to identify elements which did not belong to it. Not only does it make the task of the historian of popular culture difficult but also lands him in confusion. Besides, neither Hinduism nor Islam could boast of an institution like church, with its priestly orders, and the immense bodies of documentation, about matters sacred and profane, which they generated. If French historians of popular culture could provide many insights into the mental structure, beliefs and various rituals, it is precisely because it was very easy for them to identify elements which did not belong to the orthodox religious system, namely Catholicism, heretic sects, beliefs (witchcraft, magic) attitudes towards death, life, sex and the state could be studied with an ease.

It is difficult to locate an institution like church in India which was an orthodox institution with its body of doctrine. As we have already pointed out, the religious system called Brahmanism itself was very flexible and under the process of change. A look at the changes which Brahmanism has undergone and compromises it made reveal to us how flexible Brahmanism was and how difficult it is even today to point out what it is and what it is not. Even Rigveda's compilation, the bedrock of Vedic civilization apart from, *Yajurveda, Samaveda*, and *Atharvaveda*, presuppose several centuries of interaction with local population and cultures.[31] Both the priest and *parivrajaka* (ascetics) of Harappan civilization were successfully absorbed into the fold of Indo-Aryans. Three *yatis* who survived the slaughter were given protection by *Indra* according to *Pancavimsa Brahmana*. *Atharvaveda* talks about *vratyas*, who were priest of non-Vedic fertility cult, being admitted into Aryan fold through *vratyastana* by paying heavy *dakshinas*.[32] Efforts were made to convert them into Aryan faith and find a room for them in orthodox cult.[33] Increasing economic and military requirements forced Aryans to draw the indigenous tribes living on the periphery of this land into their fold.

It is precisely in this way the tribe of Sudras who were probably living on the banks of *Sravasti* was absorbed and was given official recognition as the fourth *varna* by *Purusasukta* which was incorporated in *Rig Veda*.[34] Some liberal attitude prevailed against *Nisadas* another local tribe and their leaders were recognized as followers of *Ksatradharma* by Mahabarata.[35] When Jainism and Buddhism emerged on the scene, challenging Brahmanism which got its sustenance from Vedas and animal sacrifices, then efforts were made for compromise, non-violence plank of Jainism and Buddhism was taken over by Brahmanism and they incorporated Gautam Buddha as the ninth incarnation of Vishnu. The castes proliferated into numerous sub-castes. Later on Greeks, Shakas, Parthians and Kushans were absorbed in Indian society as Kshatriyas, in the post-Maurya times. Huns ultimately came to be recognized as one of the thirty six clans of Rajputs.[36] Many tribal people were absorbed into brahmanical society through the process of land grants. However, tribal chiefs were given a respectable origin. But most of their ordinary kinsmen were condemned to a low position, and every tribe became a kind of caste in its new incarnation.

Brahmanical sect also made compromises with *Bhagavatism*. *Narayana* was originally a non-Vedic tribal God. He was called *Bhagavat*, and his worshippers were called *bhagavatas*. *Narayana* was supposed to bestow shares or good fortunes (*bhaga*) on his *bhakta* or worshippers. *Bhaktas* or worshippers offered their loving devotion or *bhakti* to him. Vishnu was merged with *Narayana* and Vishnu, who was a minor god in vedic times, came to be known as *Narayana Vishnu* by second century B.C. Again *Krishna Vasudeva*, a legendary hero of *Vrishni* tribe living in Western India, was also merged with Vishnu. Nowhere is this more clearer than in the great epic Mahabarat where efforts were made to show that Krishna was identical with Vishnu.

The foregoing discussion is enough to point out how difficult it is to categorize between what is 'sacred' and what is 'profane'. A similar process can be discerned in medieval Andhra society. The earliest reference to Andhra occurs in '*Aitareya Brahmana*' and in this work, Andhras are said to be a tribe.[37] Gradually Brahmanism, heterodox sects like Jainism and Buddhism competed with each other in winning over new converts. Brahmanism with its concept of *Varna* was trying to gain foothold in Andhra society. However, both Jainism and Buddhism appealed more to Andhras at that time. Later Buddhism started becoming strong even eclipsing Jainism. *Mahasangika* school of Buddhism gained foothold with *Dhanyakataka* as its nerve centre.[38] When Brahmanism assimilated Buddhism, admitting Buddha as the ninth incarnation of Vishnu, the decline of Buddhism was accelerated.[39] In order to wean away both peasants, who improved their economic position through *arthasiri* system (where the cultivator retained one half of the produce in *Agrahara* land) and merchants, who also become powerful economically, Brahmanism had to make compromises between ritualism and devotional theism.[40] As a result Bhakti-centred temple culture was revived to check the progress of

Jainism. Brahmins revived devotional theism and temple culture into which sudras could be drawn by allowing them active participation in it.

Bhakti cult, more precisely, *Srivaishnavism* and *Virasaivism*, which were more radical in their outlook in medieval Andhra also came to be identified as popular religion. Because they appealed to Sudra and other lower social groups and tribes, who were otherwise deprived of some religious rituals by Brahmanism.[41] Rituals associated with these cults also allowed participation of lower caste and tribes on a large scale. Besides worship of village gods and goddesses, rituals, festivals connected with them also assumed popularity. Myths and legends, and various forms of entertainment can be easily classed into popular culture, that were in practice in medieval Andhra during the period of study.

Later on with the entrance of Islam into this region *Khanqa, Dargah* (a tomb shrine of a sufi-saint) also became important in popular perception. People from all walks of life made pilgrimage to these shrines irrespective of their creed, caste and race.[42] They played a significant role in the religious life of the people as Sufi saints were supposed to have spiritual powers, to heal sickness, to bestow children to barren women, to prevent any danger and calamity. As a result they became very popular in medieval Andhradesa and formed integral part of the popular culture.

References

1. Peter Burke, 'What is the history of popular culture ? in Juliet Gardiner (ed.) *What is History Today .....?*, London, 1988, p.122.
2. In the recent past the literature on popular culture of various regions has grown but in India particularly to its medieval period the subject has not received much attention. There are number of works carried on this subject in Europe. The work of Peter Burke is the most pioneering one. For details see Peter Burke, *Popular Culture in Early Modern Europe*, London, 1978.
3. Dai Smith, *What is History of Popular Culture*, op. cit., London, 1988, p.123.

4. For a brief explanation of the concepts of 'Great' and 'Little Traditions' , please see Peter Burke, *Popular Culture in Early Modern Europe,* London, 1978. pp. 23-24.
5. Zev Barbu, 'Popular Culture: A Sociological Approach' in C.W.E. Bigsby (ed.) *Approaches to Popular Culture*, London, 1976, p.42.
6. Ibid., p.42
7. Morag Shaich, *Discourse on Popular Culture: Class, Gender and History in Cultural Analysis, 1730 to the Present*, London, 1989, p.35.
8. Peter Burke, *Oblique Approaches, o*p cit., p.70.
9. R.M.Isherwood,' Entertainment in the Persian Fairs in the 18th century' , *Journal of Modern History*, Vol. XXI, 1981, pp.27-30.
10. Ibid.
11. R. Issac, *Transformation of Virginia 1740-1790,* 1982, New York, p.104.
12. Barry Reay, *Popular Culture in Early Modern Europe,* London, 1985, p.17
13. P.Bourdiev, 'Outline of a sociological theory of art perception' *International Social Science Journal*, Vol.XX, 1968, p.27.
14. N.Birnbaum, *The Crisis of Industrial Society,* London, 1969, p.133.
15. R.Escarpit, *Sociology of Literature*, trans. E.Pick, Paines-ville, 1965.
16. Zev Barbu, 'Popular culture: A sociological approach' in Bigsby (ed.) *Approaches to Popular Culture*, London, 1976, p.59.
17. Ibid.
18. Ibid., p.60.
19. See Eileen Yeo and Stephen Yeo (eds.), *Popular Culture and Class Conflict, 1590-1914: Explorations in the History of Labour and Leisure*, Brighton, 1981, pp.1-27.
20. Peter Burke, *Popular Culture in Early Modern Europe*, London, 1978, p.28.
21. For historical growth of this school of thought, please see, Raphael Samuel's Introduction in Raphael Samuel (ed.) *People's History and Socialist Theory*, London, 1981.
22. Stuart Clark, 'French Historians and Early Modern Popular Culture', in *Past and Present*, No.100, Aug., 1983, pp. 62-99.
23. Ibid.

24. Emmanuel Le Roy Ladurie, *Carnival in Romans*, New York, 1981; see his other work, *Montaillou: The Promised Land of Error*, Trans. Barbara Braes, New York, 1979.

25. Carlo Ginzburg, *The Night Battles: Witchcraft and Agrarian Cults in 16th and 17th Centuries*, tr. by John & Anne Tedeschi, Routledge & Kegan Paul, 1967.

26. Carlo Ginzburg, *The Cheese and the Worms: The Cosmos of 16th Century Miller*, tr. by John & Anne Tedeschi, New York, 1982.

27. Romila Thapar, 'Imagined Communities? Ancient History and the modern search for a Hindu Identity' in Romila Thapar, *Interpreting Early India*, O.U.P, 1995, p.60-88.

28. Ibid., p.62.

29. Irfan Habib, 'Medieval Popular Monotheism and its Humans: The Historical Setting', in *Social Scientist*, Vol. 21, No.34, March-April, 1993, p.29.

30. Renov Louis, *Hinduism :An Anthology*, 1961, p.18.

31. Bridget & Raymond Alchin, *Rise of Civilization in India and Pakistan,* London, 1982, p.183.

32. R.P.Chandra, *Survival of Prehistoric Civilization of Indus Valley*, MASI, No,41, Calcutta, p.131.

33. A.L.Basham, *The Wonder that was India*, Calcutta, 1982, pp.234-44.

34. B.S.L.Hanumantha Rao, *Socio-cultural History of Ancient and Medieval Andhra,* Hyderabad, 1995, p.93.

35. *Santiparva*, 133, 3.

36. Romila Thapar, *A History of India*, Vol.1, Penguin Books, 1990, p.121.

37. B.S.L Hanumantha Rao, op. cit., p.23.

38. Ibid.

39. Romila Thapar, *A History of India,* Penguin Books, 1990, p.132.

40. B.S.L. Hanumantha Rao, op. cit., p.27.

41. Ibid.

42. S. A. A. Rizvi, *A History of Sufism in India*, Vol. I. Delhi, 1978; R. Soma Reddy, *Hindu and Muslim institutions of Andhradesa 1300-1600 A.D.,* Hyderabad, 1984; K. Satyanarayana 'Religion and Society under Qutbshahis of Golconda' in *APHC*, 1978, p.46.

2

VARIETIES OF POPULAR CULTURE AND THEIR APPROPRIATION

The social format of medieval Andhradesa was extremely complex. Brahmanism was at its height in Coastal Andhra at the time of the establishment of Kingdom of Vengi. Proliferation of castes was a marked feature of medieval Andhra society, Brahmanas were no exception. Brahmanas got divided into two major sub-castes, depending on the profession they followed; one was *Vaidikis* (those who followed *Vaidika vritti*) and the other was *Niyogis* (those who followed *Lavkikia vritti*). The inscription from *simhachalam* dated 1393 A.D. bears testimony to the existence of subcastes among Brahmanas. In the same way Brahmanas differentiated on the religious sect they followed. *Jaina* Brahmanas, *Vaishnava* Brahmanas belong to this category. And yet another group of Brahmanas came to be named after the region they resided, like *Velanati* Brahmanas, *Venginati* Brahmanas, *Kammanati* Brahmanas and *Pakanati* Brahmanas.

Since the dynasties of the age were either of local aboriginal origin (*Iksvakus, Anandas* and *Visnukundins*) or of foreign extraction (Salankayans and Pallavas), they depended heavily on Brahmanas for gaining social respectability for their families and legitimacy for their political authority.[1] This was sought to be achieved through *Agraharas* or *Brahmadeyas*. Though some kings did not perform *vedic* sacrifices themselves, yet they provided wherewithal to Brahmanas for their performance in the *agraharas*.

Proliferation of *agraharas* was also due to the compelling economic situation. *Brahmadeyas* became nerve centres of remarkable socio-economic developments. Since Brahmadeyas were essentially agricultural villages, the demands of expanding agriculture warranted some changes in the *varna* system. Expansion of agriculture increasingly brought many aboriginals of neighbouring forest and hill-tracts into intimate contact with centres of civilized life."[2] And they were gradually absorbed into different *varna/jati* of the society according to their respective positions in the tribal organisation. This is clear by the fact that many names of Brahmanas which occur in inscriptions sound non-Sanskritic and aboriginal.[3] This was allowed even by a law given by Bodhayana.[4] This process of acculturation naturally led to the rapid growth of Brahman population and they were compelled to pursue other professions other than learning and teaching etc.

Addhiyamanussa or *arthasiri* system i.e., division of produce equally between a donee as well as a tenant in gifted lands (*Agrahara/devoghoga*) gradually improved the economic condition of the peasants. Expectedly, peasants looked for a corresponding social recognition. Since a Brahman became a role model for peasants, they began to ape him in food habits and religious practices.[5] However, they were denied space in orthodox Brahmanism. It was but natural that they turned towards Jainism, and devotional cults of *Vaishnavism* and *Saivism*.

As many aboriginal tribes were assimilated into caste structure, particularly peasant class, the ranks of sudras swelled. Already, acculturation of *Boyas* through economic and religious developments has been suggested by Eastern Chalukya records. *Boya* priests started emulating their counterparts in Brahmanical society in mastering *vedic* learning and performing vedic rituals.[6] Ketana, a poet of 13th century says that Brahmins became teachers of Boyas. To consolidate their frontiers and to win the support of Boyas, eastern Chalukyas employed them as officials. An inscription of great Chola king Rajendra Chola mentions a *Boya* chief, called *Mahamandaleswara* Gunda Boya as a lord of 480 villages and that he owned allegiance to the Chola king.[7] In the same way many tribes were absorbed into caste structure due to the compulsions of expanding agriculture and military requirements which were in great demand because of constant warfare. This was how Boya *Kottams* of *Pakanadu* and Telugu *codas, Banas* and *Vaidumbas* emerged out of aboriginals as political forces probably to the exigencies of the time.[8]

Under such circumstances it was not surprising that hardworking peasant class was converted into a fertile recruiting ground from which came the bulk of the army. These recruits attended to agricultural activities during normal times but fought wars of their kings and lords whenever they were called for. This kind of soldiers are found even during Kakatiya period and are known as *Ekkatlu* or *Ontarlu*. We have already discussed *arthasiri* system in *Brahmadeya* lands. Improved economic condition together with services in the army and court gave rise to a strong peasant-warrior class.[9] From about the middle of the Vengi Chalukyan period such families appear in responsible administrative posts and as holders of military chiefs. The Matsyas, the Durjayas and Pattavardhanis are some of them. Even Kakatiyas in Telangana had almost a similar origin. The *Banas*, the *vaidumbas* and Telugu Codas emerged into political prominence during the period of Pallava-Rastnakuta conflict which was continued by their successors. Even Recerlas, the subordinates of Kakatiyas, claimed equality with *Raghuvamsa*.

Most of the ruling families described themselves as of *caturthavaya*. Having improved their position economically and occupied positions of political power, these *sudras* naturally aspired for corresponding social status. It is only against this backdrop, we would be in a position to analyse meaningfully why devotional cults such as *saivism* and *vaishnavism* became popular.

Verasaivism

This sect emerged in twelfth century in Karnataka. Basava is said to have founded this sect. He served as Prime Minister of

Kalachuri king Bijjala. He was a great socio-religious reformer. He based his doctrines on the twenty eight Agamas and developed *Sat-Sthala* system of philosophy. What made it distinguishable from other *Saiva* sects was its religious militancy and the obligation it placed on its followers to carry the insignia of Siva, the *linga* on their bodies.[10] *Virasaivas* believed that Siva was the supreme God and all should worship only him. Basava was strongly opposed to the caste system. It has been argued that Basava combined the social cosmopolitanism of Jainism, devotional theism of Agama - Puranas and most likely the religious fervour of Islam.[11] Soon it spread to Andhradesa and found many followers. *Pasupatas*, a *Saivite* sect and its leader *Lakulisavara*, are mentioned by inscriptions in Coastal Andhra.[12] However, *Kalamukha* subsect of *pasupatas* became more popular in Coastal Andhra.[13] *Aradhya* sect is also mentioned along with these two sects.

Karusa or *Kalanana* was the founder of *Kalamukha* sect. Much information is not available about this sect. We get the impression that *Laḳulisvara-Agama* is the text of *Kalamukhas* as well. *Acharyas* of this sect sometimes added suffix *pasupati* to their names.[14]

Kalamukha sect was more liberal in their social outlook. They had already set up their *simhaparisats* in ancient temples (*Puratana devayatana*) of Amaravati and Bezawada and built *mathas*. *Kalamukhas* played a significant role in the socio-religious life of medieval Andhra. By their scholarship and piety *Kalamukha* teachers became popular. They became priests in temples. They chose the most frequented *ksetras* (pilgrimage centres) such as *Vemulavada, Daksarama, Amaravati, Bezawada, Cebrolu, Nadendla, Alampur* and *Srisailam* to attract people and popularise their sect. They established or took over *ghatikas*. Through the concept of *Diksha*, they opened before *sudras* both religious and secular learning. This institution of *diksha* has been likened to *upanayana* of Brahmanas.[15]

In the *Ghatikas* set up by *Kalamukha Saivite Sudra* rulers and officers should have received education and training. Early

Kakatiyas leaving Jainism and switching over to *Kalamukha* saivism is a case in point. By conferring *Diksha, Saivism*, almost recognised ritual status of these families. These *Sudras* who rose to higher echelons of political authority and gained ritual status distinguished themselves from peasants and peasant-warriors as *satsudras*. Several sections of *Panchanamvaru* (artisans) and *Komatis* (merchants) also appear to have shifted their loyalty from *Jainism* to *Saivism*.[16]

The opening of *Virasaiva* sect to all people is brought about by many contemporary poets and writers. Nannechoda talks about the association of *Parvati*, the wife of *Siva*, with *Yerukalas* in the forest.[17] Many tribals gained access to Veerasaivism through *Diksha* (initiation). At Srisailam temple, chenchus (a tribal group) played an active role.[18] That the *Saiva* sect opened its ranks to all caste and tribes is borne by *Kannapa* story in *Basavapuranam*. Although *Kannappa* was a tribal, he would be able to please *Siva* through his innocent way of worship. *Kannappa* became popular as *Bhakta Kannapa* in Andhra region. Durjati, a Telugu poet of 16th century, in his work *Kalahastimahatyam* describes *Kannappa* as the son of a *Boya* chief.[19]

As Basava denounced caste system and ritual concepts of purity and pollution it paved the way for the betterment of lower castes. They were inspired by his teachings. As a result people of all castes joined this sect as they had a degree of respect in this sect. Gates were opened for even *panchamas*. We come across *panchamasali* which literally means a weaver of *panchama* community. It is not unlikely that *panchamasalis* were members of weaving community who belonged to Mala caste and became the followers of Basava.[20] Many other devotees referred in their work were *Kata Kota (Golla), Machayya (Chakali* or Washerman) *Gundayya* (Kumari or potter) a gold smith. They stressed on social equality. In sattara, (choultry), attached to Golaki *Matha* at Malkapura, food was offered from Brahmanas to *Panchamas*.[21]

Srivaishnavism was also popular during the period under study. Before the rise of *Srivaishnavism* there was an attempt at rapprochement between *vedism* and *prabandism* (Compilation of teachings, and compositions of Alwars). This gradually led to rise of *acharyas* distinguished from *alwars*. These Alwars based their teachings completely on *bhakti* and preached in Tamil. But acharyas on the other hand were scholars in both Sanskrit and Tamil. It is these acharyas, who combined *bhakti*, *karma* and *Jnana*, developed the *Srivaishnavism* sect. Nathamuni and Yamunacharya are said to be the earliest preachers of Srivaishnavism. Their teachings received a systematic exposition in the hands of *Ramanujacarya*. *Srivaishnavas* started moving into Andhradesa and made *Bhavanarayanaswamy* temple of Baptla as their centre for proselytising activity. An inscription from Baptla records the presence of *Srivaishnavas* at this place.[22]

Srivaisnavism also opened its ranks to all castes. They also believed in the spiritual equality of its believers. Brahmanayudu, the minister of the Haihaya king of Macherla was a staunch supporter of *Srivaishnavism*. We are told that he was so radical in his outlook that he began to denounce caste system. Tradition would have us believe that Brahmanayudu married girls of all four castes and adopted Kannamadasa, who belonged to fifth caste, as his son. He is said to have opened the gates of Chennakesava temple at Macherla to *Panchamas*. He also insisted on inter-caste dining or *chapakudu*. In fact, this inter-caste dining is said to have caused Karempudi battle. Brahmanayudu also gave *Vaishnavadiksha* by making the prospective convert eat his *uchchista* and by changing his name into *Dasa*.[23] Kannamanedu, was made commander-in-chief of his army.[24] As his approach was more radical, this sect has been described as *Viravaishnavism*.

Even many tribal people appeared to have responded to *Srivaishnavism's* liberal ideology. Srinatha, a Telugu poet of medieval Andhra, talks about a *Yerukalasani* (a sooth-sayer, a woman who belonged to *Yerukala* tribe) who prayed to *Vishnu* for the success of Brahmanayudu in the war. *Sukasaptati* indicates that some tribal people had begun worshipping *Narasimha*.[25] That ritual status was also conferred upon tribal people is borne by a story of Valmiki. He was a tribal man living as a robber, but after penance, he received the blessings of Rama and became a *rishi*.[26]

Even Srikrishnadevaraya's *Amuktamalyda* mentions how all castes and tribal people started following *Srivaishnavism*.[27] Famous as he was, he was hailed by his contemporaries as *Sahiti-samarangana sarvabhauma*, one who excelled in a gathering of literature as well as on the battle field: one equally skilled in literary craftsmanship and warfare. The main theme of the poem is the devotion of two *Alvars*, *mystic* poet-saints of *Vishnu* in Tamilnadu. This poem was written in Telugu. It weaves together the cultural strands of three different regions in South India namely Tamil, Kannada and Telugu. This poem is very important because it contains a myth namely *Mala-Dasari* Myth.

Worship of Village Deities

Pluralism characterised the religious life of the medieval Andhra people. Worship and propitiation of *Gramadevatas* or village deities was an important feature of popular religion. People believed that the *gramadevatas* were the guardian deities of the land who protected them from famine and pestilence, evil spirits and evil effects. Even today the cult of these goddesses is very popular in southern India and no village is found without the shrine of the *Gramadevata*. It is estimated that eighty per cent of the people of South India address their worship to such minor deities.[28]

Ethnological studies conducted during British period give us a detailed information about the nature of worship of these *gramadevatas*. Medieval literature, inscriptions, also bear witness to the existence of this worship during the period under study. Whitehead who conducted a study of these village deities remarks, "Every village in South India is believed by the people to be surrounded by evil spirits, who are always on the watch to inflict diseases and misfortunes of all kinds on the unhappy villagers. It is also commonly believed that they lurk everywhere, on the tops of Palmyra trees, in caves and rocks, in ravines and chasms, fly in the air like birds of prey, ready to pounce down upon any unprotected victim, and Indian villagers pass through life in constant dread of these invisible enemies. Eventually the poor turn towards these goddesses for protection against evil spirits and epidemics of cholera, smallpox or fever, cattle diseases, failure of crops, childlessness, fires and all the manifold ills that flesh is heir to in an Indian village".[29]

In all parts of South India these seven *matrikas*, who are regarded as sisters, and their worship was popular. They worshipped numerous other deities, too. These seven sisters were also referred *to as sapta matrakas*. But the names of the seven vary according to the locality and even localities quite near together having different name for them. Their number increased with the passage of time.

The deities possessed some special features by which they could be identified as the part and parcel of the village life through the ages. Most of the time these deities have got no *Vedic* background and at the same time the presence of non-Sanskritic rites and customs in their daily and annual worship have proved their antiquity in the cultural history of the country.[30] These village deities were specially to be found in association with the lower caste people and the participation of these people in the worship and festival of the deities was very much greater in comparison to those of higher caste people.

The village deities may or may not have possessed any particular form. Most of the time a piece of stone or a small brick building three or four feet high or a small enclosure with a few rough stones in the centre; and often there was no shrine at all.[31] These village deities were rarely found inside the temple; they were characteristically seen under the open sky and at the foot of trees, on the embankments of the tank or even in the paddy fields. These village deities were specially meant for the general welfare of people. At the time of problematic situation in relation to the life of the inhabitants, the villagers unhesitatingly approached the deities for immediate solution. Their names, forms and rituals varied from place to place according to regional vernacular, but their functions seem to be quite constant.

The village Gods and Goddesses worshipped during this period were *Poturaju, Kakati, Ellamma, Posamma, Mulaguramma, Kunalamma, Errapolanna, Ennemma, and Balamma* etc. The names of the some of the female Goddesses differ from region to region. For example, *Mahuramma* was called as *Maremma, Ellamma, Renuka and Ekavira*. Some of them belonged to certain castes in the society.

Later on efforts were made to incorporate these local village Goddesses into Brahmanical fold. The aniconic images and the local cults were integrated first within *Saiva* and then within *Vaishnava* pantheons. The interaction of Brahmanas and localized peasant folk constituted the primary cultural nexus of medieval South Indian peasant society. Consequently, Brahmanical cultural traditions were seen to have transformed Dravidian 'folk' culture. According to the earliest evidence both traditions modified each other. Evidently Brahmanas were increasingly drawn to rural areas by the political powers-that-be through *agrahara* and *devabhoga* lands. It prompted Brahmanas to Sanskritize village Goddesses. The myth of *Ellamma*, who was an untouchable woman, with Renuka, the wife of a Brahman *rishi* (sage) is a case in point. It was this compelling reason which made village Goddesses acceptable to Brahmanas. Because Brahmanas had to interact with non-brahman population on the one hand and the sphere of village culture on the other.[32] Such a phenomenon was perhaps a natural corollary to the emergence of *agrahara* settlements in the countryside and the consequential politico-social order achieved through alliance between sections of Brahmanas and the dominant land controlling peasantry.[33]

Here we shall briefly discuss village Goddesses, their symbolic and functional aspects. These village deities were considered powerful, creative, active and transcendent female beings. They were worshipped under numerous names. All these female deities came to be treated as forms of *shakti*. They were considered both malevolent and benevolent. Another important feature of the worship of these village Goddesses was participation of lower castes as priests in the rituals associated with these deities, such as, *Malas* and *Madigas*, who were described as *Panchama* caste and untouchables and castes associated with pollution works such as *Chakali* (washerman) and *Mangali* (Barbers).

Ellamma

She was described as the Goddess who bestows children to barren women and also protects children from diseases. Tradition has it that she was Renuka the wife of *Jamadagni*, a sage. When *Parasurama*, her son, beheaded her on the orders of his father, the head fell in the street of *Bavanis* and she became their Goddess. There is another variant of the myth. This has been treated in the next chapter in detail. *Kridabhiramam*, mentions that *Bavani's* were singing the story of Ellamma in those days.[34] She is also known as *Mahuramma, Akkalidevi, Ekavira and Renuka*. This literary work further says that *Bavanis* used to bring a neem branch in procession to the shrine of *Ellamma* at the time of festival making sounds with their drums. *Bavanilu or Baindlavaru*[35] would tell the stories of Ellamma and Parasurama playing Javanika, an instrument. Bavani women used to sing before *Ekavira* idol even during Kakatiya period. As this poem reveals:

> "*vaadya vaikhari kadu nervadiyanaga*
> *Eekavira mahadevi yeduta nilchi*
> *parasuramuni kathalella proudipade*
> *charutara keerti bavaneela chakravarti*"[36]

She was believed to protect people and would give children to barren women. When people suffered from eyesore, skin diseases, fever, stomach-ache, they would make a vow to this Goddess. Even if they saw a snake in dream they thought Ellamma appeared to them.[37]

Posamma

In Andhradesa, she is the goddess of small-pox. In Tamilnadu her counterpart was *Mariamma*. When small-pox broke out, people thought that Posamma came to them. She was supposed to be angry and expressing her anger by inflicting this disease. She is also known as *Ammavaru, Atapatalamma and Poleramma*. In Buddhist literature she is *Hariti*. We are told that Buddha converted her as a protector of children from her previous character of destruction. We come across the temple of *Hariti* during Ikshwakus at Nagarjunakonda for the first time. Goddess *sitala* is her counterpart in North India. Over the period they came to be identified as one and the same.

The shrine of *Posamma* was usually outside the village. Shrine was usually very crude, sometimes built with stones and mud. At other times it consists of stones, two or three feet long, set upright in the ground on three sides of a small square, the fourth side being left open. On the top was placed a flat stone. Within the shrine was found one small plain stone of no particular form, set upright in the ground. This was image of Goddesses. British Ethnographer, W.T. Elmore[38] observed the shrines of village Goddesses and their mode of worship in Nellore district. In fact it is he who threw much light on these otherwise neglected goddesses.

Apart from being the Goddess of small-pox, she was also considered to be responsible to some extent for all other troubles in the village such as cattle disease, drought and sickness among the people. However, the name *Ammavaru*, a respectful title for a woman, is a generic expression among people for small-pox.[39] People thought that there was no medicine for small-pox. Even if they took medicine, they thought disease would become worse and Ammavaru would get angry in which case there was risk to life, the only way out was to propitiate her by sacrifices.

Poturaju

He is represented by a small stone placed at some distance from the shrine of village Goddess. Another British Ethnographer, who studied the phenomena in South India says, "Poturaju is a mysterious person in the Telugu country; sometimes he is described as the brother, sometimes as the husband of village goddess, and sometimes as only an attendant. I have never met with him as an independent deity, and have always been told that sacrifice is never offered to him alone, but always in conjunction with one or more of the goddess".[40]

Kridabhiramam mentions that *Gangamma* and her brother *Kallipotullayya* were being worshipped in *Gurajala* in Palnadu.[41] However, we find that he was worshipped throughout medieval Andhra. Also, people believed that barren women could get children if they performed circumambulations around the shrine of Poturaju.

Poturaju was revered as *Koyyadu* by some tribal people. He repeatedly flogs and whips those who don't fulfil the vows taken. The agony of a repentant devotee who hurries up to fulfil a vow is depicted in the following song:

Oh my lord koyyodo, koyyoda
Don't be angry if I call you koyyada
Don't whip and don't flog me so,
This is heartless, merciless, oh koyyoda
I looked at the red sky
And saw the forest ablaze
I saw destruction all around
My heart sank within me
And I thought of you my saviour, oh koyyoda
I will keep my vow koyyodo, koyyoda
I am going straight now, to samalamma
I am going to Peddapuram
To buy a block of sweet jaggery
To mix it with a potful of water And make a rice sweet drink for the Goddess
I get a handful of cotton to make a wick
To present the light as homage to the Goddess
Oh my Lord Lpuupda Lpuupda
Don't whip, and don't flog me thus.[42]

Literary works of medieval period, too, talk about various Goddesses who were guardian deities and disease causing spirits.

Simhasanadwatrimsika, a literary work of 15th century by Koravi Goparaju, refers to the worship of Goddesses such as *Kamakshi, Mahakali, Candi, Nakkajiyya, Kali, Ambika, Vindhyavasini and Ekavira.*[43]

Kridabhiramam mentions other Goddesses who were worshipped such as *Camundeswari, Maisanamma*, and *Gangamma*. Srinatha in *Palnativeera Charitra* refers to *Ankamma* and *Poturaju*. He describes how people of Planadu were worshipping several Gods and goddesses. *Bhimeswara Puranam* also talks about various goddesses like, *Gogulamma, Mandatalli, Nukamba, Ghattambika and Maurikadevi*.

Later on these village goddesses were Sanskritized. We can see both upward universalization (carrying forward of religious contexts which were already present in little traditions to the level of literate Sanskritic great traditions) and parochialization (downward devolution of great traditional elements and their integration with little traditional elements).[44] Besides, as the kings' authority extended more and more into rural areas, these village deities under the patronage of ruling dynasties became *rashtra devatas* (state deities). For example, a temple was erected to *Mulaguramma*, a family deity of Reddi kings of Kondavidu, at *Mulaguru*. Even today there is a temple in Ammenabad in Phirangipuram mandalam of Guntur district. Inscriptions also inform us that special temples were errected to goddesses like *Yellamma* temple at Saundatti,[45] *Caudeswari* temple at Colasamudram,[46] *Irukulamma* at Nellore,[47] *Polaladevi* of Mangaluru,[48] and *Mukambikadevi* at Kolluru.[49] Further there were also special temples for *Akkaladevi* of *Karimadula*,[50] *Nukalaparamesari* and *Gangaparameswari* of Donakonda,[51] *Ekkaladevi Amman* at Padavedu, *Vutalamma, Gana Kalidevi, Ankalamma* and *Nancharamma.*[52]

Deification of Dead Spirits

Central to these beliefs universally encountered in traditional societies was the conception that the cosmos was inhabited by benign and malevolent spirits. In order to live and survive the contemporaries construed that one must be closely associated with merciful spirits and seek to pacify the vengeful ones. Among malevolent spirits, they also counted the spirits of dead women. As a result, there emerged a number of female deities over the period. The legend of *Kankadurga* is a case in point. Kanakamma, a woman, was believed to have become shakti after her death and began to inflict sickness and pain. So people started worshipping her to get relief from sickness. Now a temple exists for her in Vijayawada. There were instances of even human sacrifices at this temple.[53]

Worship of *Kuladevatas* (Caste Deities)

Apart from *Gramadevatas*, each caste had more or less its own deity. Generally a Kuladevata would be a female belonging to that caste. Either because of some magical powers attributed to a woman or something extraordinary contribution of her to their caste, she would be deified after her death. *Kakati* of Kakatiyas, *Mulaguramma* of Reddis, *Ellamma* of Madigas, *Gonti* of Malas, *Gangamma* of Gollas (a shepherd) caste, and *Idemma* of Gowdas (toddy-drawers) are caste deities of the respective castes.

If we study the metamorphosis of *Vasavikanya* from an ordinary maiden to caste deity (*kuladevata*) we shall come to know the process through which *Kuladevatas* came into existence. *Kanyakapuranam* which belongs to 15th century gives her story at length. It says that a certain king called *Vishnuvardahan* of Rajamahendravaram, while on tour, came to Penugonda and happened to see *Vasavikanya*, the daughter of Kusuma setti, the chief setti of Penukonda. He fell in love with her and asked her hand. However, his request was turned down. But the king insisted on his desire. Realising that they could not withstand his power, some komatis of nearly one hundred and two *gotras* and *vasavikanya* entered into fire pits and died. *Vasavikanya* became *kuladevata* of *vaisyas*.[54]

The story of *Vasavi* appear to have Jain overtones. The story does not have any historical basis, however. The family of *Vasavi* was of Jain faith and from her childhood *vasavi* developed indifference to worldly pleasures. When there was a proposal in the family for her marriage, she disapproved of it and committed *sallekhana* in true Jain fashion. Since then she has been worshipped as the caste Goddess by *Komatis*. When *Saivism* became popular she was given a *savitie* twist and treated as a manifestation of *Durga*.

Worship of Trees

Trees, too, were worshipped. People used to plant a pipal and a margosa tree side by side, usually at the entrance of a village. They would perform marriage of both the trees symbolically, two trees representing bride and bride-groom. The neem leaves were integral parts in the propitiation of village deities.[55]

Snake Worship

Another aspect of popular religion was the worship of snakes. Worship to hooded cobra on the fourth day of the bright fortnight in the month of sravana was considered important. People believed that snakes (*nagas*) were born in *sravana* month[56] This day was known as *Nagulacaviti*. On this day women used to fast and pour milk over ant hills in which cobras were believed to reside or *Nagakals* (stones on which figures of snakes were carved in relief). It was believed that worshipping *Nagas* would get children to barren women. A number of *Nagakals* of the period under study could be seen in a Saiva temple at Hampi.

Self-torture and Immolation

Another belief which persisted among people, particularly *saivites* was that a true devotee should sacrifice everything, even his life, as a mark of the depth and sincerity of his devotion. This belief gave rise to a number of religious rites and practices such as offering of one's own head, getting crushed under the wheels of the chariot carrying the image of the deity, and hook-swinging. These practices shall be discussed in chapter four in detail.

Sati Sahagamana

The practice of widows burning themselves on the funereal pyre of their husbands was another kind of self-immolation performed only by women. People believed that a wife who died along with her husband would attain *Moksha, svarga* and *vaikunta*. However, pregnant women or mothers of young children did not seem to have performed *sati*. Even Epigraphs recording the performance of *sati* state that woman who performed sati along with her husband obtained *Mukti* or attained *vaikunta* or gained the world of Gods. Thus great religious merit accrued to the departed souls and the woman who performed *sati* became a *sati* or *mahasati*. According to an inscription dated 1376 A.D. second wife of *Beci Gauda*, by name Muddi Gaundi performed sati on her husband's death.[57]

Many foreign travellers who visited Vijayanagara noted this custom in their travelogues. Barbosa described sati in the following lines. He says, "the practice of burning themselves with the corpse of their husbands was an ancient custom. In case a woman was poor, she threw herself into the same fire where her husband was burning, of her own accord. But for a woman of wealth and rank the procedure was different. Soon after her husband's body was burnt, a banquet accompanied by music, singing and dancing was arranged in honour of the deceased where all the kith and kin joined her. Richly jewelled, she went around the city on the back of a horse and when she returned to the burning ground, a great fire was prepared on the edge of the pit, where her husband was burnt. Ascending the few steps of the wooden scaffold specially erected for the purpose she distributed her jewellery to her relatives as well as friends, made a speech explaining the significance of sati, threw pitcher of oil into the fire and plunged herself after it.[58]

Nicolo Conti who visited Vijayanagara around 1421 A.D. wrote about this custom. He observes, "the inhabitants of this region marry as many wives as they please, who are burnt with their dead husbands. Their king is more powerful than all other kings of India. He takes to himself 12,000 wives of whom 4,000 follow him on foot wherever he may go and are employed solely in the service of kitchen. A like number, more handsomely equipped, ride on horseback. The remainder are carried by men in litters, of whom 2,000 or 3,000 are selected as his wives on condition that at his death they should voluntarily burn themselves with him, which is considered to be a great honour for them".[59]

Caesar Frederick, another traveller, says, "she carrieth in her left hand a looking glass, and in her right hand an arrow".[60] Nuniz, another traveller, who witnessed sati says, "the widow carried a mirror in one hand and in the other a bunch of flowers".[61] Barbosa, who saw performance of *sati* when Venkatapati Raya I died, says, "His body was burned in his own garden with sweet scented woods, sandal, aloes and such like, and immediately afterwards three queens burned themselves".

Among the *Lingayats* or *Vira Saivas*, who did not burn their dead but buried them, women who wanted to commit *sati*, were entombed along with her husband. An epigraph, dated 1509 A.D. states that when Harur Gauda's son, Bomma Gauda went to Svarga, (heaven) his wife Bommi Gauda sitting in the same tomb went to *Svarga*.[62] Nuniz also observes, they go with much pleasure to the pit, inside of which are made two seats of earth, one for him and one for her and they place each one on his own seat and cover them little by little till they are covered up and so the wife dies with husband.[63] Barbosa observes, this custom was prevalent among those people who wore Tambarane round their necks.[64] It is important to note that in spite of *Basava's* reformist attempts, which even encouraged widow remarriage, this custom continued to be observed by *vira saivas*. When *Bullideva*, the acharya of the *siddesvara* and *panchesvara* temples at Kudigere and a master of *Parama Siva Agamikas*, went to *svarga*, his three wives gave his body to the tomb. Here, three wives did not seem to have committed *sati*. It seems that *sati* was not universally present among *vira saivites*.[65]

Sati was glorified by the erection of what may be called *satikals* or *Mastikals*. They are found in and around temples of

Hampi and Krisnapuram. In sculptures, they are represented with a pointed pillar or post, from which is shown a woman's right arm bent upwards at the elbow. This is referred to in inscriptions as *tolu-kayi* meaning have given arm and hand.[66] Another variety of sati stone is a *sati* cum *virakal*. These *virakals* set up in honour of the fallen hero also contained sculptural representation of his wife or wives who committed *sati*.[67]

Virula Worship

Other worship which was popular during this period was *virula* worship or Hero worship. The people who did some extra-ordinary works were revered after their death and they became the objects of worship. The heroic deeds of these martyrs were commemorated by the erection of hero stones or *virakals*. These hero stones were set up either by their master or by their near relations or by the public. The *virakals* were set up with great enthusiasm by the people amidst song and music.

Kridabhiramam says that Macherla Chenniah, Kallu Pota Raju died and took the form of *Bhairava*. Pratapa Reddy holds that Chenniah was none but Brahmaiah Naidu.[68] These hero stones were worshipped with devotion and this was developed into a cult by the fourteenth century. Special shrines were built for heroes or *Virapurusulu*. A certain ojakka built a shrine for heroes in 1406 A.D.[69] A merchant built a temple for *Virakoti* at Karempudi, legendary place where famous war of Palnadu took place in 1424 A.D.[70] *Palnati Veera charitra*, a medieval Andhra literary work, has some references about *Virula* worship.

> *Veerulu, Divyalingamulu, Vishnuvu Nayuda Kallipotara*
> *Jaraya Bhiravundu, Tuhinadhri, Jayankamu, Nirmalambunai*
> *Keredu Gangadhara Madugemani Kanyaka yanni Bhangulan*
> *Garemapudi pattanamu kaseesumi kanugonnavarikin.*[71]

The heroic deeds of *Palnati Virulu* or the Chiefs of Palnad who perished in the fratricidal war known as the war of Palnad became the theme of a ballad sung by 'itinerant bards.[72]

In the same way another record dates to 1428 A.D. *Devappa*, son of *Mancegauda*, died in a fight. The inhabitants of *Kuku* village installed a *virakal* amidst sacrifice, songs, beating of drums before an assemblage of the people in accordance with custom.[73]

People who received worship as *Veerulu* could be divided into three categories. First category was the people who died on the battle-field or in fighting cattle thieves, second category was the people who immolated themselves for the protection of property and rights of a temple, third category was the people, who killed themselves or offered some limb of their body in fulfilment of a vow or to attain some sacred object. In 1365 A.D. a certain *Nayaka*, fell fighting in *Birammale* and *Cikka Nayaka* set up a *virakal* in his memory.[74] Some *Gaudas* of *Capparadahalli* fell fighting in the service of Hariyappa vodeyar. A *virakal* was set up in their honour in 1344 A.D.[75] Another *virakal* was set up in memory of *Vardan* who died fighting against a cattle lifter by name *Gramarasar* in 1337 A.D.[76]

Third category *Virakals* were found in the Tripura Sundari Temple at Tripurantakam. In this temple a number of *virakals* were arranged representing human figures in various postures; some with a dagger thrust into their neck or abdomen and some driving their daggers into the left thigh with one hand, and raising a weapon with the other in order to stab themselves in the chest. It was believed that these representatives were of bangle merchants who were swallowed by the Goddess as they passed by her shrine.[77] Sometimes the families of the heroes who sacrificed their lives for good cause were rewarded with grants to their families of land and cash payments. These *vrittis* were called *Ratta-Kudangai* or allowance given for shedding blood. A village called *Siru Nallalam* was granted as a *Ratta-kudangai* to *vajinjan* in 1369 A.D. as he scaled the fort and died fighting.[78]

Dargahs (Tomb of a Sufi-Saint)

The fourteenth century provided a new dimension to the political, religious and social institutions of the Deccan by heralding an era of Muslim domination in South Indian polity, which is evident in the establishment of Muslim provincial states such as *Bahamani* and later *Berar*, *Bidar*, *Ahmadnagar* and *Golconda* of *Qutb Shahis*. Islam had started gaining foot-hold from fourteenth century with the Muslim invasion of the Deccan. This also resulted in the infiltration of new Muslims and proselytization in the area.

Many renowned Sufi saints of the period came to have tomb-shrines built by their disciples. They are called *Dargahs* and *Khanqas*. These shrines became in course of time important centres of worship and pilgrimage for not only their spiritual disciples but also to laymen. For a popular saint is believed to attain *baraka* (God's blessing) which he perpetually radiated both during his life time and after his death. Therefore, they played a significant role in the religious life of the people, irrespective of their creed, caste and race.[79]

These *Sufi* saints were revered in almost all localities without religious distinctions. For people believed that these saints possessed supernatural powers: to bestow a child, provide protection from evil spirits, cure an illness, bring relief to a disturbed person, help sick cattle to recover, or to overcome vicissitudes of every sort. Hence people approached these saints seeking solutions for their problems both spiritual and mundane.

The tomb of *Baba Sharfuddin*, situated on a high hill six miles from the city of Hyderabad, was thronged both by *Hindus* and *Muslims*.[80] The *dargah* of *Qazi Zaiuddin Multani* and the *Dargah* of *Syed Shah Jamal Bagdad Warangali*, both situated in the villages near Modern *Warangal*, where *urs* are celebrated even today, belonged to this period. The name *Kazi* is said to have been derived from his name.

Dargah of *Gali Saheb* at *Rajkonda* (Nalgonda district) and the *Dargah* of *Baba Fakuruddin* of *Penugonda*, *Shah Ali Pasha dargah*, established in fourteenth century at *Alampur* (Mahaboobnagar district) became very popular during this period.

Even today *urs* are conducted at these *dargahs* in the month of *Jalikat*. The legends illustrating the life and miracles of these Sufi saints helped in fostering what Natalie Zemon Davis calls a 'religious culture'.[81] It was this articulation of such a religious culture in medieval Andhra that undoubtedly accounts for the active participation of individuals belonging to different denominations in what seemingly was a cult-centred around a Muslim *pir*. People made a pilgrimage to these dargahs ostensibly to have children to receive cure from sickness and to seek protection from any calamity and danger through the mediation and blessing of these Sufi saints.

Part of the answer to the popular faith in village Goddesses and Sufi saints may be found in the indigenous societies cognitive framework of illness and healing. It is well-known that conceptions of illness would have a crucial bearing on modes of healing. In Medieval Andhradesa a central feature in the etiology of illness was the belief that epidemics like small pox, cholera and plague would be caused by the wrath of some Goddess or the other and also the belief that some evil forces or sakti involuntarily would take over an individual's body, triggering disease. The only remedy was propitiating the goddess with bloody offerings thereby pacifying her or in case of evil force, it could be overcome, but this required divine intervention or the assistance of persons endowed with the capacity to invoke the divine power.

State of Medieval Medical Knowledge

Belief in village goddesses or Sufi saints was also partly because of the contemporary medical knowledge. Basavaraju, a medieval medical authority, refers to a verse in *Siddharasarnava* which says that '*masucika*' was the result of the wrath of the Goddess '*Mahasakti*'.[82] Indrakanti Vallabhacarya, the author of *Vaidyachintamani* mentions that the disease known as *spotaka* (small-pox) is the result of the sin committed previously by that person. Besides he tried to rationalise the disease. For *spotaka and Masucika*, he prescribes the juice of cloves, coriander-seeds, cumin and grapes with hot water four times a day. He opines that after drinking this juice, patient would be normal.[83]

Some travellers were also witnesses to some of the epidemics. Linschoten, the Dutch traveller of sixteenth century observed that Indians would cure epidemics with herbs, bhasmas, and other ointments and ease themselves from plague and flux. Many Portuguese fell victim to these epidemics.[84] Pedro Teixeira, another traveller who visited India during 1510-91 A.D. says that people were getting cure from *Maremma* or Cholera by using some medicinal stones.[85]

So even physicians, while considering the epidemics along with other diseases, did not refute the popular practices like worship of village deities. Interestingly they gave the names of the diseases in their medical works as they were popularly known among common people. Their prescriptions such as *dhupas* with medicinal substances fanning with herbal leaves to the affected person, diet regulations and hygienic steps could be seen in the form of propitiatory and purificatory activities during the worship of the epidemic deity.

The medieval state was very conscious of the developments which were taking place in the religious plane. It is not surprising that the medieval state was eager to utilise these new religious movements and cults for the legitimation of its rule. The state achieved this through Brahmanization of forest, village and pastoral gods and goddesses (folk deities). On the one hand the folk gods were made the incarnations of *Siva* or *Vishnu*, the great gods of the Brahmanical pantheon. These Goddesses were universalised as their consorts and as the manifestations of the great Goddess *Durga-Kali* on the other. This Sanskritization of the popular and Bahmanical belief systems was the most vital of the ritual processes that integrated many tribal and autochthonous people with the state. Various traditions, myths, legends and rituals which existed side by side with Brahmanical pattern show the metamorphoses of these forest deities, through village deities into the state deities. The kings and queens became the patrons of these deities and the political authority of the sacral and divine kings, in their respective frontiers has been validated and perpetuated by annual or periodical ritual-festival congregations at these cult centres. This legitimation process shall be discussed in a greater detail in the last chapter.

The royal visits to these cult centres enhanced the status of these centres[86] which, in turn, served as a tool for propagating and making accept royalty. This process was also accompanied by the construction of monumental architecture (temples, towers and forts) and gift making (*dana* and *dakshina*).[87] The Vijayanagara kings Harihara the second and Krishnadevaraya visited Srisailam temple and constructed the eastern tower (*gopura*) and the outer hall (*mandapa*) on the car street respectively.[88] Srikrishnadevaraya had installed bronze images of himself and his queen in the temple of Venkateswara at Tirumala. At Kalahasti he granted precious jewels and ornaments to Lord Kalahastisvara and constructed a *satram* or choultry. Again he also visited *cokkanathasvami* and his spouse *Minaksi* and presented ornaments to the goddess.[89] The *Velama* chief Anapota Nayaka constructed steps to *Patalaganga* at both Srisailam and Ahobilam temples.

Even the tribal mode of worship was also appropriated by Brahmanical worship: the forest produce such as (in Vernacular) *ippapulu, veduru biyyam, itapallu, velaga pallu, Neredu pallu, kondamamidi pallu etc.* became some of the ingredients of the ritual offerings (*naivedyam*) in the temples.[90] The idols of deities were bestowed with regal insignia, the most important of which were the crown studded with precious stones (*kirita*), umbrella (*chatra*), fly whisk (*camara*) and palanquin (*pallaki*),[91] and royal titles like *cakravartin, Maharaja* etc. were conferred on these deities.[92]

Vijayanagara state in spite of its rhetoric of protection of Hindu culture and its projection as protector of *Varnashra-madharma* and tradition could not carry out their rule without Muslims. Because of military compulsions, Devaraya recruited Muslims both as officials and soldiers in the army. He himself ordered the construction of mosque in the capital and allowed Muslims freedom to carry on their religious duties without any hindrance.[93] In fact the capital city had a Turkish quarter, a mosque and Muslim tombs.

In addition, Vijayanagara rulers also patronized popular Sufi saints. For instance, in 1638-39, Venkata II, renewed certain grants of villages to the *dargah* of Baba Fakuruddin of Penugonda. Many people used to visit Dargah.[94] For *urs* celebrations of Sufi saints at Khuttagulla (kadri Taluq in Anantapur dist), Hindu *basavis* used to perform dance before the *urs* participants. For this purpose, they were granted *inams*. Similarly barbers were also granted *inams* for doing free services like shaving to the descendants of saint and performing music at the time of annual *urs*. In the same way even washermen were given *inams* for cleaning the clothes of the descendants of the saint.[95]

Right from the beginning of Muslim rule, the rulers started depending upon the Sufi saints for political legitimacy since the support of religious sanction was necessary to sustain their rule. Qutb Shahi rulers sought to achieve this through Dargah and temple. The contemporary political situation, after the fall of Vijayanagara Empire, and the finality of the establishment of political dominance of one religious community (Muslim) over the other (Hindu) in itself might have necessitated the activisation of forces conducive to peaceful co-existence of the two. Peace was a necessity for both. Perpetual strife was not in the interest of either. The message of universalism and oneness of all religions as given out by some medieval *Sufi* saints, could provide a leverage to both communities to ensure the required peace and a conscious drive to establish and get legetimacy, to the other, for survival with dignity and a willing adjustment with new political structure. *Sufi* saints of medieval Andhra must have contributed in their own way towards a political rapprochement and concordance between two warring communities.

The state adopted a patronizing attitude toward Sufi saints because they acted as a medium for percolating down the power of state deep into the trust of masses. So Qutb Shahi state gave stipends to the *Dargahs* in its dominions. The statement of revenue and expenditure of the Golconda Kingdom for 1686-88 A.D. cited in *Tarik-i-zafarah* shows that the Qutb Shahi government spent Rs.397,801 as *Nadhar* (gift or stipend) to Miran Shah Raju (Shah Raju II, Sufi saint of Khanqa at Hyderabad) who was patronised by the last Sultan Abul Hasan and Rs.64,925 as allowance to Hindu temples.[96]

The liberal attitude of Qutb Shahis was to maintain status-quo in the society. However, since they wanted legitimacy for their rule, they and their subordinates gave many land grants to Hindus. Land grants and other finances given for the functioning of religious institutions show the patronizing attitude of rulers toward them in order to fulfil their aim of political legitimacy. Religious men made acceptable to the people the policies of the rulers as they yielded enormous influence over people. In turn, rulers kept them satisfied with economic gains in the form of land grants. These land grants served as legitimizing apparatus to the rulers. They tried to win over dominant religious institutions. An epigraph 1586-87, from Masayapeta village (Nellore district) which records the grant of village as *Agrahara* to several Brahmins by a Muslim official Lalkhan to promote the liberality of Quli Qutb Shah.[97] This is the way in which the popular culture was appropriated by both the Brahmanical religion and the medieval state.

References

1. B.S.L. Hanumantha Rao, *Socio-Cultural History of Ancient and Medieval Andhra*, Hyderabad,1995, p. 123.
2. Ibid., p.108
3. Goginaja of Kondamudi plates, *E.I.* V. p. 186, Ganamadija of the Mayidavolu recrod *E.I.* p.84-89, Vilasarma of Pikira plates, E.I. VIII, p.159, are some of the names.
4. Pravra Prasna, 54.
5. Burton Stein, *Peasant, State and Society in Medieval South India*, Delhi, 1980, pp. 207-208.
6. S.I.I. X. 90.

7. B.S.L. Hanumantha Rao, *Social Mobility in Medieval Andhra*, Hyderabad, 1995, p. 120.
8. Ibid.
9. For a complete discussion on social mobility of various castes, please see, B.S.L. Hanumantha Rao, *Social Mobility in Medieval Andhra*, Hyderabad, 1995, p.121
10. Krishna Sharma, *Bhakti and Bhakti Movement: A New Perspective*, New Delhi, 1987, p. 230
11. B.S.L Hanumantha Rao, Socio-Cultural History, Hyderabad, 1995, p.133.
12. S.I.I. No. 129 of 1917, S.I.I. iii No. 18, S.I.I. X, No. 334; S.I.I.VI.No. 144, No.226 of 1937-38, TTDI,I.No.36.
13. B.S.L. Hanumantha Rao, *Socio-Cultural History*, 1995, p.131
14. E.I. XXXIII, p.161.
15. B.S.L. Hanumantha Rao, *Socio-Cultural History*, Op. cit. 1995, p. 132
16. Ibid,p. 132
17. Nannechoda, *Kumarasambhavam*, 6-37.
18. Palkurki Somanatha, *Panditaradhya Charitra*, p. 237.
19. Durjati, *Sri Kalahasti Mahatyam*, canto 3, Hyderabad, 1961.
20. Konduri Sarojini Devi, *Religion in Vijayanagara Empire*, 1990, p.56.
21. P.S. Kanaka Durga, '*Radical Saivism: Its Impact on Society of Medieval Andhra*' (10th Cent. to 14th Cent. A.D.), *APHC*, 1988, p.84.
22. S.I.I. VI, No. 139, this inscription is dated 1023 A.D.
23. *Palanati Viracharitra*, 1961, pp. 125, 1102, 1105.
24. Y. Balakrishnamurthy, *Andhrula Samkshipta Charitra*, (Telugu), 1964, p. 113.
25. Palavekari Kadiripati, *Sukasaptati*, 1-101
26. Raghunadhanayaka, *Valmikicharitra,* 2-136.
27. Veldanda Prabhakaramatya, *A Commentary on Amuktamalyada*, p.112
28. Madras Government Museum, Bulletin, V.No.3, p.174.

29. Henry Whitehead, *The Village Gods of South India*, O.U.P., 1916, pp. 43-44
30. Koti Suryanarayana Murthy & S.V. Jogarao, *Gramadevatalu* (Village deities) Telugu, *Bharati*, 1989, No. 8, p. 23
31. Henry Whitehead, op. cit. p. 16
32. M.L.K. Murthy, 'Social and Economic history as reflected in the folk traditions and Myths in Andhra Pradesh', in *A.P.H.C.*, 1988, p.11.
33. Burton Stein, *All the Kings Mana: Papers on Medieval South Indian History*, 1984
34. *Kridabhiramam*, (ed.) Ananda Murthy, V. Manimanjari, Hyderabad, 1988, poem. 130
35. Also known as *Bavaneendlu* or *Pambalavaru* are untouchable Madigas, Please see S. Pratapa Reddy, *Andhrula Sanghika Charitra* (Telugu) 1949, p. 27
36. *Kridabhiramam*, 1988, poem 130. The original poem reads:

    మాన్యా ప్రైభరి కడు నేరవాదియనగ
    ఏకవీరా మహాదేవి యెదుటు నిల్చి
    పరశురాముని కథలెల్ల ప్రౌఢి పాడి
    చారుతర కీర్తి బవనీల చక్రవర్తి

37. R.Premlatha, *Janapada Sahityamu - Puranangathalu* (Telugu), 1983, p. 192.
38. W.T. Elmore, *Dravidian Gods in Modern Hinduism* (1913), Delhi, Reprint, 1984
39. In some places, *Peddamma*, meaning a great woman, is used for small-pox and *chinamma*, meaning a lesser woman, is used for *chickenpox*.
40. *Madras Government Museum*, Bulletin, V. No.3, p. 111
41. See P. Hymavati, '*Religion and Medicine in Popular Culture*', A paper presented in a seminar on Religion in Deccan: Ideology and Consciousness, held in the University of Hyderabad, 12-14 Sept. 1991, p.12.
42. B. Rama Raju, *Folklore of Andhra Pradesh*, 1978, p. 21.

43. G.R. Sarma (ed.) *Simhasana dwatrimsika* by Korivi Goparaju, Andhra Prdesh Sahitya Academy, Hyderabad, 1982.
44. For complete discussion of these concepts please see, Mic. Marriot (ed.) *Village India*, Chicago, 1955, p. 171-222.
45. Madras Epigraphy Report, 1935-36, 63, (Hereafter MER).
46. MER, 1912, 87.
47. MER, 1953-54, 80.
48. MER, 1928, 376.
49. MER, 1928, 403, S.I.I. IX, Pt. II, 460, 470.
50. MER, 1956-57, No. 60.
51. MER, 1956-57, 68, 70
52. MER, 1930-40, No. 18, 1915, No. 418, 423, S.I.I. Vol. XVI, No. 99, 129, 185, 236.
53. S. Pratapa Reddy, *Andhrula Sanghika Charitra* (Telugu), 1949, p. 82.
54. *Sri Vasavi Kanyakapuranam*, 1951, Chapter 32, Stanzas, 12, 13.
55. E.C. III. MI.22, Introduction, p. 21.
56. Sivaratrimahatyamu, Ch. IV, V.25.
57. E.C. VIII, Sb. 106
58. Barbosa, 1, pp. 213-16.
59. R. Sewell, *A Forgotten Empire*, p. 82.
60. Purchas, *His Pilgrims*, X, pp. 94-96.
61. Sewell translated accounts of both Paes and Nuniz, *A Forgotten Empire*, pp. 372-73.
62. E.C. VIII, Sb, 165.
63. Sewell, *A Forgotten Empire*, p. 373.
64. Barbosa, 1, pp. 218-19.
65. E.C. VII, SK, 93.
66. E.C. III, Md. 103.
67. Longhurst, *Hampi Ruins*, Fig. 11.
68. S. Pratapa Reddy, *Andhrula Sanghika Charitra*, p. 82.
69. MER, 1950-56, No. 66
70. MER, 1909, No. 557.

71. The original poem reads:

వీరులు దివ్యలింగములు, విఘ్నపు నాయుడు, కల్లిపోతరా
జీరయ భైరవుండు, ముసానమ్మ జయంతియు, నిర్మలాంబునై
కేరెడు గంగధార మడుగే మణికర్ణిక, యన్ని భంగులన్
గారెయపూడి పట్టణము కాశిసుమీ కనుగొన్న వారికిన్

72. *Kridabhiramam*, VV,116-126.

73. E.C. IX, CP, 162.

74. E.C. Vol. IV, Ng. 61.

75. E.C. H.S. 114.

76. E.C. Vol. IX, Ht. 98,99.

77. MER, 1909, Para 73.

78. E.C. IX, H1, 103 A.

79. R. Soma Reddy, op .cit. p.48.

80. H.K. Sherwani, '*Deccan: The region of co-existence and integration' in Medieval India - A Miscellany*, 1977, Vol. 4, p. 147.

81. Natalie Zemon Davis, "From 'Popular' to religious cultures" in *Reformation Europe: A Guide to Research* (ed.) Steven Ozment, St. Louis, 1982, pp. 312-43.

82. *Basavarajiyamu*, 1-135.

83. *Vaidyachintamani*, part I, pp. 353-73.

84. Purchas, *Pilgrims*, X, pp. 253-54.

85. Kaul, H.K. *Travellers India: An Anthology*, O.U.P. Delhi, 1980, p. 298.

86. Duvvapadu Kaifiat, *Mackenzie Manuscripts*, Vol. III, No. 100, *Epigraphica Indica*, Vol.3, p. 291.

87. *South Indian Inscriptions*, Vol. 16, Nos. 11,12, 21, 26, 33, 39, 42, 43, 522; *Warangal district inscriptions*, Nos. 46, 50; *Epigraphica Indica*, Vol. I, pp. 71.

88. Srisailam Kaifiyat, *Mackenzie Manuscripts*, 127, No. 964, S.I.I. Vol. 16, No. 63, 86, 87, *Epigraphica Indica*, Vol. 3, p. 291.

89. K. Sarojini Devi, F.No. 153

90. M.L.K. Murthy, 'Environment, Royal Policy and Social Formation in Eastern Ghats of South India, A.D. 1000-1500', in *P.I.H.C.* 53rd session, Warangal, 1993.

91. S.I.I. Vol. 16, No. 50,53, Duvvapadu Kaifiyat, *Mackenzie Manuscripts*, Vol. III, No.100, Ahobilam Kaifiyat, *Mackenzie Manuscripts*, Vol. 100, No. 526.
92. S.I.I. Vol. 10, No. 504.
93. N. Venkataramanayya, *Further sources of Vijayanagara History*, p. 107.
94. A.R.E. 1911-12, pp.89-90.
95. Syed Basha Biyabini, 'Impact of early saints of Khuttagulla of Anantapur district, 16th cent. A.D.' in *APHC*, 1991, p.104.
96. H.K. Sherwani, *History of Qutb Shah dynasty*, 1974, p. 654-56.
97. Ibid., p.655.

3

POPULAR RELIGION IN PERCEPTION

The attempts to Sanskritize the local forest and village Gods and Goddesses gave rise to a large corpus of myths and legends in medieval Andhra. As we have already noted in the previous chapter, local manifestations of divine were often incorporated into Brahmanical religion through incarnations either as *Siva* or *Vishnu*. Local Goddesses were integrated with *Durga* or *Shakti*. This necessitated a lot of myths which explained and redefined the relationships at popular level.

This myth making was not confined to any particular sect. *Saivism, Vaishnavism, Brahmanical* sects vied with each other, to incorporate many local, aboriginal Gods and Goddesses. With the incorporation of these local deities, it became easy for caste oriented society to assimilate many autochthonous elements who worshipped these deities. This acculturation was facilitated by the concept of *Bhakti* which transcends caste, creed and other barriers. *Bhakti* also assured *svarga* or *vaikunta* (heaven) to all people including *Panchamas*.[1] Illustrating some of these myths becomes essential here before we proceed to discuss their relevance in relation to popular culture.

Mala Dasari Myth

In Telugu the word *mala* means, among other things, a *panchama* (one born in the untouchable caste) and dasari means a devote of *Vishnu*. Hence *mala-dasari* indicates an untouchable man by birth who is a devotee of *Vishnu* by choice. It is, of course, a common name, and his actual name is not mentioned anywhere in the poem.[2]

When Vishnu descended to the earth as *Varaha* (the wild boar incarnation) he dwelt for sometime in a village called *Kurungudi* in the Tamil country, and hence the temple there acquired great sanctity and came to be regarded as *divya desa* (sacred place), as *Alvars* sang the praises to Lord, he manifested there.[3]

This story is actually related by no less a person than *Vishnu* himself in his *Varaha avatar* (wild boar incarnation) to *Bhudevi* (Goddess of earth). It occurs in *Varaha-purana* also. Srikrishnadevaraya writes this myth to drive home the point that caste was no bar to receive ever flowing grace of *Vishnu*.

Panchama devotee was greatly attached to the God in the *Kurungudi* temple and visited it early in the morning every day and sang songs extolling him in the *Mangala-Kaisiki raga*.[4] He did not, of course, enter the shrine, but stood outside the edifice, and sang songs to the accompaniment of a stringed musical instrument, dancing in ecstasy all the while. He would thus offer worship to the Lord through songs of praise, especially in a *raga* dear to *Vishnu*, till noon, drank the water that flowed from the sanctum sanctorum as *tirtha*, received food-offering (*prasada*) from some *sudra* devotee, and returned home, after consuming the sacred food. Though he was untouchable by birth, his conduct was noble, wherein he resembled a ruby which is not stained even when held in a soiled cloth.[5]

It so happened one night that a cat entered a hen-coop in his neighbourhood and so the roosters began to crow. The *panchama* devotee mistook the noise as a sign of the approaching dawn. He rose at once and got ready to go to the temple at *Kurungudi* to wake the Lord there with his songs in the *raga mangala-kaisiki*.[6] It was still dark, however, and on the way he trod on a creeper, which people believed led travellers astray. So he lost his way, passed through a dreary region, and ended up near a huge banyan tree, where the stench of corpses, skulls and raw, untanned skins fouled the air, indicating the presence of the evil spirit in the vicinity.[7]

The devotee saw before him a *Brahma-rakshasa* (a Brahmana demon) named *Kumbhajanudu* very huge and grotesque in appearance. As the *panchama* was hefty and had served in the army at one time, he tried to offer resistance to the demon for sometime, though he realized full well the futility of his struggle. Not only was he a trained fighter, but also a learned man, when the demon was about to kill him for food, he lectured to him on the undesirability of consuming flesh. But it was in vain that he quoted scriptures, for the demon said,

> "Do not kill us with your learning. Have we
> not studied all these *sastras* and *vedas*?
> All this effort of yours will only end
> in my feeling that the flesh of the learned
> fellow is quite tasty".[8]

The devotee realised the futility of argument with a man turned demon. Instead, he made an appeal to his sentiment, he told him about his vow of singing the praises of the Lord in the temple at *Kurungudi* before dawn everyday. It was getting late for the discharge of the sacred duty, so he pleaded with the *rakshasa* to allow him to visit the temple and offer devotional service to the Lord through music, earnestly assuring him that he would return to the place promptly after the act of *kainkarya* (service) and offer himself as food to his benefactor.[9]

When the demon heard this plea, he was greatly amused. He touched the devotee of Vishnu playfully on the cheek and said,

> "You are pretty clever, my dear fellow! Did
> you not indulge in highway robbery for your
> living for decades and became a dasari
> only recently? I surely admire you for

> your temerity in trying to cheat me and
> escape from my clutches.
>
> Is there a land somewhere in the world where
> a man heeds such an appeal and lets off
> a fellow who is within his grasp as
> food? And is there also a land on earth
> where a man returns of his own accord
> to get consumed as food, just to keep
> his word? It is obvious that I shall not
> let you go just to please you, and equally
> obvious that you will not return, if
> I allow you to go. Why, therefore, this discussion,
> these words, regrets and grief?"[10]

As soon as he heard these words of the demon, the devotee closed his ears (for fear that he might have to hear such outrageous talk still further), uttered the word "*Narayana*" (to purify himself from the sin of hearing such blasphemous utterances), and promptly made pledge.[11] He said:

> "If I don't return to you after my morning
> prayers, I shall have committed the grievous
> sin of considering some other God as the equal
> of Vishnu, at whose glance this world is created,
> in whom it finds its sustenance, and again,
> in whom it ends."

The *rakshasa* was impressed by those solemn words, and let the devotee go. After delighting the deity with his songs, especially in the *mangala kaisiki raga*, the *dasari* came back hastily to the demon and offered himself as food, the demon was awe-stuck by the truthfulness of the man, and at once made circumambulation (*Pradakshina*) to him, fell at his feet, and pressed him in reverence.[12]

Then the *rakshasa* burst into eulogy, and said,
"I know of many Gods, demons, kings and sages
in this wide world who received just praise
for keeping their word in other matters, but
there never was man like you till now
who kept the unusual pledge of offering his own
body as food. I have lived long,
and known the world quite well. I solemnly
declare that there is none on earth comparable
to you in truthfulness."[13]

It was now the turn of the devotee to praise the demon. He embraced him, and said,

"I feel a sense of fulfilment because you so graciously allowed me to go to the temple and offer worship to *Hari* (God). Pledges after all, are fickle, and a man in danger makes a million promises. Letting a man go, when he is ready at hand for consumption, is most unusual. You alone have shown such consideration, there is none so virtuous as you.

Though you were hungry, you allowed me
to go so that I might observe my vow.
We are food ordained to you by Brahma.
There is nothing wrong in your eating
human flesh. So, go ahead now and eat me."[14]

The demon was shocked at the suggestion. He told the devotee that while leading a despicable life all these years, he had been cherishing the hope that some day some saint, some ascetic, might come his way, and release him from the demonical bondage through his grace. Where is salvation found for such wretched creatures as he, if pious souls like the *dasari* do not take pity on them and make them pure.[15] A Philosopher's stone instantly turns into a gold knife, innocent of human blood, and a sword, used in killing a Brahmin, without distinction. Likewise, pious men should be equally consecrate towards the virtuous and the wicked.

He asked the devotee to be compassionate and transfer to him the fruit of singing the praises of Vishnu at *Kurungudi* that morning, so that he might be freed at once from the curse that transformed him into a *Brahma rakshasa*.[16]

The devotee did not readily agree to the plea. How can one think of giving away the fruit of singing *Vishnu's* glory in exchange for one's life.

> "How often were we not born as the guardians
> of the cardinal points (*dik-palas*), and soon
> thereafter as beggars? How often were we not
> born as lions and then as insects? Were we
> not born as elephants and then as mosquitoes
> several times? Were we not born as kings now,
> and then as slaves several times? We were born
> many times as performers of *yajnas*
> (ritualistic sacrifices), and as birds, snakes, and
> devils. Only, we have never before been born as
> devotees of *Vishnu*. Giving up the fruit of offering
> musical service to Vishnu to save one's life
> is sheer madness, like exchanging camphor for salt."[17]

The demon then begged for at least half a share in the merit acquired by the devotee through his prayers that morning. Votaries of *Sri Vishnu* must be compassionate, he pleaded. *Mala-dasari* should show him compassion as *Ramanuja* and *Vedant Desika* showed their compassion for others.[18]

Mala-dasari was moved by the pathetic appeal of the demon and wanted to know how he happened to become a *rakshasa*. The demon told him that originally he had been a scholarly *Brahmin*, named *Soma Sarma*, living in the Chola Kingdom.[19] Pride of learning went to his head and led him to become a trickster. He drifted to *Mathura* and fell into the company of some *Brahmins* who turned into money-lenders. Giving up the austere living dictated by his birth, he became greedy, and amassed wealth. During a journey he was caught on the way and murdered by highway robbers. As he saw that horrible robber before his death, as the last sight, he became a fierce demon, and was dwelling on that Banyan tree.[20]

After telling his past history, he pleaded with *Mala-dasari* to grant him at least the fruit of the last song he sang in the *Mangala-Kaisiki* raga that morning, as that would be enough to release him from his present despicable state.[21]

The devotee replied that the fruit of singing hymns is known only to the Lord, and that it was not for *prapannas* (devotees) who had offered self-surrender to his feet, to measure the merit they acquire through devotional service. He assured the demon that the Lord would surely show him grace. That very moment *Soma Sarma* lost the dreadful form of *Brahmarakshasa*, and assumed the form of a *Vaishnava*.[22] After professing gratitude to his benefactor, he went on a pilgrimage to holy places like *Badari-Narayana kshetra* in the Himalayas, and, by ardent devotion to *Vishnu*, attained liberation (*moksha*) at the end.[23]

When the Lord in *Varaha* incarnation narrated this story of *Mala-dasari* to *Bhudevi* (the Goddess of earth), she decided to descend to earth in the form of *Goda Devi* to serve him by composing and singing songs in his praise, an act most pleasing to *Vishnu*.[24]

This myth can be analyzed in a better way with reference to *Ashrma* ideology,[25] and by understanding the process how different caste categories were conceptualized in medieval Brahmanical thought.[26] *Mala-dasari* belonged to *Mala* caste which was considered as an untouchable caste. In Medieval Andhra, *panchamas* (untouchables) were known as '*Gosagangulu*' and their status was denoted by the word '*Lenka*' which meant a serf.[27]

They faced discrimination of an extreme form—as polluting castes. They have, for centuries, remained rigidly segregated from the main body of the Hindu village community by way of residing outside village precincts, being denied access to village well and so forth.[28]

Although he belongs to *Mala* community, he is said to have acquired spiritual merit by his singing everyday before the idol of *Vishnu* in *Kurungudi* temple everyday. As we have already noted earlier, *Mala-dasari* seems to be parallel to *sanyasi* in that his spiritual merit is acquired and not inherent as in the case of *Brahman*. In the case of sanyasi, he gets his spiritual power by austerity which was replaced by bhakti. In other words, what sanyasi achieves through austerity was achieved by *Maladasari* through *bhakti*. It means that *bhakti* is equal to serve austerity. Through the spiritual power which *Mala-dasari* achieved by devotion or *bhakti* he was able to turn *Brahma-rakshasa* (a brahmana demon, namely Soma Sarma) to a Vaishnavite *brahman*. While this myth reveals some mobility of some untouchable castes, it also justifies *varnashanama-dharma*. This aspect is clear when we see the life of *Mala-dasari*.

Although *Mala-dasari* was a pious *Vishnu* devotee, he still was untouchable.[29] As such he had to observe caste rules of eating and drinking and other related rules. We are told that everyday he would go to the temple early morning to sing before *Vishnu's* idol. However, he never entered precincts of the shrine but stood outside the edifice and sang songs. Again he did not receive *tirtha* (sacred water) from the officiating priest. Neither did he receive *prasada* (food-offering) from the priest. Interestingly he drank water that flowed from sanctum-sanctorum and received *prasada* from some *sudra* devotee and not from a *brahman* priest. By the logic of *Ashrama* ideology, a *sanyasi* has no rights and obligations either as a member of his *varna* or his household.[30]

As we know only *dvija* (twice-born) were allowed to wear sacred thread which signifies initiation into caste. Therefore, *sudras* and other untouchable castes did not wear this sacred thread as they were single-born. So *Mala-dasari* also could not wear it. In the case of *sanyasi* his renunciation to his caste was symbolised by his taking off sacred thread. In *Mala-dasari* case this question did not arise because he did not have this sacred thread. So, while treating his bhakti devotion equal to austerity through which a *sanyasi* acquired spiritual power, he could not be treated as dead symbolically. This was the reason why he retained his *varna* distinction and had to observe caste rules and taboos. The reason why he was eulogized was not only because of his *bhakti* but also because of his observance of *Varnashrama-dharma*.[31] Hence, it becomes very clear that *Mala-dasari* was not rebelling against the system but he was to trying to adhere to the caste based social norms.

Vaishnavism made lot of compromises and gave space to people of all castes in the face of rivalry with *saivism* and also threat from Islam which entered Indian soil and was trying to take root. Interestingly, it appears that *Vaishnavism* made compromises not only in medieval Andhra but also in medieval India in general. As such *Mala-dasari* case was not an isolated incident. In other parts also, *Vaishnavism* did indulge in integrating lower social groups, *Namdev*, the *simpi*, a tailor and Raidas in North India are a case in point.[32]

Kannappa Legend

Dhurjati, court poet of *Srikrishnadevaraya*, was a *saivite* by faith. He wrote two beautiful poems *srikalahasti mahatyamu* and *Srikalahastisvara satkamu*. The former contains a lot of stories relating to snake and elephant, *Natkirudu*, Yadava king, daughters of a prostitute and story of *Kannappa*. *Dhurjati* wrote all these stories only to drive home the power of Srikalahasti, and its religious significance. However, we have taken the story of *Kannappa* for our discussion.

Dhurjati says that this story occurred in *Kali* age. *Kannappa's* original name was *Tinnadu*. He was born in a tribal village called *Vudumuru*. His father was *Nathanathudu* and mother was

Tamde.[33] Actually *Tinnadu* was no less a person than *Arjuna* in *Dwapara* age. As he could not attain *svarga* because he killed his own kith and kin, *Siva* ordered him to be born as the son of *Kirata* (Tribal) king.[34] He grew up and went for hunting to the forest one day. He was tired in hunting and fell asleep under a tree. Then he had a dream. In that dream he saw a *Jangama* (saivite priest) who told him that there was a *Siva Linga* in the vicinity and asked *Tinnadu* to go and worship *Siva*. Then he woke up from sleep and started searching for the *linga.*[35] When he found *Linga* he felt very happy, then he worshiped linga and asked *Siva* why he was in the forest. He requested *Siva* to go to his house. However, *Siva* did not reply. So, *Tinnadu* thought that Siva was willing to stay in the forest. Therefore, he also decided to stay back in the forest and worship him.[36] Everyday he would carry roasted meat strung together on an arrow, mouthful of water and few flowers tucked on to his hair. On reaching *linga*, he would spit over it from his mouth, take flowers out of his hair and put them on the top of *linga* and place roasted meat and thus would perform his worship. *Siva* was pleased with his worship.[37]

At the same time there was a *Brahman* who worshiped *Siva* in his *Brahmanical* way, one day he noticed roasted meat and other things. This desecration, as the Brahman considered it, gave moral pain to him, and, in his extreme distress of mind, he appealed to Siva himself as to who brought about this desecration and why *Siva* should have suffered it. *Siva* appeared to him in a dream and pointed out to him that *Boya* hunter Tinnadu's devotion to Siva was so whole-hearted and hence was more pleasing to him than even that of those who had offered him excellent prayers with a mind prepared by the long study of the Vedas and *Vaidika-Agamas*. *Siva* directed much distressed *Brahman* to remain in hiding and see for himself.[38]

As usual *Tinnadu* brought meat and requested *Siva* to eat, *Siva* did not eat meat. He was trying to figure out why *Siva* did not eat meat. He wondered why *Siva* did not eat meat and expressed his feelings in these words:

> "*Kaalova, krovvavo, madam*
> *galeno, chavigavo kammagavo, Neekun*
> *jaalavo yalavadava tina*
> *Velakarakutlu? Parvateesvara! cheppuma*"[39]

It means that husband of Parvati, is this meat not roasted; or not fatty, or is it completely fried? or is it not tasty? Is it not going to satiate your hunger, or do you eat meat or not? If not why are you not eating this meat. He does not leave *Siva* here, he goes on asking, why don't you eat? are you not hungry, or don't I have devotion (*Bhakti*); please eat this meat without making me sad.[40] In the meantime water started coming out of one of the eyes of *Siva*. Then *Tinnadu* thought that *Siva* had got some eye infection. So he brought some herbals to cure his eye, but to no avail.[41] Then blood started oozing out of one of the eyes of *Siva's* idol. First *Tinnadu* fainted at the sight of it and when he came back to himself, he took his bow and arrows and looked about for those who might have done this harm. Unable to find anybody he sat about thinking as to how exactly he should cure it. Do what he might the blood still continued flowing. Then it struck him that the best way to cure such a disease was to put flesh for flesh and eye for eye. He pulled out with an arrow his own right eye and put it in the place of right eye of *Siva*. He found that the bleeding stopped.[42] He was so delighted with his performance that he danced in sheer joy. *Siva* made his other eye bleed. When *Tinnadu* was about to pull out his other eye to substitute it for the bleeding one of *Siva, Siva* put forth his arms from the Linga and took hold of his hands and cried at "eye friend eye" (*kannappa, kannappa*) and this ejaculation of *Siva* gave him the name *kannappa*. Then Siva told that *Brahman*, called *Sivadvijudu*, about *Tinnadu's* bhakti. *Siva* asked both of them to ask for some boons. Then both of them asked *Siva* to be united with them. So *Siva* agreed and they were united with *Siva* at that very moment.[43]

Kannappa's myth reveals the interaction and consequent syncretism, which was a natural corollary , of *brahmanical* sect with tribal people. These tribal people were variously described by medieval inscriptions and literature as *Kirata, Atavika, Sabara, Chenchu, Yerukala, Polinda, Boya, Manyamjanulu* etc. It is to be noted that our sources rarely make distinction among tribes. They almost treat all these names as synonyms. These people have been described as living in their own settlements, which were isolated areas. Some other tribes made this living by hunting-gathering, others took to pastoralism and still others took to agriculture, over the period they came into contact with rural and urban areas through many processes.[44]

With the conquering and annexation of many forested and pastoral landscapes by the state the forest peoples (hunter-gatherers like *chenchus, Boya, Yerukala*) and pastoralists (*Goll* and *Kuruba*) became important in the political, economic and social milieu on the one hand, in the organization of settlement frontiers on the other.[45]

The acculturation and integration of *Boyas* a hunter-gather tribe, is classic example of how many tribes have been effected through acculturation and gradually became integrated with *varna* based society. *Boyas* were a warlike autochthonous people of *Andhra Pradesh*. They primarily lived in thickly forested mountainous tracts of *Prakasam, Nellore* and *Chittoor* districts. They were known for their tenacity in hunting and never missed their mark. In some medieval inscriptions the homeland of Boyas was referred to as *Boyaviharadesa*,[46] *Boyavidu*[47] and *Boyavila*.[48] Boyaviharadesa of inscriptions roughly corresponds to eastern taluks of *Nellore* district viz., *Kanigiri, Atmakur* and *Udayagiri*. *Boyas* hold that they were the legitimate children of *Nisada*, mythical king and son of *Vanaraja* who was depicted in the puranas. They treat *kuruvas, yanadis* and *chenchus* as his illegitimate children.[49]

The eastern Chalukyan records of seventh century A.D. suggest that the *Boya* priests started emulating their counterparts in the Brahmanical society in mastering *Vedic* learning and performing Vedic rituals. Most of them added the suffix *sarma* to their names which may be taken to mean 'Vedic Scholar'.[50]

As we have already pointed out with the annexation of forests and pastoral landscapes the people who lived in those areas also were integrated in the power structure.[51] This gave rise to new institutions such as *Kavaligars* and *Polygars*. *Kavaligars* were appointed to safeguard the villages, pilgrims and trade routes in the hilly and forest area. *Gujjala Paramappa Naidu*, a *Boya* was appointed as Kavaligar of Adoni, Gutti and Kurnool areas.[52] In the same way villages which were founded along the hilly and forested area were organized into *palems*; these were given to the forest peoples, pastoralists and the dominant peasants with hereditary rights. The prominent among those who were holding *palems* as (*polygars*) were *Boyas*, *Gollas*, *Kapus* and *Reddys*.[53] *Boyas* were also drawn into the temple service as cattle keepers.[54] and as the staff of the temple service,[55] and *Boya* girls were admitted into the *Sani Munnuvuru*. An inscription from *Nadendla* mentions that the grand daughter of *Peddana Boya* as the *sani* of the temple of *Mulasthaneswara*.[56] We have already noted that some boyas reached higher echelons of power like that of *mahamandalesvaras*. *Golla polygars* claimed themselves as *Yadavas* like those of *Kunkanur*, *Dukikonda* and *Maddikera*.[57]

It is only against this backdrop that we can analyse the above myth, namely *Kannapa* myth. In the myth, Tinnadu was said to be son of a *Yerukala redu* (king) in one verse,[58] in another verse as the son of a *Chenchu redu*,[59] and in yet another as being born to a *Bhilla Nayaka* chieftain due to a boon given by Siva. The author of *Sri Kalahasti Mahatyamu* was not clear exactly as to what tribe he actually belonged. It is natural that he did not concern about his tribe. Because his purpose in writing this poem was different. His main purpose in writing this was to provide sanctity to *Sri Kalahasti* as a pilgrimage centre. As such all the stories and myths which he gave in this work were intended to project *Sri Kalahasti* as a special sacred place where God was supposed to stay, where forgiveness for sins could be obtained, where barren women could get children, where people irrespective caste, could get *Kailasam*.

Secondly, there are clear attempts to win over tribes like *Boya*, *Chenchu*, *Yerrukala* etc. to this sect. *Saivism* and *Vaishnavism* competed with each other to propagate their creed among tribes. *Dhurjati* tries to co-opt Boyas through the myth of Kannapa. Accordingly Kannapa was said to be *Arjuna.* in his *purvajanma* (previous birth).[60] Simple worship of Tribal people and organised religion of Brahmanas were contrasted here. Kannappa's bhakti, however rudiment it might appear, was considered greater than that of a learned Brahman. Siva liked the way of the worship of both *Kannappa* and *Sivadvija* although the former's worship was non-brahmanical and latter's brahmanical. As we have seen in the previous pages, tribal people became very important in the power structure as the state kept on annexing many forests and hilly areas, during medieval Andhradesa, many tribes achieved social mobility and also became an apparatus in the administration. Many *Boyas* were employed as *talaris* for performing police duties such as reporting crime and illicit distillation, catching robbers and punishing murderers.[61] However, some of them also emerged as powerful *polygars* during *Vijayanagara* period. With the downfall of Vijayanagara Empire, these *polygars* carved out their own little kingdoms. So Kannappa's myth was an attempt by Brahmanas come to terms with forest tribes, as the Brahmanas started interacting with tribal people. Above all some *Boya* chieftains with economic prosperity and rise in social hierarchy, made gifts of cattle, money and land to the temples.

Narasimha (Man-Lion God) Myth

Sukasaptati, written by *Palavekari Kadirepati* around 1660 A.D indicates in a context that some tribals namely *Chenchus* and *Yerukala* tribal people were worshipping Narasimha. Many folk songs connected with this narrate episodes in which Narasimha, the man-lion God wanders into the forest of *Nallamal* Hills and falls in love with the daughter of a *Chenchu* king who was on a hunting prowl.[62] Then a dialogue takes place between Narasimha and Chenchu maid. This myth is preserved in their folk songs as follows:

Narasimha:

Who art thou, o damsel. Figure of pure gold?
Who is our peer in this whole world
What handsome features, delicate frame,
Enchanting form and winning face,
Why stand'st thou firm and far from me
While with cupid's fury stand I transformed.

Chenchu Maid:

What is it to thee who I am?
Come not near me or cross my way.
Speak from a distance, in courtesy.
If not, thou shalt taste soon enough
The sharpness of the arrow from my bow
O thou of cheeks so large with protruding teeth bulging eyes
And unruly whiskers,
Forehead marks long and straight
And matted hair and rounded waist.
Stop, where thou art,
Frightened am I not,
Thou will be vanquished in no time
By the fury of my kith and kin.

Narasimha:

O lass, why roamest thou in the wilderness
And direct not thy glance at me?
What crime have I committed
That thou shouldst be so hard hearted?
Cluster of glittering diamonds art thou
My tongue has no words to utter,
In praise of him, who created thee,
Come on as thou art, cruel or kind

Treading the woods, climbing the hills,
But dodge me not.

Chenchu Maid:

Figure of lion and man combined
How art thou worthy of me?
Away with thy dalliance
Beware of my piercing dart
Flee to thy mountain fast

Narasimha:

O girl of graceful gait
With bodice of rubies and pears
My chest heaves
To hold thee in embrace
I am the Lord of *Bhadra* Hill
The daughter of the mountain,
Kind *Parvati* is all praise for me
The king of the Gods, Lord *Indra*
Offers worship unto me
But parted from thee, I cannot remain
Awake, I cannot endure,
And sleep will not come to my eyes

As the dialogue continues slowly both of them are drawn to each other. Love quickens their hearts, they speak in dalliance.

The song is continued:

Chenchu Maid:

Canst thou climb the trees?
Canst thou clear the shrubs?
Canst get honey
Guarded by the buzzing bees?

Narasimha:

Trees can I climb,
Birds can I hit
And sweet honey from the bees
Can I get thee for certain

Chenchu Maid:

Canst thou pierce the jungle growth?
Canst thou get into the thickest tough?
Canst thou strike the elephant
With a fist blow, O lion of Man?

Narasimha:

I can foot the woods all over,
Every kind of fruit will I bring
And all the hill streams can I swim
Everyday water fowl and beast can I hunt
To the Lord of Chenchus will I bow
With Chenchus folk in amity shall
I live

Chenchu Maid:

Canst thou get me the peacocks
With their slant and curved necks?

Narasimha:

Certainly my beloved,
Believe me, I swear here and now
I shall ever by thy word abide[63]

Finally the following song concludes the wedding of Narasimha and Chenchu maid. Thurston gave English translation of this song. This song is sung by two men and a woman.

Wedding:

The Tali was *avaram* leaves[64]
Oh the Lord of *Chenchus*
The *Basikam*[65] was made of the leaf of wild tree leaves
Oh the lord of *Chenchus*
Wild turmeric was used for the *Kankanam*[66]
Oh the Lord of *Chenchus*
Wearing a garment of the leaves of the paru tree[67]
Oh the Lord of *Chenchus*
Wearing a bodies made of the leaves of the *Pannu* tree[68]
Oh the Lord of *Chenchus*
Roaming over inaccessible hills
Oh the Lord of *Chenchus*
Wandering through dense forests,
Oh the Lord of *Chenchus*
Committing acts that ought not be done.
Oh the Lord of *Chenchus*
Obulesa's[69] marriage is celebrated,
Oh the Lord of *Chenchus*
A four cornered dais was made
Oh the Lord of *Chenchus*
On the dais arrows were struck
Oh the Lord of *Chenchus*
Bamboo rice was used to throw on the heads of the bridal pair
Coconut shells were placed over the pointed arrows.
Oh the Lord of *Chenchus*
The marriage was thus celebrated[70]

According to another version, it is not *Chenchu* maid who test *Narasimha*.[71] When *Narasimha* sought the hand of *Chenchu* maid, chenchu woman reciprocates and seeks her father's consent for the marriage. The *Chenchu* king, to satisfy himself that *Narasimha*, a stranger, will be suitable husband for his daughter puts him to several tests: he was to show his prowess in hunting, climb tall trees and precipices and extract honey, and dig out termite mounds and collect queen termites (a favourite food item for the *Chenchus*). *Narasimha* accomplishes these tasks competently and wins the hand of the *Chenchu* woman. In these folk songs, *Narasimha* is a non-brahmanical pastoral folk God and pleads with the *Chenchu* girl to accept him.[72]

Parallel to this *Brahmanical* version, in this version Narasimha goes in the *Nallamala* forest in a rage, after exterminating the demon *Hiranyakasipu*. He chances upon the beautiful chenchu girl (the daughter of the *Chenchu* king) and thinks that she is his consort *Lakshmi*, and follows her to the *Chenchu* settlements.[73] Even when he is told that she is not his wife, he solicits her hand, marries her and takes her to his heavenly abode. She has become *Chenchu Lakshmi*. In these two versions Narasimha is an incarnation of *Vishnu*.

In the same way *Chenchus* of southern part of *Nalamala* Hills, where famous *Ahobilam* temple exists, think that Narasimha is the brother-in-law of the *Chenchus*. For the God *Mallikarjuna* of *Srisailam* (northern part of *Nallamala* Hills), is fondly called *Srisila Mallanna* (incarnation of Siva, a *Chenchu* beauty is his favourite wife). *Srisaila Mallanna*, likewise is also the brother-in-law of *Chenchus* of this region. At *Ahobilam* and *Srisailam* temples *Chenchus* have special rights in the ritual performances.

This myth clearly shows an attempt by *Brahmanical* religion to incorporate *Chenchus* in to its fold. *Chenchus* like their Boya counter-parts also entered administration as *talaris* (watchmen).[74] *Vaishnava* sect tried to incorporate *Chenchu* tribe through *Narasimha* myth. Narasimha who was basically a non-brahmin folk God was given *Brahman* colour as an incarnation of *Vishnu*. *Vishnu*, who is a *brahmanical* God ran after a *Chenchu* maiden. Although she refused him at first, he persisted to win her hand. As we have seen in the dialogue, *Vishnu* did not mind to adopt the living conditions and food habits of *Chenchus*. This shows the flexibility of *Brahmanism* to adjust to any condition in order to survive and maintain its hegemony.

Ellamma Myth

She has got different names such as *Mahuramma*, *Akkalidevi*, *Ekavira* and *Renuka*. There is an interesting myth about this goddess. *Kridabhiramam* says that people worshipped *Ekavira* along with *Kakati*, the *Kuladevata* of *Kakatiyas*.[75] *Renuka* was the wife of *Jamadagni* a famous *Rishi* (Vedic seer) and to them was born *Parasu Rama*, one of the incarnations of *Vishnu*.[76] *Renuka* was so chaste in mind that she could carry water in a mass without any vessel, and her wet cloth would fly up into the air and remain there till it was dry. One day, as she was coming home after bathing, some of the *Gandharvas* or heavenly singers flew over her, and she saw their reflection in the ball of water in her hand. She could not stop admiring their beauty, and, through this slight lapse from the perfect ideal of chastity, she lost her power, the water flowed down to the ground, and her cloth fell from the sky.[77] So she arrived home with no water and with a wet cloth. The *rishi* questioned her as to the meaning of this and she confessed her fault. Her stern husband ordered his son *Parasurama* to take her into the wilderness and cut off her head. So the son took his mother away, but when they came to the appointed place *Renuka* met a *madiga* woman, and in her longing for sympathy embraced her in her arms. So *Parasurama* cut off both their heads together and went back in great sorrow.[78] Another variant of myth says that when *Parasurama* beheaded her on the order of his father, the head fell in the street of *Bavanis* and she became their goddess.[79] *Bavanis* are identified with *Madigas*, an untouchable caste. Parasurama's father promised him a reward he chose to ask in return for his obedience. So *Parasurama* asked that his mother might be restored to life. The father granted his request and gave him some water in a vessel and a cane, telling him to put his mother's head on her body, sprinkle the water on her and tap her with cane.

In his eager haste he put his mother's head on the body of a madiga woman and vice-versa, and restored both of them to life. The woman with Brahman head and madiga body was afterwards worshipped as *Renuka*,[80] while the woman with madiga head and

Brahman body was worshipped as the goddess *Yellama*. To Yellamma buffaloes are sacrificed; but to Renuka goats and cocks but not buffaloes.[81]

Posamma Myth

According to the tradition, *Posamma* is the daughter of Siva. She is the goddess of small-pox. As soon as she is born, she asks her father to celebrate her birthday. At first *Siva* says that he is too busy to celebrate it. Then in order to show her power, she causes *Siva* to suffer from small-pox. Unable to bear this he requests her to cure him. Then she cures him with neem leaves. She is so powerful that she can influence her own father.[82]

These two myths are interesting in that it shows the ritual process through which syncretism of both Dravidian cults and *Brahmanism* has been brought about. It suggests quasi-brahmanization of the village goddesses; they are made acceptable to the *brahmans* who were increasingly drawn into interaction with the non-brahmanical communities on the one hand and the sphere of village culture on the other.[83] We have already noted that under *Vijayanagara* rulers, *Devabhoga* grants were on increase.[84] The *amaranayakas*, who were military officials, were mostly of the dominant peasant castes. The *sudras* and other tribal people were given a place in temple rituals and share in temple honours. Some tribal and untouchable castes became part and parcel of *Ayagara* system. They were also included in twelve *Ayagars* who were twelve professional caste people to serve village society. So such a phenomenon as Sanskritization of forest and village goddess was perhaps a natural corollary to the emergence of *Agrahara* and *Devabhoga* grants in the countryside.[85]

Festivals: Tirunals, Jataras and Vratas

Festivals were part and parcel of the religious life of the people during this period. They were celebrated by all people. It was also one of the overlaps of popular culture. We are not in a position to ascertain as to what was the origin of these festivals. Neither can we establish the functional aspects of these festivals. By and large these festivals were observed by people according to their belief system. Religious significance apart, these festivals gave a tremendous boost to the growth of trade and artisan production. Besides, some common festivals, sectarian festivals were also observed by different sects. For example, some festivals were considered particularly sacred by *Saivites* or *Vaishnavites*. Some temples also conducted festivals.

Vaisakha Paurnami

This is celebrated on the full moon in *Vaisakha*, third month in Telugu months of lunar cycle (April-May). As the seeds which were sown earlier started sprouting after early showers, peasants celebrated this day as a festival. People used to visit temples on this day and celebrate it as a *molakala punmnami* (sprouting full moon). On this day people used to celebrate *Rathotsavam*, (chariot ceremony) in the local temples, and would donate many things. An inscription records the gifts made on this day.[86]

Sivaratri

This festival falls in the month of *Magha* (January-February) and was very popular during medieval *Andhradesa*. *Sivaratri Mahatyamu*, which was written by the celebrated Telugu poet, *Srinatha*, talks about the significance of *Sivaratri*.[87] The plot of this work is weaved around a Brahman youth, the son of a minister to king *Hemangada*, the ruler of *Ratnapuri*. The *Brahman* youth named *Sukumara* fell bad ways and addicted to wine and women at a tender age and indulged in all sorts of vices. On reporting his behaviour to king, he was banished from the kingdom.

During his banishment he reached *Hevna Mandala*. However, his banishment did not bring out any change in his mind set. So he developed illicit relations with a low caste woman, *Chandalika*. He ate meat cooked by her and finally eloped with her to another region. He had four children by her and when she died he violated the chastity of his own daughters. He also got two sons through them.[88]

One day he went to the *Siva* temple to steal some flowers from the garden for the use of his daughters. He had the *darshan* of Lord when he went into the temple. As it was *Sivaratari* day, many devotees gathered in the temple. They spent the night in the exposition of *Siva Puranas*. In this way they were keeping the holy vigil. *Sukumara* waited for an opportunity to steal flowers until midnight. However, he could not steal flowers, went home. From that day onwards he gave up his evil ways and took to good life. Finally, when he died, he went to Siva Loka – *Saivite* heaven. This is the significance of *Sivaratri*. Although he committed many unpardonable sins he went to heaven only because he observed *Sivaratri*.

Srinatha relates the same kind of story in his *kasi khandam*. In this story, another *Brahman* boy, *Gunanidhi*, like *Sukumar* fell bad ways. However, unlike *Sukumara*, *Gunanidhi* tried to flee after stealing from a Saiva temple. But he got killed in the process and went to *Sivaloka*. *Siva* sent *divyavimana* to bring *Gunanidhi*. Just for worshipping *Siva* on Sivaratri day Lord *Siva* granted him a second life.[89]

Another medieval *Andhradesa* literary work, *Basava-puranam* says that devotees spent the night in listening to the stories of *Siva*, going round the temple singing and dancing, witnessing cock fights and ram fights. The temple was decorated on the *Sivaratri* day with garlands of leaves made of copper, trunks of plaintain tree, etc. On *Sivaratri* day people from all parts of the empire went in large numbers on pilgrimage to celebrated *Saiva* centres like Srisailam and Kalahasti.[90]

Navaratrulu

It was a nine day festival in honour of Goddess *Durga*. It started on *Asvayuga Sudha Podyami*, and lasted for nine days. The tenth day was celebrated as *Vijaya Dasami*. This festival became very popular during Vijayanagara Empire. It was celebrated both by the King, his courtiers and common people. The worship of Devi was of three kinds: *Satvika*, *Rajasa* and *Tamasa*: *Satvika* was performed with *Japam*, *mantra* and rice offerings; *Rajasa* required animal sacrifices; *Tamasa* was with offerings exclusively of liquor and flesh without any *Mantra*.

Domingos Paes witnessed the celebrations of this festival when he was travelling in the *Vijayanagara* Empire. According to him, celebrations commenced on the first day with installing of *Kalasa* or the idol. The *Kalasa* was made of gold and was embowered in roses. It was placed on the richly ornamented throne, standing on a dais in the house of victory within the palace enclosure. King offered worship on all nine days with the assistance of *Brahmanas*. He also worshipped eleven horses and four elephants which were beautiful and richly caparisoned, then twenty four buffaloes and one hundred and fifty sheep were slaughtered.[91] This is interesting in the sense that both *Saivism*, *Vaishnavism* and *Brahmanism* did not subscribe to animal offerings. Although some *Vijayanagara* rulers were either *Siva* or *Vishnu* followers, they also gave animal sacrifices to *Durga*. We have already pointed out that all village Goddesses were worshipped with animal sacrifices. It is precisely because they were conceived as malevolent spirits who were responsible for some diseases and epidemics. These local Goddesses were also treated as manifestations of *Durga*. It seems that even some sections of elite appear to have shared the same belief. *Homa* or lighting of the sacred fire was also a part of worship. During worship king threw consecrated powder into the fire.[92]

During these celebrations many professionals displayed their skill. Dancers, musicians, wrestlers and acrobats, poets and *pandits* exhibited their skills. The dancing girls (probably *Devadasis*) dressed in fine silks, richly embroidered and decked with ornaments made of gold in laid with precious stones, impressed the on-lookers. Wrestlers and acrobats, experts as they were in their fields, presented breath- taking feats. All these performances constituted its afternoon programme of each day.[93]

At night, many torches were lit which illuminated the whole scene. These lights made night as though it was day. Many items of amusements were also introduced. There was a parade before the king in the manner of a march-past.[94] A tableau in the parade consisted of men on horse-back engaged in a mock battle, "these horses like the hobby horses made in Portugal for the feast of the *Carpo de Dios*". Others come with casting nets, fishing and capturing the men that are in the arena. At the end of the amusements were many rockets and different sorts of fires, also castles that burn and fling out from themselves many bombs and rockets.[95]

After amusements, there was a march-past of the triumphal cars belonging to the captains, covered with fine silks exquisitely embroidered in intricate patterns. Then there was a display of horses covered with cloth of very fine stuff of the kings' colours, with floral decorations on their heads and led by the state horse, the state horse was decorated more elegantly than the others and carried two state umbrellas.[96] After parading them round the arena twice, the horses were arranged in five or six lines with the state horse in the leading position and all facing the king. Then the high priest of the king offered them worship with a bowl of coconut, rice and flowers. Other Brahmanas followed him carrying a pot of water in their hands.[97]

Then fair and young as they were, sixty women, dressed in fine silks and wearing priceless jewels, went a little forward carrying in their hands vessels of gold containing lighted lamps. When women retired, the king offered his final prayers to the idol. This was followed by the sacrifice of a large number of buffaloes and sheep.[98] Then the king would have his supper for he fasted on all the nine days and ate only at midnight. This routine was followed on all the nine days of the *navaratri* festival. Paes further says that festival came to an end with the slaughter of two hundred and fifty buffaloes and four thousand five hundred sheep.[99]

The king held a review of all his armed forces in the presence of the presiding deity at the end of nine day festival. The military personnel of the king headed by their captains, clad in rich clothes, arrayed themselves according to their ranks. The king reviewed the troops on his state horse accompanied by attendants carrying two umbrellas of state gilded and covered with crimson velvet. In front of all, the idol which was worshipped during *navaratri* was carried in a very large cage, close to the king.[100]

Vasantotsavam (Spring Festival)

Vasantotsavam or spring festival was another major festival which was conducted annually with great enthusiasm.[101] The festival was celebrated in the name of *Kama* or *Madana*, the God of love and his associate *Vasanta*.[102] According to tradition, as Siva assumed *Pasupata Vrata* and absorbed himself in *Yoga*, *Parvati* grew restless over his prolonged *Samadhi*. It was also because *Siva* took to this *vrata* immediately after their marriage. She requested *Indra* to help her and he sent *Manmatha Rati* and *Vasantha* to disturb Siva's penance and make him obey the dictates of Natural law. So these three started their job. When *Siva* felt disturbed, he opened his eyes and found *Manmatha*, with his bow made of sugar-cane stalk and fitted with *Puspaka Bana*, taking aim. Siva got angry and opened his third eye from which emanated deadly fire which reduced *Manmatha* to ashes.[103] Rati, Manmadha's consort, was plunged in grief. Realising that she was responsible for the catastrophe, Parvati appealed to *Siva*. *Indra* and other *devas* also appealed to *Siva*. Moved by their appeals *Siva* agreed to revive *Manmadha*. However, his revival was subject to a condition that only one day in the year (the thirteenth day of the bright half of the month of *chaitra*) he would assume the bodily form and that for the rest of year remains without any physical form. Thus *Vasanta* festival commemorates the resurrection of *Manmadha*.[104]

On this day dramas were enacted to win royal patronage and admiration of the public. Srikrishnadevaraya's *Jambavati Kalyanam* was enacted before the king and a large number of people assembled to witness *vasantotsavam*. Contemporary records reveal the way in which this was celebrated. The ministers looked after the arrangement of the festival. An elegantly and elaborately decorated pavilion with golden arches in which were set up a number of altars decorated with precious stones, on which were placed the images of *kama*, *vasanta* and others. Various designs were drawn with camphor on the floor of the *vedi* and beautified with *purnakalasas* or vessels filled with water.[105] Then the king seated on the back of his state horse in great splendour, followed by his army, poets, musicians, dancers, jesters, knights and others retinue, marched out to the accompaniment of music. The king's procession after crossing the city gate reached a nearby garden. As the king was taking stroll in the garden, his *vidusaka* composed a verse on a mango leaf saying that the possession of *rasala* or sweet mango tree helped to conquer *kama*, the God of love.[106]

In the meantime some of the damsels in the party played a sport with their lovers, namely, hide and seek among flower plants singing songs with joy, while some others prepared flower garlands and presented them to the king. This was followed by the presentation of tributes by his *samantas* and *amaranayakas*. The tributes consisted of girls, horses, precious stones and other jewels. Then the king in the company of young damsels entered the pavilion where the deities were installed and worshipped at the end of the function, the king sported with beautiful damsels, sprinkling camphor, sandal paste and other perfumed things. All subjects assembled followed him and played *Vasantotsavam*. After finishing bath in Lotus tanks, the king with his queens gave audience to his subjects in the same park under a tree.[107]

Sankranti

This festival was in honour of Sun and was observed by all and sundry. It signified the movement of the sun from one *rasi* to another- in which the Sun enters is designated as Sankranti of the particular rasi.[108] There are twelve *sankrantis* in accordance with twelve rasis. *Devi Purana* identified *sankranti* with Goddess Durga. It says that *Devi* was all pervading and merged herself with year, *ayana*, season, month, fortnight and day.[109] Taking bath in a river on *Makara Sankranti* day was considered to be of great merit.[110] Three days or one day fasting on *Makara Sankranti* was recommended.[111]

The festival was celebrated for three days, i.e., *Bhogi*, *Sankranti* or *Surya Pongal* and *Kanuma*. The *Bhogi* celebrations start with the putting of the fire in front of the house. The second day is called *Surya Pongal* or *Pongal* of the *Surya* and is set apart in honour of the Sun who is regarded as the health-promising God. The third day, i.e., *Kanuma* is the festival of the cattle. A big vessel is filled with water, they put some saffron, the seeds of cotton (*pratti*) and leaves of margosa (*Vepa*). After mixing this well, they go round all the cows and oxen belonging to the house, sprinkling them with water many times, as they turn to four cardinal points. However, women are kept away from this ceremony. Cattle were also decorated with turmeric and flowers on their necks which were aimed as a protection to cattle against malignant *grahas,* evil spirits and poisonous creatures.[112]

Ugadi

It was celebrated as a Telugu new year on the first day of the month *Chaitra* (March-April). One special feature of this festival was preparation of *ugadi pachchadi*. It has also some medicinal value as the ingredients included neem flowers, juice of tamarind mixed with jaggery, small pieces of mango and sugarcane and cumin seeds. An inscription also bears testimony to the observance of this festival.[113]

Somavara Vrata

This *vratam* was observed on the first Monday of either *Sravana*, *Vaisakha*, *Kartika* or *Magha*..[114] On the day of Vrata, Siva was worshipped and total fast was observed. If the person who performed this *Vrata* was a king, he would donate some gifts to local temple.[115]

Kartika Vrata

People observed this in the month of *Kartika*.[116] During the entire month a person, after taking bath in a river, should perform the *Gayatri* mantra and eat only once in the day of sacrificial food or havisya. The lighting of lamps by the performer in the temples of *Siva*, *Candi*, the Sun and other Gods was considered meritorious, eating food in a garden or *vanabhojanam* was considered good.[117]

Dhanurmasa

This was considered important by *Sri Vaishnavas*. All the thirty days of *Magha* were considered *Dhanurmasa*. Everyday the performer of *vrata* should get up early in the morning, offer prayers and *naivedya* to Lord *Vishnu*. A devotee would get a lot of blessings by observing *vrata* even on a single day. *Govindasani*, the daughter of *Polu Nayakkam* of *Sajjarautu* family, provided for thirty *tiruponakam* on the thirty days of the month of *Margali* in *Govindaraja* temple at *Tirupathi* for *Dhanurmasa puja* in 1534.[118] Another person *Rayasam Ramachandra Diksitar* arranged for an offering in Nammalvar's shrine at Tirupati on the thirty days of *Dhanurmasa* in 1535 A.D.[119] In fact, an inscription records the observance of all these festivals.[120]

Pilgrimages (Tirthayatras)

People visited many holy shrines and places which have great sanctity. Places such as *Srikalahasti*, *Ahobilam*, *Srisailam*, *Srikurmam* and *Tirumala* became very important pilgrim centres. It was considered meritorious to visit these holy places on festive occasions, lunar eclipses and other days of religious significance and make gifts to temples and *Brahmanas*.[121] *Krishnadevaraya*, the great emperor of *Vijayanagara* visited *Tirupati* and installed the bronze image of himself and his queen in the temple of *Venkateswara* at Tirupati.[122]

Sri Kalahasti Mahatyamu describes the greatness of *Kalahasti* as a *Saiva Kshetra* and how men and animals reached *Kailasam*. There are many stories such as spider, the serpent and elephant and myth of *Tinnadu*.[123] People believed that if they visited some holy places, their sins would be expiated and would also receive children.[124] People used to bring *lingas* and images of God from holy places and install them in their towns and villages. Travel was also very tedious in those days without proper facilities. So people travelled in groups to escape from robbers and wild animals. Rich people used palanquins as a conveyance. Poor people might have used bullock carts or went on foot. To provide water to the pilgrims, *chalivendras* (water-supplying centres) were set up at many places. This was referred to as *prapa* or water-shed in literary works.[125]

References

1. *Panchamas* were untouchable castes of Medieval Andhra.
2. This myth is taken from *Amuktamalyada* which was written in Telugu by Vijayanagara Emperor Srikṛishnadevaraya, see *Amuktamalyada*, Vijayawada, 1997, p. 98-100.
3. Ibid., p.99
4. *Amuktamalyada*, p. 100
5. Ibid., p. 100
6. Ibid., p. 101
7. Ibid., p. 101
8. Ibid., p. 106
9. Ibid., p.107
10. Ibid., p. 107
11. Ibid., p. 108
12. Ibid., p. 108
13. Ibid., p. 108
14. Ibid., p. 109
15. Ibid., p. 109
16. Ibid, p. 109
17. Ibid, p. 110.
18. Ibid., p. 111
19. Ibid., p.112.
20. Ibid., p.113
21. Ibid., p. 114
22. Ibid., p. 115
23. Ibid., p. 115

24. Adapa Rama Krishna Rao, *Krishnadevaraya,* Sahitya Academy, 1955, pp. 66-72.

25. *Ashrma* ideology is often characterized as division of the individual life span into four successive stages; *brahmacharya* (of the student), *grihasta* (of the house-holder), *Vanaprastha* (of the hermit) and *sanyasa* (of the ascetic). In the last stage, the individual renounces the world totally and has no rights and obligations either as a member of his varna or his household. His renunciation as a member of his varna is symbolized by his giving up the sacred thread and the break with his family is symbolized by the performance of his funeral rights by his immediate kin. After this he is considered to be symbolically dead to his family and caste. However, this pattern applied only to upper castes, and even so it remained largely a theoretical argument. See for details Veena Das, *Structure and cognition: Aspects of Hindu caste and ritual*, O.U.P. 1997.

26. This changing conception of Brahmanas about caste categories is best illustrated in the rise of the concept of 'fallen kshatriyas'. This was used to assimilate many non-Indo-Aryan origin groups such as Greeks and Shakas because they had political power. As such they could not be treated as outcastes. This 'fallen kshatriya' status conferred on them was a shrewd manoeuver. See Romila Thapar, *A History of India* (Vol.I, N. Delhi, 1966); similarly many sudra families such as Reddi, Velema etc who wielded political power were conferred kshatriya status by Brahmanas during medieval Andhra. In the same way komatis, who had obscure origin, were given vaisya status when they became powerful economically in medieval Andhra. For a discussion on social mobility in medieval Andhra, see B.S.L. Hanumantha Rao, *Social Mobility in Medieval Andhra* (Hyderabad, 1995).

27. P. Lakshmikantam (ed.), *Palnati Veera Charitra*, Vijayawada, 1961, p. 89 and 123. Malas provided labour services to agricultural operations.

28. Agricultural work apart, they also took to spinning and weaving which gave them extra-income, see N. Venkataramanayya, *Studies in the History of Third Dynasty*, p. 361.

29. This is clear from his observance of caste taboos.

30. William de Bary, et al, *Sources of Indian Tradition*, Delhi, 1958, p. 235.

31. Bhakti was not a unified or homogenous movement, this is because the religious modes and organizational aspects of the sects, ideological positions that were taken by different *bhaktas* show a wide range of variations. In fact *Bhakti* covers a number of religious movements—each with its own distinctive features and ethos. Some of them were antithetical to one another, notwithstanding their professed faith in *bhakti* or devotion. *Nirguna bhaktas* like Kabir and Nanak denounced caste hierarchy and all social conventions based on caste distinctions whereas *Saguna bhaktas* like Tulasidas upheld the sanctity of caste system & supremacy of *Brahmanas*. Thus *Saguna* school actually advocated the preservation of existing social order and socio-religious norms. For details see Krishna Sharma, *Bhakti and the Bhakti Movement: A New Perspective* (New Delhi, 1987).

32. *Cokhamela*, a mahar of pandharpur was another untouchable, who became famous as a devotee of *vitthala (Vishnu)*. In this case, interestingly the officiating priest, after resisting the entry of *cokhamela* for some time, led *cokhamela* himself into the temple. After his death, he was buried right in front of the temple. His tomb became a shrine and people even now seek the blessings of this *mahar* saint, see Charlotte Vadueville, *Myths, saints* and *legends in Medieval India*, O.U.P. 1996, p. 229.

33. Dhurjati, Srikalahasti Mahatyamu, 3-19.

34. Ibid., p. 3-105

35. Ibid., p. 3-107

36. Ibid., p. 3-108

37. Ibid., p.3-108.

38. Ibid., p. 3-109.

39. *Sri Kalahasti Mahatyamu*, p.3-888. The original poem reads:

" కొలవో, త్రొవ్వవో, మూడం
గాతెనో, చవిగాదో, కమ్మగాదో, నీకున్
జాలవో, యులవడువో, తిన
వేలా కబళముట్లు? పార్వతీశ్వరా! చెప్పుమా "

40. Ibid., p. 3-89.
41. Sri Kalahasti Mahatyamu, 3-110.
42. Ibid., p. 3-111
43. Ibid., p. 3-112.
44. B.S.L. Hanumantha Rao, *Social Mobility* in *Medieval Andhra*, 1995, p. 80.
45. M.L.K. Murthy, 'Environment, Royal Policy and Social Formation in the Eastern Ghats, South India', A.D. 1000-1500. in *I.H.C.* Warangal, 1993, p. 19.
46. *N.D.I.* Vol.1, Atmakur, 32, dated 1409 AD
47. Ibid, Kandukur, 10, dated 1415-16 AD
48. Ibid, Atmakur, 37, undated
49. Thurston, *Castes and Tribes of South India*, 1975,p. 187-188.
50. In the same way Boya chieftains were known as Doras or Simhasana Boyas. They organized themselves into Kottams. Kottam was a sub-division of Nadu. By ninth century these Boya Kottams were conquered by Pallavas and Vengi Chalukyas. Consequently Boyas were dispersed from their strongholds, see, B.S.L. Hanumantha Rao, *Social Mobility in Medieval Andhra,* Hyderabad, 1995; Following different occupations, Boyas gradually entered the main stream of the socio-politico-economic life of the land. Their settlement in new lands also appears to have helped them in rising quickly even in social status. From about twelfth century we come across many inscriptions recording gifts of cattle, money and land made by Boyas to temples and priests. It is again about this time that we find *Boyas, taking Sanskrit* names such as *Bhima Boya, Canadana Boya, Surya Boya* (S.I.I. V, 188), Trikoti Boya (S.I.I. X, 33) and giving up tribal suffix in preference to honorifics like *Nayaka*, *Reddi*, *Nayudu*, *Nedu* and *Raju*. The *Kompula* or *Koppula* family used different honorific suffixes Reddy, Naidu, Naik by different individuals of that same family (S.I.I., IV, 765). Many inscriptions talk about the enhanced position of Boyas.
51. The medieval Telugu poets like *Peddana* used the term *Boya* in the sense of cruel or merciless, (*Manucharitra* IV, Verse, 87). Another poet Cintalapati Yarranaraya in his *Tarakabhyudayam* describes a Boyavidu on the outskirts of a forest. In Amuktamalyada, the Vijayanagara emperor *Srikrishnadevaraya* advocates a policy of

cautious appeasement towards hill and forest tribes which included the *Boyas* (*Amuktamalayada*, Canto. V. Verses, 204, 223). Another text , *Rayavachakam*, says that army of *Srikrishnadevaraya* consisted of *Boya* Lords from Eighteenth *Kapanas*. In the course of his eastern campaign, *Krishnadevaraya* is said to have let loose on the districts of *Vinukonda*, *Bellamkonda* and *Kondavidu* the *Boyas* and other tribesmen; For further discussion see, C.Ramachandraiah, *Further studies on Srikrishnadevaraya,* P.114.

52. Kapatrala Kaifiyat, *Mackenzie Manuscripts* (hereafter M.M) Vol. 110, No.789, Pandikonda Kaifiyaat, M.M, Vol. 95, No.574, Panyam Kaifiyat, M.M, Vol. 120, No.897.
53. Maddikera Kaifiyat, M.M, Vol. 168, No.1201; Aspari Kaifiyat, M.M, Vol.123, No. 923; Nandyal Kaifiyat, M.M, Vol.110, No. 793; Rollamaduga Kaifiyat, M.M, Vol. 108, No. 738.
54. S.I.I.IV,735,765, 766, 780, A-V,156, 172, 188, VI,96, 905, 910, 921.
55. S.I.I.IV,107, 60.
56. S.I.I, X, IV, 1248
57. Kunkanur Kaifiyat, *M.M,* Vol.123, No.928, Dudikonda Kaifiyat , *M.M*, Vol. 146. No.1149, Maddikera Kaifiyat, *M.M*, Vol.116, No.855.
58. Kasivisvesvarasastri, K. (ed.), Dhurjati's *Sri Kalahasti Mahatyam*, Vijayawada, 1985, p. 81.
59. Ibid., p.84.
60. Ibid., p. 84.
61. Thurston,E., *Castes and Tribes of South India,* Vol. 2, pp.28-29.
62. Thurston, a British Ethnographer collected a lot of information about castes and their culture. He also collected this myth. For a complete information please see, *Castes and Tribes of South India,* Madras, 1909.
63. Ramaraju who worked on folk culture collected these folk songs. For information on Narashimha myth, please see B. Ramaraju, *Folklore of Andhra Pradesh,* New Delhi, 1978.
64. Cassa Auriculta
65. Auspicious chaplet worn by the bridal pair during wedding period.
66. A sign of purity and regimen
67. Erythrina Indica

68. Alexandrian Laurel
69. Narashimha is known as *Obulesu* in folk perception.
70. B. Ramaraju, op.cit.
71. M.L.K. Murthy, 'Forest peoples and historical traditions in the eastern ghats, South India' in Bridget Allchin (ed.), *Living Traditions : Studies in Ethno-archaeology of South Asia*, New Delhi, p. 215.
72. Ibid., p. 215.
73. Ibid., p. 215, this story is so popular in Andhra region that a film was made on this theme in Telugu vernacular in 1960s with the title *Chenchu Lakshmi.*
74. Talaris were paid in kind and cash, besides being granted land free of tax. Some of the *Chenchu* headmen to this day have the appellation *talari* and they are respected by their tribesmen.
75. *Kridabhiramam*, V.128.
76. W.T. Elmore was a premier British Ethnographer, who actually collected and observed many rituals in early part of 20th century, for a complete picture, please see his work, *Dravidian Gods in Modern Hinduism*, (1913), Reprint, 1984, p. 86.
77. Ibid., p. 87.
78. Ibid. p. 87.
79. *Kridabiramam,* p. 128.
80. Ibid., 130.
81. S. Pratapa Reddy, *Andhrula Sanghika Charitra,* 1949, p.27, there are different folk stories about her, please see, R. Premalatha, *Janapada Sahityam: Puranagathalu,* 1983, pp. 189-200.
82. R. Premalatha, op. cit., 1983, pp.178-184.
83. M.L.K. Murthy, 'Social and Economic history as reflected in folklore traditions and myths in Andhra Pradesh' in *A.P.H.C,* 1988, p.11
84. Burton Stein, *Peasant State and Society in medieval South India,* 1985, p. 372.
85. Ibid., p. 372.
86. P.V.P. Sastri (ed.) *Inscriptions of Andhra Pradesh: Cuddapah District*, Vol. 2, p. 105.
87. *Sivaratrimahatyamu*, 1968, 182-196.

88. Ibid., IV Chapter.
89. *Kasi Khandamu*, 1958, p. 182-196
90. S.I.I, Vol. IX, pt.11, No.407, 521, MER 1937-38, No.197, MER 1915, No.40.
91. Sewell translated the writings of both Paes and Nuniz. For the account of Paes who actually witnessed the celebrations of Navaratrulu, see Sewell's *A Forgotten Empire,* pp.255.
92. Ibid., p. 256.
93. Ibid., p. 257.
94. Ibid., p. 257.
95. Ibid., p. 260.
96. Ibid., p. 260.
97. Ibid., p. 261.
98. Ibid., p. 262.
99. Ibid., p. 262.
100. Ibid., p. 268.
101. Epigraphica Indica, Vol.1, p. 370, MER, 1921, No. 371, S.I.I., Vol. IX pt.11, 466.
102. T. Ramachandra, *Hindu Festivals*, p. 314.
103. Ibid., pp. 292-293.
104. Ibid., pp. 294-295.
105. K. Sarojini Devi, *Religion in Vijayanagara Empire*, p. 276.
106. Ibid., p. 276.
107. M.S. Sharma, *History of the Reddy Kingdoms,* p.356.
108. Madhava, *Kalaniranya,* p. 331.
109. Hemadri, *Catarvargacintamani on Kala*, pp. 418-419.
110. Madhava, *Kalanirnaya,* p.339.
111. T T.D.I, Vol.11, Nos. 30, 31, S.I.I Vol.IX, pt.11, Nos. 625, 627.
112. Abbe, J.A, Dubois, *Hindu Manners, Customs and Ceremonies,* pp.284-285.
113. Cuddapah District Inscriptions, p. 328.
114. Ibid., p. 328.

115. Kumara Kampana perfomed this vrata and granted a large village to the Somanatha temple, *E.C.,* X, K1, 222.

116. *Cuddapah District Inscriptions,* p. 328.

117. T.T.D.I, Vol.IV, Nos. 12, 18, 100, Ibid., Vol.111, No.11, 118, *Padmapurana*, 111, 3-13.

118. T.T.D.I, Vol. IV, No. 33.

119. T.T.D.I, Vol.IV, No.59.

120. *Cuddapah* District Inscriptions, p. 328. The original poem reads:

– సోమవారం, శుక్రవారం మొదలుగాగల ఉత్సవాలు
మహాశివరాత్రి, కళ్యాణ మహోత్సవము, సంవత్సరాది, వసంత
నవరాత్రములు, శ్రావణమాసము ఆశ్వీజమాసము
నవరాత్రములు కార్తీకమాసం అభిషేకాలు, సంవత్సర
పుష్యమాసము ధనుర్మాసాల సంవత్సర మొదలుగా గలందులకు
శ్రీ భ్రమరాంబ మల్లేశ్వర.... కు సమర్పించినది. "

121. MER, 1927, No.374, 385; 1937-38, No.197.

122. T.T.D.I, Vol. 111, No. 65, E.C, IX, No.42.

123. Ch. 11, VV, 94-155, Chap. 111, VV, 3-130.

124. L.S. Yagnavalkya Sarma, *Srikalahasti Mahatyam: Janajeevanam* (Telugu), 1997, p.99.

125. Panduranga Mahatyamu, Ch. IV, V.16; MER, 1937-38, No.217, Ibid., 1926, No.414.

4

POPULAR RELIGION IN PRACTICE

The previous chapter discussed peoples' perception of cosmos that was inhabited by benign and malevolent spirits. In order to live and survive, they thought that vengeful goddesses must be propitiated. This pacification of these malevolent goddesses was also thought to be a protection against calamities and dangers of life. Even to get a child or to protect them from dangers and sickness, people took recourse to worshipping these village goddesses. Therefore we focus our attention on various rituals and customs practised at popular level in medieval Andhra. Various festivals associated with popular culture are also under our purview in this chapter.

Medieval Andhra people thought diseases like small-pox, cholera, plague, failure of crops, cattle diseases were the result of anger of one or the other village goddesses. To them it were these goddesses which inflicted and cured some diseases. The key to understand various rituals connected with these goddesses lies in their belief pattern. It is only against this backdrop that we can understand the meaning of these rituals.

Whenever small-pox broke out in a village, people used to say that *Ammavaru* (goddess) came to them. She was supposed to be angry, and expressing her anger by inflicting the disease. Since it was her wrath which caused the dreaded small-pox epidemic, devotees exercised considerable caution to contain her anger.[1] Medieval literature has not much to say about these rituals except some pieces of information. Only during British time, premier ethnographers like Henry Whitehead and W.T. Elmore, recorded some of these therapeutic rituals.[2]

Elmore, who observed these rituals thoroughly and meticulously, says that before a general *Jatara* or offering of bloody sacrifices to appease goddess takes place the small-pox afflicted person performed certain propitiatory ceremonies. The first thing done was to place some cactus leaves on the wall near the gate. Sometimes cactus was placed over the door. This was done also for cholera and at times for other diseases. The intention in this was that *Ammavaru*, seeing the cactus, would think the place uninhabited and pass on, since cactus would not be allowed to grow on the walls of an inhabited house. Then a sheep or small buffalo was tied to the leg of the cot on which the sick man was laying. If the people were very poor a chicken would be substituted. This animal was a votive offering and it was hoped that with this promise *Ammavaru* (goddess) would satisfy and leave the house.

Within a few days the dedicated animal was taken outside and sacrificed. Two pots of food were prepared, some of the food was placed on the decapitated head of the buffalo or other animal sacrificed and the head with the food on it was left outside the boundaries, with the hope that *Ammavaru* would be pleased to remain outside. The remainder of the food was taken home by the one who offered it and was eaten at home. Many families which were not affected by small-pox would also perform these ceremonies as a precautionary measure.[3]

Sometimes it becomes difficult to identify which Goddess was believed to be responsible for a particular disease. Because in some places *Mahuramma* and *Maremma* was regarded as the goddess of cholera. Yet another places, *Anakamma* was Cholera goddess. In Coastal area Ammavaru, in Rayalaseema *Poleremma* in Telangana area *Posamma* were believed to be small-pox goddesses.[4] So we find that no single goddess was thought to have been affiliated a particular disease throughout medieval Andhra.

However, the under current of belief is that diseases were caused by wrath of one goddess or the other.

There were no fixed dates for *Jatara*. Usually they would be celebrated once in a year and generally immediately after the harvest. However, when epidemics break out, cattle were down with disease or during famine conditions, they thought that village goddess was angry and should be propitiated immediately.

When the epidemic disappeared from the village, a general '*jatara*' was arranged, for *Jatara* was a popular festival connected with bloody sacrifices of village goddesses. Other festivals were indicated by the terms *Tirunalla*. First the announcement of coming *Jatara* was made and offerings solicited. This was usually done in this manner. When epidemic broke out, village headmen assembled and discussed ceremonies to be performed to avert the wrath of that particular goddess and to make vows to offer to the deity. Sacrifices of animals and food-stuffs according to their capacity and the nature of the epidemic were also offered. Then potter was asked to prepare the clay-idol of the goddess and a carpenter was asked to prepare a small wooden-cart. After bathing the image of *Ammavaru*, a procession was formed led by the *Madiga* (an untouchable) *asadi* or story-teller, a village servant (*Yetti*) and washerman (*chakalli*).[5] Taking new pots, these three would go about the village from house to house announcing coming *Jatara*. At each house they receive a small amount of food and butter-milk, which later they divided among themselves. They then went to the centre of the village, and took a new pot they placed in it small coins of money, some turmeric, charcoal and rice. The *asadi* now told the story of *Ammavaru*, describing her powers and the dangers which might come from neglecting her. Wrought with fear, people then made vows to her to be fulfilled at the time of *Jatara*. The pot was then tied to a tree and left until the time of worship. And a buffalo was chosen as chief victim for the sacrifice.[6]

The *Jatara* usually occupies four days.[7] *Jatara* was also known as *Devara* or *Kolupu*. The customs and rituals might vary from place to place. However, sacrifice of goats and buffaloes was common everywhere. On the day one the pot was taken from the tree and carried in procession through the village, accompanied by the beating of drums. As it was carried past each house, the inmates came out and bowed in worship before it. All the people then brought pots of food and went to the house of head-man, they spread leaf-plates and made an offering of food, the *asadi* summoned all the elders to witness, calling each one by name. He publicly announced the various vows made to the goddess. A sheep was then sacrificed to seal the promise made in vows. Once again the procession formed and the pot was carried around the village, food being collected at each house. The *asadi* recounted the stories of Gods as they went, telling of their various wars and exploits, in order to arouse people to take a proper part in the worship. After collecting the food the procession went outside the village to the temple of *Ammavaru*. Then temple was purified with various ceremonies. *Ammavaru* was bathed and the pot of food and some offerings were placed before her.[8] In *Sukasapatati, Kadiripati* mentions religious processions known as *gangagudi* and killing of sheep-fowls on this occasion.

The procession formed now anew and went to the water, a well or irrigation tank, where the royal staff and the snake's hood was kept in water over night. These were taken from the water and carried to the temple after a sheep was offered. After placing these two in the shrine of *Ammavaru*, another sheep was offered. This usually marked the completion of ceremonies of the first day.[9]

On the day two, there were still more processions about the village, and food was offered in front of the house of a shepherd. A sheep was sacrificed and story telling continued as on the first day. On the day three, they started the procession earlier, and more food was collected. Those who collect the food, ate it themselves, after offering it to the Goddess. In the afternoon all the people left their houses, and went to some suitable spot outside the village near the temple of *Ammavaru*, they cooked food and ate it offering it to *Aammavaru*.[10]

Thereafter, the merry-making part of the *jatara* began. The villagers brought their carts and oxen, the carts being gaily decorated for the occasion and formed a procession to go around the temple. There was a definite order for the carts, according to the wealth of the owner, and his social standing in the community. At times when the number of carts was large, there was great confusion and the beating of drums, and shouting of the people made oxen frantic. However, accidents did not occur. Then people brought sheep, goat and chickens and offered them to *Ammavaru*, carrying away the carcasses to be eaten later. This marked the end of ceremonies on the third day.[11]

The fourth day was the greatest day of the festival. On this day the buffalo, usually a small buffalo of one year, was sprinkled all over with yellow turmeric while garlands of margosa leaves were hung round its neck and tied to its horns. In the afternoon it was conducted round the village in procession to the sound of music and the beating of drums. Two sections of *panchama* castes *Malas* and *Madigas* took leading part in the sacrifice and conduct the buffalo from house to house.[12] One *Madiga* went ahead with a tom-tom, to announce that "the buffalo devoted to the goddess was coming". The people then would come out from their houses, bow down to worship the buffalo, and poured water over his feet, and also gave some food to him and the people in procession. The buffalo was brought to an open spot in the village and tied up near a small canopy of clothes supported on bamboo poles, which has been set up for the reception of the goddess. All the people in the village then assembled at the same place, they went in procession, with music and tom-toms and torches, to the house of potter, where the clay image was ready prepared.[13]

Henry Whitehead, another premier ethnographer, observed and recorded all these details of rituals personally.[14] After coming to the potter's house, they poured about two and half measures of rice on the ground and put the image on the top of it, adorned it with a new cloth and jewels. All those who gathered then worshiped the image and ram was killed. It's head being cut off with a large chopper and the blood was sprinkled on the top of the image, as a kind of consecration. The potter then took up the idol and carried it out of the house for a little distance and gives it to a *chakali* (washerman), who carried it to the place where the canopy had been set up to receive it.[15]

During the procession the people flourished sticks, spears and swords to keep off the evil spirits, and for the same purpose, cut limes in half and threw them up in the air. The idea was that the greedy demons would clutch at the golden limes and carry them off, and so be diverted from any attack on the man who carried the image.[16] When the idol had been duly deposited under the canopy another procession made to the house of a *gowda* (toddy-drawer). At his house some rice was cooked and a pot of toddy and a bottle of some *arrack (kapu sara)* were produced and duly smeared with yellow turmeric and vermillion.[17]

The cooked rice was put in front of the pot of *toddy* and bottle of arrack, a ram was killed in sacrifice and then the toddy-drawer (*Gowda*) worshiped the pot and the bottle. Then he carried the pot and bottle in procession and placed them under canopy near the image of goddess. Then came yet another procession and with more pomp and éclat. The people went off to the house of village headman and brought some cooked rice in a large earthen pot, some sweets and a lamb. Margosa leaves were spread on the ground in front of the image, the rice from the village headman's house was placed upon them in a heap and a large quantity of rice, according to the amount of subscriptions was poured in a heap a little further away.[18]

Before the buffalo was sacrificed, the lamb (called *Bana gorre*) sacrificial sheep, was first worshipped and then its throat and head were cut and its blood was mixed in the heap of boiled rice and grains (*Kumbham*). A ram was next brought and placed over the first large heap of rice and was cut into two, through the back, with a heavy chopper, by one of village *chakali* (washerman). The blood poured out over the rice and soaked it through, one half of the ram was then taken up and carried a few yards off, where a body of *asadis* were standing ready to begin their part in the ceremonies. The other half of the ram was left lying on the rice. The *asadis* then began to sing about the powers of the goddess.[19]

For the main event, the *devara potu*[20] (sacrificial he-buffalo) was brought, tied to the sacrificial post and was beheaded by either a *Madiga* or *Chakali* amidst din or commotion (*kolahalam*) made by the votaries and on lookers who kept shouting *poliga, salipoliga, kabali and kobali*.[21] The head of the *buffalo* should fall off in not more than three strokes. The blood of *devara potu* was mixed with *kumbham* (boiled rice and grains). This mixture was called *poli* and was sprinkled in the houses of the village (by *Urapoligadu*) and along the boundary (*polimera*) of the village (by *bhutapoligadu)*. Jatara came to an end by biding send off to the goddess. For this purpose, her clay figure or in some areas wooden figure was taken in procession in a small four wheeled cart (*ratham*) from her make-shift canopy to the *polimera* (boundary) and was lodged under a tree.[22]

People performed more or less the same rituals even when they worshiped goddesses for good rains on crops. One remarkable feature of this ritual was that they never allowed people of other villages in or around this place. Because they thought if someone from the neighbouring villages took this, that village would get all the benefit that this sacrifice accrued. Even if the smallest particle of that rice taken stealthily to any other village, the fruits of the function and the prosperity of the village were supposed to be transferred to that village. So even the best friends or the nearest relatives and the highest invites of the function were kept away from this function and men mounted on horses would guard the man carrying the rice balls thrown around lest any particle of it should be stolen.[23]

In Godavari and Masulipatnam areas a different method was followed to know which crop they had to sow that year. After the buffalo head was cut, the blood was collected in a basin and nine kinds of grains were put into it. The basin was then put before the idol inside the shrine and the doors of the shrine were kept shut for three days. On the fourth day the doors were opened, the coagulated mass of blood, grain and gram were carefully washed and grain and gram were separated on the ground behind the shrine in order to see which of the various kinds of grain had sprouted. All the *ryots* (peasants) eagerly assembled to watch the result and whichever it found sprouted, was regarded as marked out by the goddess as the right kind of grain to sow that year.[24] A few taxes like *Jatre*[25] and Maharaja-*Prayojanalapannu*[26] were collected from certain localities to conduct annual festival of the village deities.

There is one legend about *kumbham* (rice balls and blood of sacrificial animal mixture). There was a person who stole this *Balikumbam* and consequently got killed. After his death, he received worship as a *Veerudu* (Hero). His stone image is at Veldi village in Manthani taluq. On one occasion of this sacrifice, a *chakali* (Washerman) of a neighbouring village, Kelledu, caught a ball of rice with response the *Bali* (let me receive ball of rice). The chakali took the rice ball and ran towards his village but the guards pursued him and overtook him a furlong from the boundary of his village. When he swallowed the rice ball they killed him and washed his intestines in the canal that watered the village fields. His body was buried where he was killed. In recognition of his heroism and love for his own village, a stone slab with his image figure in natural size was installed.[27] This image is still there for everyone to see.

When viewed superficially, the *Jataras* or festivals that centred around these village deities, appear as though they were integrating all castes of society which was otherwise highly stratified. Because these rituals required the participation of all castes, particularly lower castes, and all had role to play. As we have seen in previous pages, washerman, carpenter, toddy-drawer, leather workers, and agricultural labourers, all had some or the other role in these rituals. Even village headman, village accountant had their stint. Social, economic, religious boundaries appear to have been transcended and taken back seat at least for the time being. We see all castes, upper and lower, pure and polluting merging at one common place. All these tend to portray an integrated picture of village society.

However, when we move deeper into these rituals, we will come to understand how these rituals were used by privileged castes to construct and reinforce caste ideology and power. First, the entire management and organisation of rituals remained in the hands of village headman, who himself was, more often than not, a landlord, and other landlords. It were these people who benefited the most through timely and plentiful rains, and good crops. Because they owned almost the entire agricultural land in the village. But they could not conduct these rituals by themselves unaided. So participation of other castes became necessary. Secondly, when other castes participated in these rituals, what was the nature of participation? This participation was not on equal terms, lower caste people such as *Chakali* (Washerman), *Mangali* (Barber) *Kummari* (Potter), *Gowda* (Toddy-drawer) and *Madiga* all participated through inferior or subordinate roles traditionally assigned to them.

As we have noted earlier, a potter made clay idol of the goddess. Carpenter made a small wooden-cart. Toddy-drawer supplied toddy and arrack. *Malas* and *Madigas* conducted the buffalo from house to house. A *Madiga* also announced the coming of buffalo. Of course, cutting of buffalo's head was also the duty of either a *chakali* or *madiga*. All these occupations were traditionally assigned to the respective castes which performed the same function in these rituals. So actually these castes are not doing anything out of their *jati dharma*. No privileges accrued to these lower castes on account of these rituals. In fact, as the participants took up traditionally defined ritual roles appropriate to their caste occupations, the caste ideology and caste system whereby the higher castes enjoyed superior status and entitled privileges, were reinforced time and again, recreating the traditional authority and power. So these rituals actually served as loci for construction and reinforcement of power.

Human sacrifices also prevailed during medieval times. Usually sacrifices took place in *shakti* shrines. They were called *champudugullu* (sacrificial temples). People thought *shakti* would sometimes be satisfied only with human sacrifices. There are some pieces of evidence which point to the prevalence of human sacrifices even in 1880s.[28] By making human sacrifices, they believed that they could get the grace of god for themselves and for their crops.[29] However, this belief was by no means confined only to tribal, peasants and lower castes. It appears that people belonging to all sections of people shared this belief. An incident which happened during Vijayanagara period and reasoning of brahmanas reveals it very clearly. Dominigos Paes, a Portuguese merchant, stayed in Vijayanagara during the years 1520-22 A.D. in the reign of Srikrishnadevaraya. His narrative *Chronica dos Eeis di Bisnaga* contains an incident which happened during his sojourn in Vijayanagara. He says, "when a tank burst two or three times, the king asked his *brahmanas* to consult the idol as to the reason why it burst so often, and the brahmanas said that the idol was displeased and desired that they should make a sacrifice and should give him the blood of men and horses and buffaloes. As soon as the king heard this, he forthwith commanded that at the gate of the pagoda the heads of sixty men should be cut off and of certain horses and buffaloes which was at once done".[30]

Once a *komati* (merchant) went to a shrine with his wife. They saw trunks with heads cut off and filled with awe, he exclaimed!

"*champudigudi Ediyani ee*
dampatulu kalebaramula talalumganitat
sampadita bhayaroudra
kampithudai setti chegadi kannulumusen"[31]

(A komati (setti) couple saw mutilated dead bodies in a temple. They closed their eyes with fear and exclaimed that it was a sacrificial temple).

Another ritual called *sodi* was practised for fortune telling. People believed that *Yerukalasanis* (fortune-telling women who belonged to *Yerukala* tribe) would reveal past and future and their predictions would come true. *Yerukalasanis* were respected a lot. They would wander in the villages telling people about their past and future. Palnati Veera Charitra tells us that one *Yerukalasani* forecast about the impending war to Brahmanaidu. Believing very strongly in her words, Brahmanaidu made preparations for the war.[32] *Sukasaptati*, too, mentions about *Yerukalasanis* moving in villages.[33]

People also believed that some tribal people were bestowed with special faculties such as reading past, and future and some magical powers. These *Yerukalasanis*, as they were nomads, moved from village to village forecasting for the people. Their magical power was thought to be so powerful that it could prevent a person from going by a particular road (*Darikattu*) and could make a woman submit herself to the wishes of man who desired her.[34]

However, over the period, many other castes took up this profession. There were both *vaishnava* and *siva* followers among this community. These *sodi* women announce their coming in the streets. Usually women folk would invite them. They started their narrating future by invoking several goddesses. A bamboo stick was held by her at one end and she asked the women to hold it at the other end, as she explained some symbols that she was going to use all through her narration. These women, while foretelling, smear turmeric powder on their faces, made a big mark of vermilion (*tilak*) on the forehead and started telling future. They invoked a number of goddesses to the *shruti* (scale) of a *Kinnera* or an *ektara* in a sing-song way. They also carried a bamboo basket which contained a small bag of turmeric powder, nine shells, an old palm-leaf manuscripts and a brass idol of *Mahankali* of Ujjain. Sometimes they would also give medicines for diseases, for sterility and for driving away evil spirits.[35]

Other Rituals

As we have already noted, people's belief system was marked by heterogeneity. They believed in a number of gods and goddesses, although *srivaishnavism* and *veerashaivaism* were making steady progress. Since people believed in miracle working, disease curing goddesses, they expressed their devotion to these Goddesses and Gods in a variety of ways. Villagers used to arrange religious processions from time to time to various gods' shrines. In *Sukasaptati*, Kadiripati describes these religious processions as *Gangagudi*.[36] *Hamsavimsati* also narrates these religious processions. Besides, it also tells us that what kind of musical instruments were used during these processions such as *veerana, pamba jamidika, tappeta, nagasvaramu, singinadamu* and *pillana grovi*.[37] *Kridabhiramam* also mentions that people went to the shrine of *Ekkavira* in a procession. People also worshipped *Bhairava* and *Mylara*, aggressive manifestations of *Siva*.

Kanumari ritual was performed for appeasing Gods in extreme forms. *Kridabhiramam* describes about the ferocious acts of sacrifices made by villagers. They used to cut their hands, breasts, heads, ears, necks and chest. *Kridabhiramam* says that sometimes devotees also walked on fire to fulfil their vow which had been made when they were afflicted with diseases such as epidemics. It says about fire-walking in these works,

> "*Rava ravamandu nerrani chandra mallela*
> *chodyampu gundala chochchuvaru*"[38]

(They go through embers)

Tenali Ramakrishna, one of the eight poets of (*Ashtadiggaja*) Srikrishnadevaraya, also describes many rituals of villagers during *Jataras*. He says that men and women of lower classes, particularly, in the rural areas, took an oil bath, put on new clothes, adorned themselves with garlands of flowers and margosa leaves and chewing betel walked across the fields to the temple of *Ganga* situated on the outskirts of the village. Men and women would get drunk, streams of blood flowed from the cut off necks of a number of goats killed to propitiate Goddesses. Some devotees started jumping into pits filled with blazing coals or vaulting into pits of fire.[39]

Pandurangamahatyamu further says that women also walked on fire and danced on tender plantain-leaves. In case of illness or other trouble people used to make a vow to walk on fire.[40] When this was to be done, a trench was dug in front of the shrine and washed with a solution of cow-dung to purify it. A cart-load of fire-wood was then spread over the trench, set alight and left to burn till the wood became a mass of red-hot embers. Whitehead, the premier British ethnographer, observed this ritual during his stay. He says that when all was ready, the people assembled and the *pujari*, whose turn it was to conduct the worship, first bathed himself to purify and then amid the deafening din of trumpets, tom-toms and symbols and the clapping of hands walked with a bare feet slowly and deliberately over the glowing embers, the whole length of the trench toward the shrine of the goddess. After him some women also walked over red-hot embers with lighted *aratis* on their heads.[41]

Sometimes women would dance on tender plantain-leaf as a part of *Jatara* ritual. Many references are there. This kind of dance has been referred by *Pandurangamahtmyamu* and it says that women danced on tender plantain leaves like lotuses on water weeds.[42] Sometimes they would express their devotion by practicing *mounavrata* or silence. Or they would cut off their bits of flesh from their haunches and offered the same to the deity or *marugalu* (one offering sacrifice on behalf of another). The devotees who resorted to this kind of extreme devotion were called *Mailarubhatas*.[43]

Finger and tongue offerings also formed part of this ritual. Various kinds of rituals performed by *mailarubhatas* are described in Kridabhiramam. It says,

"*Karavadi yulugula ganapa patarlalo*
nutti cherulu gosi yurukuvaru
katiki honnalambu gandakattera batti
misimintulunugaka mringu varu
sandulanu navasambula salupuvaru

yadama kudicheta naratulichchvaru
sahasamu murtigaikonna saranivaru
dheera hrudayulu mylaru veerabhatulu"[44]

(Some devotees jumped from high places, some cut their tongues, some were cutting their throats with scissors, some lighted oil lamps in their left and right palms, *mylaru veerabhatulu* were looked as though they were the embodiments of adventure).

Besides all these sacrifices, the practice of cutting the last joint of the foreigner as an offering to Lord *Siva* was also in vogue. A fourteenth century inscription from Siti at *Kalabhairava* temple refers to this practice. One myth talks about the origin of this practice. According to this myth, *Bhasmasura* asked a boon from Lord *Siva* to the effect that anybody on whose head he placed his hand should be reduced to ashes. When *Siva* granted him this boon, *Bhasmasura* wanted to test the efficacy of the boon on *Siva* himself. Frightened *Siva* ran for his life even as *Bhasmasura* pursued him. *Siva* came to the hermitage of Gautama near Siti at last. Then Gautama advised Siva to hide in a cave. When *Bhasmasura* reached this spot, he lost track of Siva and enquired from a cultivator working in a nearby field the whereabouts of *Siva*. On being asked, the cultivator pointed to the hill where *Siva* was hiding with his forefinger. But *Bhasmasura* was prevented from approaching that hill by *Vishnu*, who came in the form of a beautiful damsel called *Mohini* who brought about his destruction.[45]

On relating this story of *Bhasmasura's* destruction to *Siva* by *Vishnu, Siva*, whose curiosity was excited to see *Mohini*, requested *Vishnu* to reveal his *Mohinirupa*. When Mohini appeared, *Siva* could not but fall in love with *Mohini*. This resulted in the birth of *Kalabhairava*.

Siva directed *Kalabhairava* to occupy the Siti hill. The cultivator, who showed the hiding place of *Siva* to *Bhasmasura* with his forefinger, was condemned along with his descendants to offer the last joint of the offending forefinger to *Kalabhairava* as an offering. Accordingly it became a custom among the cultivators such as *Reddis* to cut off the last joint of the forefinger and offer it to *Khalabairava*. However, as the cultivator found it difficult to do agricultural operations with his forefinger being amputated, later on an arrangement was made to offer two fingers—the little finger and the ring finger of the female in place of one finger of male.[46] The inscription further says that a regular staff was maintained in the temple to cut off the finger, dress the wound without much loss of blood. Devotees brought not only a certain amount of food, but also to pay a fixed amount of money for using the services of the staff.[47] This practice which was primarily associated with the rituals of village goddesses might have been adopted by *Veerasaivism*. Because originally cutting fingers, hands, heads, breasts, ears were the rituals connected with the worship of village goddesses.

Throat, stomach and breast piercing also took place as a ritual performance. When women did not have children for a long time, they used to perform extreme forms sacrifices. They did not mind even laying their lives to get the blessings of goddesses. *Palnati Veeracharitra* tells about it in the following poem,

> "*Ee jeevanambela Ee dehamula nekaina pranamul*
> *nekearpinthu*
> *abalalamani yencha narhambukadu netturu nemeda*
> *nindajalledamu*
> *chudu ma sahasa spurtulanuchu aagaka rosha*
> *samavesamesaga*
> *varala mattuku kattuluravadi dusi vakshasthalambula*
> *vadalakayunchi*"[48]

Palkuriki Somanatha's, *Panditaradhya charitra* also says that apart from cutting tongues, hands they would also pierce their throats, stomach, breasts with arrows. It says,

> "*Galamula gihvvala karnarandramula*
> *kadupula medala vakshamula pukkillu*
> *nalaranga penu diliyalu narasamulu*
> *galayanga nirumeyigada sandhinchi*"[49]

Another ritual that was performed during *Jatara* was called *Kavu* Ritual. It refers to the sacrifice of a goat on the last day of *Jatara*. On the last day of the ritual, a strong goat would be bathed, it was sprinkled with Turmeric and vermilion and would be worshiped. Then goats legs would be tied with ropes and three men would hold it aloof. Now a man, who drank *Kallu* (toddy) and was disguised as a tiger would be kept in a small hut. When the time came this man would come out and rip open the mouth of the goat and pluck the tongue of the goat and keep it in a platter. All people who were assembled at *jatara* would praise that man as hero. This was called *'kavu teeyatam'*. This ritual continued until eighteenth century, because in a piece of poem belonging to this period, *Neelasundari parinayam*, the heroine of the poem makes vow that if she could get *Krishna* as husband, she would have *'kavu'* arranged to the goddess *Gangamma*. It says,

> "*Goppa chimbotu kadupulagoorchi neeku*
> *kavu bettinthu chummiya ganganamma*"[50]

Some devotees showed their devotion or fulfilled their vows by piercing cheeks. To fulfil their vow of *mounavrata* (silence), they would have their cheeks pierced through and through with a wire of silver or other metal, fixed in such a manner that the mouth could not be opened without extreme pain This ritual was called locking the mouth (*Noti-talamu lichchuta*). *Panduranga-mahatyamu* also talks about *noti talalu*. This ritual was often protracted through the whole day. It says,

> "*Kanta yokartu moopuna kandalichche*
> *marugalichche noka sudhamadhuravani*
> *lalana yokartunori talambulichche*
> *shakti jatara sadbhakti sektulesaga*"[51]

Pingali Surana, one of the *Ashtadiggajas* of Srikrishna-devaraya, too, says in his work *kalapoornodayam* that some devotees closed their mouths with mouth-locks.[52] Ganapavarapu Venkatakavi also described about this mouth-locking. He writes,

> "*Kondaru noti beegamulu dasalla pelluna*
> *norula poorulu garachuvaru*".[53]

Yet another group of devotees would have their bodies branded with *vaishnava* symbols like wheel so that these marks remained on their skin perennially. This was also done to attain some ritual purity.[54]

People thought that some devotees would be possessed by the spirit of goddesses. This was called *Sigamugadam*.[55] Whatever the spirit possessed devotees, people believed them to be true. This was a common ritual during *jataras*. According to *Sukasapatati*, all those spirit possessed people were given a lot of respect and were treated as representatives of Goddesses. These spirits possessed people would say something about future or past, people would give them grain as a gift. *Sukasaptati* says,

> "Sivamu puttinchi yapudu checheta dhisikoniye puttetudu
> vittulu"[56]

Many people of medieval *Andhra desa* followed extremely severe forms of devotion. No matter what kind of ritual they practiced the basic belief which underlined these rituals was to appease the goddess whose anger was thought to be the cause of many evils which were afflicting both men and physical world. One of these rituals was hook-swinging—a custom that was quite common among lower castes during medieval *Andhradesa*. This ritual can be very briefly described as a practice involving suspension of the body on hooks and some kind of movement which may increase pain or stress such as the act of being swung in rotation, bounced or simply lifted or lowered several times in succession.

The earliest reference to hook-swinging in Andhradesa is found in *Kridabhiramam*. *Vallabharaya*, to whom this text is ascribed, describes, inter alia, hook-swinging. Describing various rituals such as fire-walking, throwing one's self from high places, cutting one's tongue, hook-swinging and lighting oil-lamps in palms, he noted,

> "*Galampu Konki kankala charmamu gruchchi"*
> *Yudu veedhi nuyyala luguvaru*"[57]

(Having pierced hook, they were swinging)

Tenali Ramakrishna, a poet of sixteenth century, in his work, *Pandurangamahatyamu* - also referred to many rituals that were performed by votaries during a *jatara* dedicated to goddess *Ganga*. Many rituals have been described by Tenali Ramakrishna in connection with this *Jatara*. Describing the events and rituals which took place at this Jatara, he says that many devotees took to different rituals like firē-walking, dancing on tender plantain leaves, cutting off bits of flesh from their haunches and offering the same to the deity, hanging themselves from *Sidi Mranu* (swinging post) and piercing their jaws with long and sharp needles. He writes,

> "*Ambodaramu krinda nasiyadu, nairava*
> *tiyu bole sidi vrele terava yortu*"[58]

Interpreting the *sidi mranu* of *Pandurangamahtmyamu* S. Pratapa Reddy says that :

"A long pole was planted in the earth at the end of which was fixed a round stone with a hole passed through the pole. On the stone was placed a beam which rotated round it and an iron hook hung from the beam".[59]

The earliest known European eyewitnesses account of hook-swinging was by a Portuguese traveller, Durate Barbosa, who visited Vijayanagara in the early sixteenth century.[60]

This account was followed by the publication of an increasing number of descriptions of the practice by other European observers—adventures, traders, missionaries and the like who travelled or lived in India from the early sixteenth to the end of eighteenth century. Some writers described the custom in a relatively detached and objective manner, saying nothing about how they felt. Among them was a Portuguese traveller, Pietro Della Valle, who witnessed the hook-swinging in 1623. Writing about this ritual in that year, he said:

> A sort of Gibbet is erected with a pulley at the arm, through which a line passes with a sharp hook at the end, those who have vowed to undergo this penance place themselves under the gibbet from which the rope and iron hook are let down. Thereafter benumbing the flesh of the middle of the back of the votary, they fix the hook into it giving play to the other end of the string, they hoist up to the top of the gibbet, the devotee, thus suspended by the muscles of the back. Hanging in the air while all the blood was running down from their body.[61]

However, it appears that this ritual with its underlying belief existed in other parts of India as well. There is a mass of evidence which shows the prevalence of this ritual during eighteenth and nineteenth centuries in other parts of India. A Portuguese traveller, Gaspero Balbi, also witnessed hook-swinging exhibition in 1592.[62] Sonnerat, a Frenchman also described the rite as practiced on the Malabar coast in the eighteenth century.[63]

Tavernier, a French Protestant traveller, too, witnessed this ritual and was surprised at the way in which healing took place after the body had been cut and pierced with hooks. Writing about the custom whereby a great number of 'poor people' hung themselves upon hooks at Malda in Bengal he remarked:

> " It is a surprising thing not to see a drop of blood come from this cut flesh, and not to see a sign of it even on the hook, and in two days they are entirely cured by the drugs which the *Brahmanas* give them".[64]

Edward Moon, also wrote about the existence of this ritual among Marathas in Eastern India in 1794. He found it 'very singular', 'curious' and even amusing. He wrote,

> If any records of these circumstances are kept in the swinging villages, with the causes of swinging, they would, doubtless, make a curious figure in a European dress; for we have heard of a number of causes assigned for the ceremony, that would furnish almost as diverting an essay as the well-known story of the lover's leap, if worked up by so humorous a hand.[65]

Although there was commonality in all these rituals, yet there were regional variations. In South India where temple culture was more pervasive, the swinging was conducted from or around a pole fixed on a platform on the back of a temple cart. The whole apparatus could be moved and the devotee was kept suspended in the air while the cart was dragged along, bumping its way around the temple. However, in Bengal the swinging was round a pole fixed in the ground. Alexander Dutt in 1840 described the swinging at annual *charak puja*. He wrote:

> An upright pole, twenty & thirty feet in height, is planted in the ground. Across the top of it, moving freely on a pin or pivot, is placed horizontally another long pole. From one end of this traverse beam is a rope suspended, with two hooks affixed to it. The other extremity is fastened with another rope, which hangs loosely towards the ground. The devotee comes forward, and prostrates himself in the dust. The hooks are then run through the fleshy parts of his back, near the shoulders. A party-holding the rope at the other side, immediately begins to run round with considerable velocity.[66]

Rev. Noyes, an American missionary stationed at Kambam in the Madura district of the Madras Presidency, described the first method. Recording a hook swinging at a festival he attended in 1868, he remarked:

> "The machine consisted of a four-wheeled platform car, in the centre of which is an upright post, 20 or 30 feet high, and upon the top of it a traverse beam, 40 feet long, fitted to work like a well-sweep, and also to be

> swung around in a circle. Upon one end of this beam, the hooks already inserted in the man's back are fastened by strong ropes. Long ropes are also attached to the other end by means of which several men manage its motions. The victim is first swung around in a circle, and then raised high in the air, while the multitudes below fill the air with their shouting. In going up he favours himself by catching hold of the rope with his hands, but pretty soon lets go, and is suspended by the hooks inserted in his back, being bent almost double, his head and feet hanging, and the muscles of his back being pulled out to their utmost tension. While he is hanging in this position, the car is drawn by hundreds of men, over rough ground, around the temple, the man being shaken and tossed from side to side by the motion of the car. It was a full hour, by my watch, that I saw the man thus suspended.[67]

However, Rev. J.E. Sharkey, who visited the festival at Vuyyur in Masulipatnam district on two separate occasions, wrote that the process there did not include rotation of the body. He described the sequence and different phases of the ritual—the insertion of the hooks, the raising of the beam, the suspension of the man in the air as the temple cart was drawn around and the final part such as lowering of the beam and releasing the man.[68] He also noted that the man who swung was followed by three more who went through the same preparation, 'but with this difference', that 'each was raised and lowered and set free—all in two seconds. Therefore, there was no rotation of the body involved in the ritual at Vuyyur. Later on he visited Rajahmundry and witnessed hook-swinging ceremony. Reporting about this ritual at Rajahmundry, he noted that unlike the swinging at Vuyyur, the swinger at Rajahmundry was 'swung round the perpendicular pole of the machine.[69]

According to his statement, it appears that in Andhra two forms of swinging i.e., swinging involving the rotation of the body and swinging that was essentially 'hook-hanging were prevalent.

Powell and Irwin have constructed the theories of the origin of hook-swinging, based on the assumption that one of its essential characteristics was rotation. Irwin argues that hook-swinging ceremony is 'a common misnomer for the solar rite properly called *cakra puja*, literally "the wheel form of (sun) worship,[70] while Powell holds that the *Hindustani charak means* 'wheel' or something that revolves, and that the literal translation of *charak puja* would perhaps be the 'wheel form of worship' or 'revolving ceremony'.[71] However, swinging in Southern and Western India did not take place at the *charak puja* and the terms used for swinging in other languages were different and were quite unconnected with the idea of a wheel. For example the word for hook-swinging in *Telugu* was *Sidi* and the *Tamil* word for it was *Cheddle, Chedul or cheddal* and both, literally mean 'needle'. As a matter of fact the terms used for hook-swinging process varied from place to place. Some words imply the idea of a wheel or rotation, others do not.

There were also variations in the way in which the hooks, usually two in number, were used. They were made of iron and were described by various European observers from time to time. The traveller Basil Hall remarked that the hooks used in the ritual in Madras in 1830's 'might be about the size of a small shark-hook, but without any barb; the thickness being rather less than a man's little finger.[72] After the back had been prepared by 'thumping' to produce a slight swelling, by rubbing with oil or in some other way, hooks were inserted. This hook-swinging continued in all Telugu-speaking and Tamil-speaking districts of the Presidency. Missionary and other sources also indicate that the ritual was performed in princely states such as Hyderabad, Mysore, Cochin, Travancore and the French enclave of Karikal on Coromandal coast.[73]

What is especially striking is the absence of the practice in the north and north-west of India—areas which roughly correspond with the older notion of *Aryavarta*. From a linguistic point of view, the custom was strongly entrenched among those who spoke the four major Dravidian languages of the south, namely *Telugu, Kannada, Tamil* and *malayalam*, among *Bengali* and *Oriya* speaking people of eastern India, among *Marathi* speakers in western India. It was not practiced in Assam (among north-eastern tribal groups) and was absent among *Hindi* speakers and some other groups whose languages derived from *Sanskrit*.[74]

Hook-swinging was not equally popular in all districts or subdivisions of British India. According to Madras reports of 1854, annual swinging festivals were conducted in 40 villages in Guntur, 48 in Masulipatnam, 10 in Trichinopoly, 16 in Madura and 78 in Tanjore district. Besides, the extent of the custom varied from place to place. There were also differences in both the frequency and dates of hook-swinging festivals in different parts of the country. In some place, the frequency and timing of swinging was still more varied and less predictable. This was partly because it was connected with a very much wider range of deities, many of them were of local or restricted influence.[75]

Jataras or village festivals at which swinging took place were held in different localities at different times throughout the year.[76] Under such circumstances the timing of the swinging depended on the cycle and timing of the local festival which might be held, for example, after the harvest or on some other occasion. In some other instances, swinging festivals were arranged as separate events whenever sufficient resources were available and the need arose. In Masulipatnam district, generally swinging took place at those festivals held about the full moons from December to May. In Madras Presidency in Madura district, they appear to have been done in June/July and in Tanjore district in August.[77]

This ritual was not necessarily an annual event. In some cases it was conducted only once in every three or four years or even at longer intervals.[78] It was a more common occurrence, taking place twice or even more frequently throughout the year, in other cases. The more frequent performance of this ritual was a reflection of the difficulties the village people were facing as a result of some type of calamity, such as famine or epidemic disease. The villagers, believing that their tutelary or guardian deity was angry and responsible for these events, conducted hook-swinging in order to placate the spirit, bring rain or prevent further sickness. However, Corporate calamity was not the only cause for the spontaneous and unscheduled performances of hook-swinging. Another important reason for the timing and frequency of the practice was individual need—the need for some occasion (apart from annual festivals) when men and women could perform the act for personal or family reasons.[79]

It appears that this ritual was performed only by *Sudra* and some lower castes. In Cuddapah district, swinging was prevalent among *kapus* (well-do-farmers) and *Balijas* (cultivators and traders) as well as among those who were described as 'the more ignorant and degraded people of *Sudra* castes.[80] In the Tamil-speaking areas of Madras Presidency swingers also included *Kallars* and *Maravars*. Some of them owned land or were important in village administration. L.K. Anantha Krishna Iyer says that *Nayars* (high caste *sudras*), *Kammalars* (carpenters, blacksmiths, etc.), and *Izhavars* (palm cultivators and toddy-tapers) performed the ritual in Cochin Area.[81]

Swinging was performed either by priests or victims on behalf of the village or inter-village community in Madras Presidency. However, in Bengal it was performed for the benefit of the individual, for relatives or for the patron or landlord. In South, this ritual was performed before guardian deities and inams or special grants also encouraged for its regular performance. This ritual seem to have been encouraged more by ancient ideas of blood offerings and human sacrifice, the ritual being more of a symbol or substitute for the offering of life itself.[82]

One of the commonality of this rite as performed in medieval Andhra and elsewhere was that a majority of those who performed the rite were tribal, the poor, and the one referred now as marginalised and oppressed people. In Madras Presidency, hook-swinging was performed not only by *Kallar, Marwar, Kapu* and *Balija* castes, but more often by lower status group such as *pallis* (or *Vanniyans*) who were employed chiefly as agricultural labourers,[83] *Kuruvans*,[84] a partially itinerant community of basket-makers and untouchables—notably the *pallars* and *pariahs*. The reason for the prevalence of the custom particularly among lower castes is partly explained by their powerlessness which was linked with their economic and social condition. It was also, partly related to the religious tradition and world view.[85]

Financial considerations were sometimes important for swinging in Madras Presidency. *Inams* or government grants to make village authorities possible to pay to the individuals to swing on behalf of the community existed. In the mid-nineteenth century *inams* were granted in support of the ritual existed in many parts of the Presidency such as Guntur, Nellore, Cuddapah, Rajahmundry and Ganjam in Telugu areas and Madura, Chingleput and North Arcot in Tamil speaking areas.[86]

Whether the money was available through *inams* or from some other source, rates of pay varied from place to place. According to the Magistrate of Masulipatnam, *Vetties* (minor government servants appointed to assist the village headman) or *Pariahs* of the village, most probably *Malas* and *Madigas* who had special roles at *jatara* of village deity, were the performers and received between one and four rupees from a general fund subscribed by the villagers or granted for the purpose by some public spirited individual.[87] At Vuyyur in the same district, it was customary for the village treasury to pay five rupees to any *Pariah* of the village who was willing to swing on behalf of the community, while in the nearby village of *Peddanah* the man who swung was paid four rupees.[88]

Some individuals were paid to swing as proxies for higher caste and wealthier *Hindus*. As in Bengal, in Masulipatnam, too higher castes paid low caste proxies a sum between one and four rupees (or the equivalent of between eight and thirty two days pay for unskilled labourers in the same district in 1859).[89] However, in Cuddapah, in 1838, the rate was about eight *annas*.

Financial rewards for performing the ritual were however, not the only 'worldly inducements'. The other consideration was enhanced reputation and status, particularly within the family, among peers, or in the wider caste or tribal community or in the village.[90] In some cases, status was enhanced, wholly or in part, by the fact that the performer or celebrant was seen as enacting a spiritual drama and, in doing so, becoming possessed or at least imbued with something of the deity's power.[91]

Swingers, also, were revered at times. J.E. Sharkey remarked that the swinger's body was besmeared with turmeric and his person decked with jewels. Rev. Mateer, who saw this ritual wrote that when about to sing, the swinger's ears, neck and waist were adorned with golden ornaments and a silver belt or chain.[92] Similarly in Mysore, swinger was adorned with 'floral garlands',[93] at Manarguid in Tanjore district, he was covered with ornaments of bell and flowers. In Maharashtra also swinger was ritually dressed in silk breeches and garlanded with flowers.[94]

Besides, swingers who were believed to be able to confer special blessings, flowers or fruit, symbols of blessings and fertility, showered by swingers while swinging were considered very holy and picked up by on lookers. Just as the sweat-meats distributed by *sati* just before she mounted her husband's funeral pyre, the flowers and fruits thrown by swingers were revered and picked up by the people. Rev. Hoole, while referring to the same practice of throwing flowers over spectators, noted that the people 'struggled to catch and preserve them', as though they had been blessings from heaven.[95]

There is no doubt that some individuals performed hook swinging for financial and/or social reasons and that the custom gave some of them an opportunity to improve their standing among friends, within the family, or in the larger community. All the same, one of the reasons for this increased reputation or change in status was because of the fact that the custom was regarded as a sacred ritual—the performer deriving status and sanctity from what he or she was perceived as doing at a spiritual level.[96]

Thus, while it is possible that some swingers may have used the custom for their own particular purposes without any thought for its 'religious' dimension, the usefulness of the custom derived at least in part from the fact that some people regarded it as especially sacred and as an activity which gave them access to blessings or spiritual power. Moreover, some of those who swung were, quite clearly, not interested in its financial benefits and were prepared to pay what were for them large sums of money in order to perform the rite. Hence, on the one hand people were paid to swing; the opposite was also true on the other. In some cases the people themselves paid for the privilege of using the apparatus and of undergoing the rite. For instance, at Vuyyur the cost of swinging for one's own private reasons (as distinct from swinging on behalf of the village or community) from about 1815 to 1853 was Rs. 2 per person.[97] Nearly 5,000 people seem to have paid the fee during that period. The cost of swinging at Yellamma's Hill in Belgaum was Rs. 18.

Hook-swinging was seldom if ever conducted before such deities as *Vishnu* or his incarnations, but rather before gods and goddesses who represent, to a much greater extent the more volatile, dangerous and destructive as well as creative aspects of nature. They were perhaps more the objects of apprehension and fear than of trust and adoration and usually required a great deal pleasing and propitiation.[98]

Hook-swinging in connection with the worship (or rather propitiation) of female deities was stronger in medieval South India in general and Medieval Andhra in particular. People believed that *Ellamma* ('the mother of all') would be pleased by the performance of hook-swinging ritual. As we have noted in the previous chapter *Ellamma* was believed to be the original *sakti* and cause of the universe.[99] Not only *Ellamma* of Andhra but *Mariamma*, the mother of small-pox and *Angaramma*, the goddess of Cholera and disease in general in Tamil-speaking areas and *Durgara*, goddess of cholera and *Dayamava*, the goddess of small-pox in Karnataka were worshiped with this ritual.

Swinging was also associated with *siva* or with his *shakti* or with independent and local female deities. However, by no means, *Vishnu* or his *avatars* (incarnations) were key factors in this ritual. Reports of swinging in honour of *Vishnu* or his *avatars* such as *Rama* or *Krishna* are absent.

It was felt that all of these deities could in some way be influenced, controlled or manipulated, it was presumed that all of them required some form of pleasing or propitiation. One way of propitiation was through pain and suffering. The idea of the persuasive power of self-inflicted pain was the predominant rationale behind hook-swinging. And yet, the question of how much pain was actually experienced as a result of the process is somewhat problematic.[100] Degrees of pain may also have varied depending on how far the back was prepared for the operation and the care and skill of those inserting the hooks. The hooks were, in fact, usually inserted by specialists with considerable experience, and the manner in which this was done impressed more than one sceptical European observer. In 1833, Basil Hall, the English traveller, witnessed Hook-swinging in Madras. He remarked that 'the points of the hooks being extremely sharp, they were inserted without lacerating the parts, and so adroitly, that not a drop of blood flowed from the orifices, in fact, the native, who appeared to suffer no pain, conversed easily with those about him.[101]

The extent to which performers were in a trance or 'possessed' is impossible to estimate. However, a number of descriptions, most notably of the behaviour of hook-swingers in Medieval Andhra are consistent with this condition, a state of mind or being which again explains why some swingers claimed they felt no pain. Rev. H.W. Fox observed a man who swung in 1845. He describes that the man, who performed some rituals preliminary to swinging, was also on that occasion possessed by the spirit:

> "He was now rubbed all over, from the crown of his head to his feet, with turmeric—a yellow powder—and had his feet striped with red: a small cloth around

his waist, and a small turban on his head formed the whole of his dress, while around the calves of his legs were tied strings of little bells, which rattled as he moved. He came along dancing and leaping, flinging his arms and legs about like a maniac, sometimes bellowing, sometimes screeching, sometimes shouting in praise of the goddess... the crowd of spectators were highly delighted, and called out, 'see the power of the *Ammavaru*' 'Great is our goddess!' with other like expressions, and telling us that now he was possessed by, and actually represented by goddess".[102]

Another assumption which underlined hook-swinging was not so much the idea of appeasement by pain, but the notion that the Gods and Goddesses could be appeased by human and bloody sacrifice.[103]

Nowhere is this more clearly seen than in a *Telugu* myth of origin which suggests that hook-swinging was not the original form of devotion which pleased the deity, but a substitute for human sacrifice. The myth as recorded by the District Magistrate of Cuddapah in late nineteenth century reads:

> "There were two sages called *Vasishta* and *Vishwamitra*. They fell out with one another and the latter cursed the former; in consequence of which *vasishta's* sons become *pariahs* and began to offer human sacrifices to deities in performing their vows—*vasishta* became very uneasy at the fate of his sons, and asked *Vishwamitra* to point out some means by which they could find salvation. Then *Vishwamitra* proposed the process of hook-swinging and said that it answered as well as human sacrifice as it involved human torture".[104]

Although we cannot argue that the myth proves that swinging in general had its origin in a format human sacrifice, it certainly suggests a connection between hook-swinging and human sacrifice.

There is sometimes a distinct difference between the ideas implicit in the mythology, history, content and structure of certain ceremonies and beliefs of those who participate. For instance, it cannot be assumed that all those who took part in swinging ceremonies were necessarily aware of all that the ritual implied. And yet, there was undoubtedly a widespread conviction among performers concerned with the supernatural, that the practice would, in some way, please or placate the deity; and that this was all that was necessary to know if one was to deal with problems in the present, or exercise some control over future events.[105]

The decision to swing was usually made weeks or months or even longer before the swinging took place. If an individual had done it for his or her own particular reasons (as opposed to those who acted as proxies or swung as 'victims' on behalf of the community), then the swinging was invariably the result of a vow—votaries promising to perform the ritual if the deity would grant their request. In that sense, therefore, the purpose of hook-swinging was much the same as that of pilgrimage, fire-walking or some other ritual undertaken as a result of a vow made to the deity at a time of crisis or personal need.[106]

Swinging took place only in the presence of certain deities—namely those that required frequent propitiation. As a result swinging was likely to occur or to be chosen as an option in those areas where different types of deities and different theologies, such as *bhakti* tradition, were especially influential. The specific reasons for making the vow to swing varied.[107]

There seems to have existed a connection between hook-swinging and the forces of nature. The like of which were of concern not only to individuals but to the whole community. A British administrator, Lushington commented that, in Masulipatnam district, in case of famine, cholera or other calamity, a swinging takes place for the purpose of propitiating the deity.[108] Toke Jeyaram Nayudu, a retired sheristadar in Nellore district, noted in 1893, that in some cases the practice was followed for the propitiation of the village

Goddess, when famine, cholera or other calamity occurred and when men and cattle died in numbers.[109]

It appears that the ritual was totally alien to the *Brahmanic* culture. It had nothing to do with what might be described as *Aryan* or *vedic* traditions. It is also apparent that the practice was neither mentioned nor sanctioned in *shastras* or classical Hindu texts. And one of the more striking aspects of the ritual is that there is no evidence of a single Brahman ever having swung. The communities involved were either *sudras* or more commonly untouchable or tribals.[110]

However, this ritual continued until the British Government tried to curb this practice from 1854 onwards. What people thought if they gave up the practice as a result of Government attempts to suppress the practice is reflected in petitions to authorities in Madras Presidency. In 1890's a cultivator, on behalf of his community, requested the Government of Madras to revive the practice in a certain village. He claimed that since the ceremony had been stopped, the rainfall had been deficient and the crops scanty; cholera had been prevalent; and in families where there were five or six children ten years previously, there were now only two or three.[111] It only shows how deep was the belief, that underlined the swinging ceremony, entrenched in the minds of the people at popular level.

The nature of religious practices at popular level shows clearly that the dominant social groups not only restrained from participation but presided over a religious system that entailed unimaginable suffering and loss of men and materials.

References

1. Suryanarayana Murthy & S.V. Joga Rao, 'Gramadevatalu' (Telugu) in *Bharati*, No.8, 1989, p. 30.
2. W.T. Elmore, *Dravidian Gods in Modern Hinduism,* Delhi, (1913), Delhi, Reprint, 1984. p.13.
3. Ibid.
4. Ibid.

5. Ibid., p.14.
6. Ibid., p.14.
7. This may vary from region to region and goddess to goddess. For a description of the worship of *Peddamma* please see, *Kurnool District Manual*, 1880, see, 11, pp. 50-56.
8. W.T. Elmore, op. cit., p.15.
9. Ibid, p. 16; Palavekari Kadiripati, *Sukasaptati* (Telugu text written around 17th century) (ed.) by B. Rama Raju, A.P. Sahitya Academy, Hyderabad, 1979, poem, 2-76.
10. Ibid.
11. W.T. Elmore, op. cit, p.16.
12. Ibid.
13. Henry Whitehead, *The Village Gods of South India*, Delhi (1921), Reprint, 1988, , p. 49.
14. Ibid.
15. Ibid.
16. Ibid.
17. Ibid.
18. Ibid., p.50
19. Ibid., p. 51.
20. This he-buffalo would be sometimes let loose before *Jatara*, as *devarapotu*. But this is not necessary for all *devarapotus*. But this loosed buffalo is taken into captivity as soon as the date for *Jatara* is fixed by village elders and is tied in *Madiga* area (an untouchable area).
21. People made these words to express their excitement and enthusiasm.
22. M.L.K. Murthy, *Social and economic history*, op cit, p. 10.
23. K. Suryanarayana Murthy & S.V. Joga Rao, 'Gramadevatalu' (Telugu) in *Bharati*, No.8, 1989, p.31.
24. H. Whitehead, *Village Gods*, op. cit, p. 65.
25. E.C. V. Ag.7
26. C.P. Brown, *Local Records*, 15, Gandikota, p. 127.
27. *Census of India*, 1961, *Fairs and Festivals*, Vol. II, Part VII-(b) (17), Karimnagar district, p. 61.

28. Ramalakshmi, 'The Maria practice and the East India Company', in *APHC*, 1986, p. 245.

29. Ibid., p. 167.

30. Dominigos Paes, Chronica dos reis di Bisinga, translated into English by Robert Sewell in *A Forgotten Empire*, London, 1900, p. 245; Fernao Nuniz, another traveller to Vijayanagara also endorses these views, Please see, *Narrative of Fernao Nuniz*, tr. by R. Sewell, Ibid., p. 365.

31. S. Pratapa Reddy, *Andhrula Sanghika Charitra* (Telugu), 1949, p. 82-3. The original poem reads:

" చంపుడి పడి యెదియని యా
దంష్ట్రయుల కళేబరముల త్రలులంగని చేత
సంపాదిత భయదైద్ర
కెంపియబ్బె ఘట్టి చెగడి కన్నులు మూసెన్

32. Srinatha, *Palanati Veera Charitra*, p. 304.

33. Palavekari Kadiripati, *Sukasaptati*, (ed.) by B. Rama Raju, A.P. Sahitya Academy, Hyderabad, 1979, poem: 1-99.

34. Ibid, poem, 1-100

35. M. Nagabhushana Sarma, Folk Performing Arts of Andhra Pradesh, Hyderabad, 1995, p. 147.

36. Kadiripati, *Sukasaptati*, Hyderabad, 1979, Poem, 1-99.

37. Ayyalaraju Narayanamatya, *Hamasavimsati* (ed.) by C.V. Subbanna Satavadhani, Hyderabad, 1977, Poem, 3-29.

38. Vallabharaya, *Kridabhiramam*, Hyderabad, 1960, poem, 142. The original text reads:

" అవ అవయందు నెజ్జిని చంద్రమల్లెల
చూర్ణంపు సందాల చూచ్చువారు "

39. Tenali Ramakrishna, *Pandurangamahatyamu*, (ed.) by G. Ramasubba sarma, A.P. Sahitya Academy, Hyderabad, 1984, Ch.3, VV, 73-79.

40. Ibid., VV, 73-79.

41. H. Whitehead, *Village Gods of South India*, 1988, p. 80.
42. Tenali Ramakrishna, op. cit. 3-77.
43. B. Ram Raju holds that *Mailarubhatas* were the devotees of village goddesses. Their faith and piousness toward goddesses were very barbarous and superstitious. See, his work, *Telugu Janapada Geya Sahityam*, Hyderabad, 1958, p. 438. However, it seems that these kinds of sacrifices were also performed at Saivite temples.
44. Vallabharaya, *Kridabhiramam*, Poem, 142.

" కరవాడి యులుసల గనపపోతర్లల
నుచ్చి చేరులు గోసి యుయుకువారు
కటికి వాన్యళంబు గండ కత్తెరబట్టి
మీసి మిండయులనుగాక త్రింగువారు
సందులను నాకసంబుల సలుపువారు
యెడమ మడిచేత నారయులచ్చువారు
సాహసము మూర్తి దైకొన్న సరణివారు
ధీర హృదయులు మైలారు వీరభటులు "

45. K. Sarojini Devi, *Religion in Vijayanagara Empire*, 1990, p. 267.
46. Archaeological Survey of Mysore, *Annual Reports*, 1910, p.5.
47. Ibid.
48. Srinatha, *Palnati Veera Charitra* (ed.) by P. Lakshmikantam & A. Surya Rao, Vishalandhra Publications, Vijayawada, 1961, p. 57. The original poem reads:

" ఈ జీవనంబేల ఈ దేహముల నీకైన ప్రాణముల నీకె అర్పించు
అటులలమని యెంచ నర్పింపు కాదు నెత్తురు నీ మదా నింప జల్లెదము
చూడు మా సాహస స్ఫూర్తులనుచు ఆగక రోష సమావేశ మెసగ
విరల మట్టుకు కత్తులరవడి దూసి వక్షస్థలంబుల వదలక యురిచి "

49. Palkuriki Somanatha, *Panditaradhya Charitra*, (ed.) by Ch. Narayana Rao, Telugu University, Hyderabad, 1992, poem, 409, the original poem reads:

" గళముల జిహ్వల కర్ణరంధ్రముల
కడుపుల మెడల వక్షముల ప్రక్కల
నలరంగ పెను డిలయలు నారసములు
గలయంగ నిరుమెయిగాడ సంధించి "

50. Kuchimanchi Timmakavi, *Neelasundari Parinayam*, Poem 1 - 114.

" గొప్ప చింబోతు కడుపుల హూర్చి నీకు
కొవ్వు బెట్టింతు చుమ్మియో గంగనమ్మ "

51. Tenali Ramakrishna, *Pandurangamahatyamu*, Hyderbad, 1984, Ch. 3, V.78.

" కొంత యొకర్తు మూపున కంప లచ్చె
మూరుగా అచ్చె నాక సుధా మధురవారి
లలన యొకర్తు నారి ఊళంబులచ్చె
శక్తి జాతర సద్భక్తి శక్తుతెసగ "

52. Pingali Surana, *Kalapoornodayam*, A.P. Sahitya Academy, Hyderabad, 1980, poem, 6-43.

53. Ganapavarapu Venkatakavi, *Prabandha Rajavenkateswara Vijayavilasamu*, Ch. 7, V.88.

" కొందరు నోటి జీగముల దాసళ్ళ పెల్లన
నోరుల పూరులు గలుచువారు "

54. Tenali Ramakrsihna, *Pandurangamahatyamu*, 3-73.

55. This is called '*Poonakam*' in modern times.

56. Palavekari Kadiripati, *Sukasaptati*, 2-450.

" శివము ప్రత్యించి యపుడు చేచేత వేసికొనియె ప్రత్యేడు విద్యులు "

57. Vallabharaya, *Kridabhiramam*, Hyderabad, 1960, poem, 142.

" గాలంపు కొంకి కంకాళ చర్మము గ్రుచ్చి
యుడు వీధి నుయ్యేల లూగువారు "

58. Tenali Ramakrishna, *Pandurangamahtmyamu*, Hyderabad, 1984, 3-77.

" అంబనరము క్రింద నసియాడు, నైరాడ
అయు బొటె పిడప్రేతే తెరవయొర్రు "

59. S. Pratapa Reddy, *Andhrula Sanghika Charitra*, (Telugu), 1949, p. 259.

60. Describing the marriage customs among the people in the interior of the Malabar coast, he wrote: There are amongst them young girls who desire to marry some man for whom they have a liking, and one of these will promise her idol to do it a great service if she should marry such a one whom she wishes for. And if she marries that one, she then says to him, I have to make a feast for such a god, and I have to offer my blood before I deliver myself to you. And so they appoint a day for celebrating that feast. And she takes a large wagon with oxen, and they fix it in a very high crane, such as those with which they draw after, and they fasten it to as iron chain with two iron hooks, and she comes out of her house with great honour, accompanied by all her relations and friends men and women, with much singing and playing of instruments, and many dancers and jesters; and she comes wrapped very tightly round the waist with her white stuffs, covered from the waist to the knees, the rest bare, and at the door of her house, where the car stands, they lower the crane and stick the two hooks into her loins between the skin and the flesh, and put into her left hand a small round shield, and a little bag with lemons and oranges. They then raise the crane with great shouting and sound of instruments, firing guns, and making other festal demonstrations: and in this manner the car begins its march on the way to the house of the idol to which the promise was made; and she goes suspended by those hooks fastened into her flesh, and the blood runs down her legs. And she continues to sing and shout for joy, and strike upon the shield, and to throw oranges and lemons to her husband and to her relations, who go with her in this manner to the door of the said house of prayer, where they take her down, and cure her, and deliver her to her husband; and she gives at that place great alms to the Brahmans and offerings to the idols, and a great feast to as many as accompanies her. Duarte Barbosa, *A Description of the Coasts of East Africa and Malabar in the beginning of sixteenth century*,

trans. by the Hon.H.E.J. Stanely, Hakluyt Society, Vol. XXXV, London, 1866, pp. 95-6.

61. *Travells* of Pietro Della Valle in India, Hakluyt Society, Series II, Vol. II, London, 1892, p. 259.

62. Gaspero Balbi's Voyage to Pegu', in Pinkerton, A General Collection of the Best and Most Interesting Voyages and Travels in all parts of the World (17 Vol.) Vol. IX, London, 1811, p. 398.

63. As quoted in E. Thurston, *Ethnographic Notes in Southern India*, Madras, 1906, p. 490.

64. W. Crooke (ed.), *Travels in India by Jean-Baptiste Tavernier* (First Indian ed.), Delhi, 1977, Vol. II, pp. 198-9.

65. Edward Moon, *A Narrative of the Operations of Captain Littles' Detachment...* London, 1794, p. 412-13.

66. Alexander Duff, *India and India Missions*, Edinburgh, 1840, pp. 268-9.

67. *The Missionary Herald*, Vol. LXIV, 1868, p. 408.

68. *Church Missionary Gleaner* CIZ/0222/3, Journal, 20/2/1848 and CI2/0222/9 journal, 15/2/1851.

69. *Select Documents: Extracts from the Rev. J.E. Sharkey's journal of a visit to the festival at Vuyyur, Masulipatnam District, 1848, in Geoffrey A. Oddie, popular Religion, Elites, and Reform: Hook-Swinging and its Prohibition in Colonial India, 1800-1894*, p. 178. Hereafter select Documents

70. J.C. Irwin, 'the sacred Anthill and the cult of the Primordial Mound' in *History of Religions*, Vol.21, 1982, p. 341.

71. J.H. Powell, 'Hook-Swinging in India', *Folklore*, Vol. XXV, June 1914, p. 148.

72. Basil Hall, *Fragments of Voyages and Travels*, London, 1833, p. 83

73. Geoffrey A. Oddie, op. cit, p. 24, The same author published some important documents from India Office Library and records, from Missionary Magazine and News Papers in his work. These are very important to an Indian scholar as they are otherwise available only abroad.

74. *Selections from the Madras Government*, No. VII, Reports on the swinging Festivals and Ceremony of Walking through Fire, Madras, 1854. (Hereafter Selection from Madras).

75. Geoffrey A. Oddie, op. cit. p. 28.

76. Henry Whitehead, *The village Gods of South India*, London, 1921, p. 45.
77. Selections from Madras, p. 14.
78. Ibid, North Arcot, Nellore.
79. Geoffrey A. Oddie, op. cit, p. 29.
80. IOR P/4409 M.J.P. 21/12/1893, p. 65, quoted by Geoffrey A. Oddie, op. cit., p.44.
81. L.K. Anantha Krishna Iyer, *Cochin Castes and Tribes*, P. 324.
82. For different motives of the ritual in other parts of India, see, Geoffrey A. Oddie, op. cit, p.32.
83. Selections from Madras, p.2.
84. Census of India, 1901, Madras, Vol.15, part.I, p. 164.
85. In the same way in Bombay Presidency, the prominent castes and communities who performed hook-swinging were *Kunbis* (cultivators) and *Malis* (gardeners) as well as *Mahar* and *Mangs*, two major untouchable groups in the region, besides, bills, a large tribal community. R.E. Enthoven, *Tribes and Castes of Bombay*, Bombay, 1920.
86. Selections from Madras, p.16.
87. Selections from Madras, p. 16
88. Geoffrey A. Oddie, op. cit. p.35.
89. S. Srinivasa Raghavaiyanar, *Memorandum of the Progress of the Madras Presidency*, Madras, 1893, p. cxcviii.
90. Geoffrey A. Oddie, op.cit., p. 35.
91. The Church Missionary Gleaner, 1850-51, pp. 16-19.
92. S. Mateer, p. 220
93. *Harvest Field*, Vol.3, April 1864, p. 140.
94. D.D. Kosambi, 'Living Prehistory in India', *Scientific American*, Feb. 1967, p. 111.
95. E. Hoole, *Madras and the South of India; or a Personal Narrative of a Mission to those countries*, London, 1844, p. 358, B. Rama Raju & Nayani Krishna Kumari, *Janapada Geyalu, Sanghika Charitra*, Hyderabad, 1972, p. xxxvi.
96. Geoffrey A. Oddie, op.cit.p.40.
97. Selections from Madras, p.15

98. Geoffrey A. Oddie, op.cit., p.47.
99. W.T. Elmore, *Dravidian Gods in Modern Hinduism*, Madras, 1925, p. 102.
100. Geoffrey A. Oddie, op. cit, p. 51.
101. Basil Hall, *Fragments of Voyages and Travels*, London, 1833, p. 83.
102. *The Church Missionary Gleaner*, 1845, pp. 123-5; 1850/1, p. 18 quoted by Geoffrey A. Oddie, op. cit. p. 55.
103. In Bengal a view of hook-swinging as pain and penance was dominant whereas ideas of the custom as a blood offering or a substitute for bloody sacrifice tended to predominate in South India.
104. 10RP/4409 *Madras Judicial Proceedings*, 21/12/1893, p.65, quoted by Geoffrey A Oddie, op. cit. p. 56.
105. Geoffrey A. Oddie, op. cit. p. 58.
106. Ibid, p. 59.
107. A Methodist missionary had observed that hook-swinging near Madras in 1820's took place in consequence of vows made in time of sickness or danger or for obtaining children or for some other desired object. E.Hoole, *Madras and South of India*, op. cit., p. 357.
108. *Selections from Madras*, p.14.
109. Quoted by A. Geoffrey A. Oddie, IOR P/4409 *Madras Judicial Proceedings*, 30/6/1893, p.84.
110. Geoffrey A. Oddie, op. cit. p. 78.
111. E.Thruston, *Ethnographic Notes in Southern India*, p. 498.

5

PERFORMING POPULAR CULTURE

In the previous chapter, we have discussed various kinds of rituals and customs. In this chapter let us try to examine how popular culture found expression in performance. Closely connected with rituals were entertainments, and professional groups. During medieval Andhradesa there were many kinds of entertainments. Most popular among them were: *Jangam Katha, Asadi Katha, Jamakula Katha, Pichchukuntas, Palnati Katha, Katamaraju Katha, Veera Mushtis, Tandana Tana Kathalu* which are basically narrative in character; Dance forms such as *Kolatam*; theatre forms like *Yakshaganam* and *Tolubommalata* were also a very popular.

The common thread which runs through all these forms was religious in character. Whether it was a narrative dance or theatre forms, thematic representations were largely associated with epics, puranas etc.[1] Another important feature was that a particular caste emerged as the performer of a particular art form.[2] Narration of *Palanati Katha* by *Vira Vidyavantulu* and the appropriation of this narration is a case in point.

Narratives or Ballads

Ballads are narratives meant for singing. Usually their dramatic mode of narration focuses on a single event. They are highly emotive in the sense that they arouse anger, fear and sorrow almost instantaneously. It is because the ballads, more often than not, narrate startling stories of either exceptional valour or of agonising nature, pathetic or sometimes stories containing both these were also narrated.

The tradition of ballad singing owes its origin to Veerasaiva sect, which tried to propagate saivism through these songs. The story told by *Jangams*, originally a Veerasaiva wandering sect, is known as '*Jangam Katha*'. *Jangam* ballad singers sang only stories of saivism.[3] However, over the period, other sects, taking cue from *jangams,* began singing the stories of heroic deeds of a local hero or religious stories.[4]

Jangam Katha

As we have already noted, *Jangams* were Saivite minstrels. The ballads they recited were called '*Jangam Kathalu*'. These reciters were also called *Budige Jangalu* because the main percussion instrument which gave rhythm to the narration was '*Budige*' or '*Dhakki*' or *gummeta* (a percussion instrument). Many medieval literary texts have recorded these reciters. Palkurki Somanatha's *Basavapuranam* and *Vallabharaya's Kridha-bhiramam* say that these reciters drew huge crowds with their performance during *Sivarathri* festivals.[5]

To begin with *Jangams* recited saiva stories. However, later on they started reciting many non-saivite and mundane stories as well. They were basically itinerant singers who moved from place to place singing and performing in villages. An inscription from Pedakoduru of Cuddapah district talks about *Jangamas*.[6]

Jangam Katha contains three participants: *Kathakudu* (the main narrator) and two *Vanthalu* (chorusmen) providing the rhythm and singing the refrain. The refrain was sometimes a short '*bhali-bhali', tandana-tana'* and '*ayyo-deva'* which are mood referents and sometimes a general refrian '*tandana-tandani tandana-deva nandana'* etc. which reflect the metrical length of the song. Their percussion instrument was called differently as *budige, dhakki, gummeta* etc. in different parts of the state.[7]

The main narrator wore a gown up to his ankles, a *dhotti* to his waist, a turban on the head and bells on his ankles. He had a *tambura* on his shoulder. He played on it for scale (*shruti*). He also wore *andelu* (bells) around his left thumb and the left pointing finger which gave basic rhythm to his singing.[8]

Drum, *dhakki* or *gummeta* is a clay vessel (sometimes of brass) of 10" diameter at one end and was covered by goat skin. The other end was in the shape of a jar and was not closed. The *gummeta* players used to hang it to their left shoulder. The rhythm came from the right side of the drum which was closed by striking at it with the fingers of the right hand, as the left palm opened and closed, the open end gave the varying tonal changes in the rhythm.[9]

Adidamu Sura Kavi, who belonged to eighteenth century, (1720-85) laments that many castes were squandering their money on patronising some traditional entertaining castes but no one was willing to give to poets (brahmanas). He says:

"Jangalapalu Devangula Vithambu"[10]

(It means that Devangas or non-brahmin saivites spent their riches on Jangamas)

Asadi Katha

Asadis served as priests of Goddesses. They were mainly performers of rituals on festive occasions particularly during procession. The *asadis* narrated many stories during the nightlong festivals and *jataras*. The story which was accompanied by dance took place for three nights sometimes it was even extended to nine nights. W.T. Elmore, the premier British Ethnographer observed this story telling personally. He writes that *asadis* sang the story of *Poleramma*,[11] describing her powers and dangers which may come from neglecting her. This was done during processions before *Jatara* started. Again, on the first day of *Jatara asadi* summoned all the elders to witness calling each one by name and publicly announced the various vows made to *Poleramma*. As the procession continued, *Asadi* chanted the stories of goddess to arouse the people to take a proper part in worship.[12]

It appears that in the beginning only one *Asadi* used to narrate. However, as the time passed by there emerged three persons in the *Asadi* presentation, the main narrator and the other two who provided rhythm. All the three had *jamidikas* or *bavanikas*. The leader's instrument was usually bigger than the other two.[13]

Jamakula Katha

This is a narrative recited to the accompaniment of two *Jamukas*, string instruments, one serving as shruti (scale) and the other as a percussion instrument. Performers who recited Parasurama and Yellamma were called *Jamukula Vallu*.[14] Sometimes Malas and Madigas served as priests during *Jatara* of various goddesses. *Jamuku* was called *Jamidika* in Telangana. This was also known as *Pamba*. The *Pamba* was always in pairs - one small and another bigger. In Coastal Andhra, performing Madigas were known as *Bavanilu* or *Baindlu* and narrated the ballad of Parasurama and worshiped Yellama.[15] *Kridabhiramam* tells us that *Bavani* women used to sing before Ekavira idols during Kakatiya period. It reads

"*vaadyavaikari kadu nervadiyanga*
Ekaveera Mahadevi Yeduta nilchi
Parasuramuni Kathalella Proudi Paade
Charutara Keerti bavaneela chakravarti"[16]

Malas who used to sing the ballads of *Ankamma* were known as *Pambala*. W.T. Elmore also remarks that story-tellers in the worship of Ankamma are *Pambala Vandlu* who are Malas. He further says that Madigas (*asadis*) would not be allowed to tell the story of *Ankamma*.[17] However, in Telangana, Madigas were known both as *Pambala* and *Baindla*.[18] Both Malas and Madigas served as priests of village Goddesses and sang the ballads of Goddesses to ward off epidemics and cattle diseases in villages.[19]

Medieval literature like *Kasikhandam* and *Sukasaptati* also talk about Bavanis. *Kasikhandam* says about piety of Bavanis in the following poem:

> "*Saivudai yokavela sarvangakambula*
> *bhutau rudrakhamulu dharinchu*
> *batiyinchu sregeeta parama bhagavatudai*
> *yuddati natiyinchu nokkanadu*
> *goraga mylarunu goniyada nokavela*
> *nosalipai bhamdaru pasupudalchi*
> *pranutinchu Ekaviradevi nokavela*
> *bavaneedai, samagra bhaktigarima*"[20]

Another text *sukasapati*, also, describes *Bavanis* as:

> "*kalalo devara chepperela yedutam ganpinchi neyyambu, vaa tila neepaliki devudinka, bavaneedayanchu danada, gaa valene bapana muppelaina sariya varella satkaalu, nee valegocharinchire ninne koltunanuchu nvarinchucho namtatan*"[21]

The chief narrator played on the bigger instrument while his assistant played on the smaller one. The strings used in both instruments were made of animal guts fixed into the hollow drums covered with skin on one side and kept open on the other side. In the smaller instrument the gut was permanently fixed to a wooden rod running over the outer cover of the drum forming a triangle.[22] When the string was struck with fingers or nails it produced sweet notes of *sruti*. In the bigger drum the gut at the loose end was tied to a small stick which the player held with the left palm, while striking the string inside the hollow space with the right hand fingers and produced different terrific sounds.[23] Along with the pair of *jamukus* they also used a wind instrument called *Titti*. In Costal Andhra ballad singing by these communities had become a sort of folk performing art. However, in Telangana it was ritualistic in nature. It also formed a part of tenth day ritual of a dead person, particularly among Kapus, Reddis and Yadava communities.[24]

There were three performers in the *Pamba* ballad singing. One provided *shruti* (scale) with a *titti* and the other provided rhythm with *Pambajodu* (percussion instrument). The main narrator held a long sword in his right hand and a smaller one called (*jamajala*) in his left hand. He also wore a coloured head gear and a coloured waist cloth to dress like a prince.[25] Adidamu Surakavi (1720-85 A.D.) in his *satakam* laments that Kapus were spending money on *Pambala Vallu*. He remarks,

"*Kapu vittambu Pambakani palu*"[26]

Pichchukuntas

They were also an itinerant minstrels who wandered through villages singing the caste histories to *Kapu, Reddi, Balija, Kamma* and *Yadava* communities. They were also called *Pichchukunta Vallu*. There are many references to this group in medieval literary texts. They are called *Helivaras* in Karnataka. They used to move from place to place telling Yadavas and Reddis of their family *gotrams* (lineages).[27]

They were Saivites and worshipped Mallikarjuna of Srisailam. Their spiritual preceptors were *Jangams*. They sang with the help of *titti* (a wind instrument) and *ganta* (bell). However, now-a-days, they use tambourine and *dhakki* (percussion instrument). But *dhakkis* are smaller in size than the ones used by the Jangamas earlier. They are made of brass and are covered on one side with goat skin. Adidamu Surakavi talks about the patronization of this caste by *Golla* (Yadava) caste.

He says,

"*Golla vittambu Pichchukunta palu*"[28]

The eighteenth century classical work *'Hamsavimati'* by Ayyalaraju Narayanamatya also mentions, inter alia, this group.[29]

With the passage of time they also started narrating ballad of *Palnati Yuddam*, a ballad which was traditionally sung by *Vira Vidyavantulu*.[30]

Palnati Katha

This is the earliest historical ballad cycle in Medieval Andhra. This is based on historical events which primarily pertain to a battle between two cousins. This battle was fought circa 1182-85 A.D. This was fought between Nalagama Raju and Malideva Raju, the Haihaya Princes.[31]

Palnati Veeracharitra has been built around two important personalities, Brahmana and Nagamba or Nayakuralu, who were arch rivals. These two pushed rulers of Palnadu to the background and dominated the political stage. Anugu Raja (1138-1170 A.D.) had three sons by his three wives. Brahmana, the Prime Minister, of Anugu Raja crowned Nalagama as the king of Gurijala and Narasimha, another son of his, as crown-prince.[32] Nagamba, another powerful woman in Haihaya court service won over Narasimaraja to her side. Soon she increased her influence at the court and became chief advisor of Nalagama and de facto Prime Minister.

Now Brahmana espoused the cause of Malideva, the third son of Anuguraja. Later the kingdom was partitioned between Nalagama and Malideva and his brothers. Malideva started ruling from Macherla as his capial and Nalagama with Gurijala as his Capital.[33] Cock-fight between Brahmanna and Nagamba and the defeat of Brahmanna resulted in the loss of the kingdom of Malideva.[34] After spending sometime in exile, Brahmana sent an envoy to negotiate the restoration of Macherla to Malideva and brothers. When the envoy was murdered, it resulted in the battle. This is the historical background of this ballad.

The extant *Palanati Veera Charitra*, which is the main source of information about the war, is, too, in the form of ballad. This is in a meter known as *Manjaridwipada* which is well-suited to singing.

It is attributed to famous Telugu poet Srinatha during the early half of 15th century at the Reddi court of Kondavidu. It is likely that he also based his work on the ballads that were current during his time.[35] These ballads are practically in the possession of *Panchamas* (Malas). They are called *Vira vidyavantalu.*[36] They are also known as *Dasarlu*.

C.P. Brown is said to have collected these ballads. However, they were first edited by Akkiraju Umankantam.[37] Subsequently it underwent many editions. Visalandhra *Prachuranalayamu* published a fuller and complete text and it was edited by Pingali Lakshmikantam.[38]

Brahmanna who was famous for his radical Vaishnava movement and various socio-religious reforms and sixty six heroes who fought on his behalf and sacrificed their lives in the war are worshipped even today in a five-day festival at Karempudi and in all neighbouring villages during the month of *Kartik*. At this celebration, *Viravidyavantalu* sing the commemoration ballads.[39]

Prefix *Veera* is for everything connected with Palnadu battle. The land itself is called *Veera* Palnadu. Villages where battle took place are called *Veera Gramalu*. Worship of heroes is called *Veera Puja* or *Veeragallu*. Festival is *Veerotsavam*. On this occasion *Veera Vidyavantalu*, the Mala minstrels sing about heroic deeds.[40]

These *Veera* Vidyavantalu or *Palnati Varu* were *Panchama* minstrels. They are authorised to narrate ballads by the temple trustees. It is only *Veera Vidyavantalu* who sing at the commemoration of this ballad, although there are other groups of minstrels who narrate *Palnati Katha*, particularly *Pichchukuntis*.

According to T.V. Subba Rao, *Palnad* ballad cycle consists of twenty five ballads.[41] All are related either to the actual war or preparations for the war or the genealogies of some of the heroes. *Vira Vidyavantalu*, who narrated the ballad, claim that they were the descendants of Kannamadasa who was a great *Panchama* warrior who died in the war fighting on behalf of his foster-father

Brahama Nayudu and became a martyr.[42] By 13th century, this ballad was already well-known and was narrated during the *Sivaratri* festival at Orugallu. *Kridabhiramam*, also states that ballads of *Palnati Katha* like Nagambas machinations, cock-fight and Brahmanna's '*Chapa kudu*' (inter-caste dining) were narrated by *Vira Vidyavantalu* or *Palnati Varu*.[43]

Even now the five-day festival at Karempudy is a spectacular event when people of all castes worship Heroes of their land and the weapons they used. On the fourth day, the *Matha-Adipathi*, the *Guru* of the *Peetham*, takes the costumes of Brahmanayudu to worship the Heroes and the weapons and thousands of people follow him to pay their tribute.[44] During all the five days and the subsequent fifteen days, the families whose ancestors participated in the battle will arrange for the performances of *Palnati Katha*, even at their own houses.[45]

This group consists of four members—the main narrator and his assistants. One plays on *Veera Jodu* (a pair of drums) with two bells on it, and other a *shruti* (scale) instrument known as *titti* and third *talam* (cymbals). Third man follows the ballad by filling the gaps and by repeating the lines. As the main narrator symbolises Heroes of Palnadu battle, he wears a sword and a shield.[46]

According to the tradition, the main narrator and his companions have to wear twelve components as a part of their costume: 1) a red-bordered dhoti (*kasi-kaka*), 2) a long cloth tied as turban (*talagudda*), 3) a feather in his turban (*kaliki turayi*), 4) an image of the *ummahu* bird made of silver (*Ummahu Pitta*), 5) the image of the half-moon (*chandravanka*), 6) a ring to the second finger of the right leg (*ande*) 7) a sword and a shield (katti, dalu), 8) a bell hanging to his waist (*boddu ganta*), 9) a cloth tied across form the left shoulder down to the arms (*jamjagudda*), 10) a pair of drums (*veerajodu*), 11) a shruti instrument made of calf leather (*titti*). Apart from these, the main narrator also wears *tirumani* (a long vermilion mark on his forehead, on his chest and on either side of upper arms).[47]

Katama Raju Katha

Katama Raju Katha is the second oldest historical ballad after *Palnati Veera Charitra*. The story describes the events and incidents connected with *Panchalinga Konda* and *Erragaddapadu* battles fought between Yadavas under the leadership of Katama Raju on the one side and Nellore Cholas under Nallasiddi Raju on the other. These battles took place between 1280 and 1297 A.D.

Kommu Gollalu are minstrels who belong to *Madiga* community. They narrated the ballad of *Katama Raju Katha* to Gollas or Yadavas.[48] According to the tradition, only *Kommu Gollalu* were authorised to sing the ballad of *Katama Raju*. They are also called as *Suddula Gollalu*[49]and '*Teracheera Bhaktulu*'.[50] *Hamsavimsati* gives an interesting details about '*Tellakoka Bhaktulu*'.[51] These may be identical with *Kommu Gollalu*. They also tell the clan histories of *Gollas* particularly on the eleventh day of a dead person.[52]

Warriors who belonged to Panchama community like Birnidu and chennappa fought on Yadava side. The eldest son of Polaraju, Bhaktiranna who survived the battle is said to have ordained the progeny of Birnidu to sing the glory and maintain the records of Yadavas. *Kommulavaru* claim that they were the descendents of Birnidu and as such are hereditary custodians of this tradition. This explains the fact that *Kommu Gollu* were patronised by all Gollas all over Andhra Pradesh, particularly southern parts of Coastal Andhra.[53]

Ganga has always been considered as the *Kuladevata* (caste-deity) by Gollas. Therefore, all fairs and festivals (*jataras*) were organised in her name from time to time. *Katama Raju* stories sung at the time of these *Jataras*. We also find that the idols of *Katama Raju* are often located in the temples dedicated to Ganga, their *kuladevata* (caste-deity).[54]

Since the narrtors use *Kommu* (a hollow horn) at the beginning of their story-telling, they came to be called *Kommulavaru. Kommu* is variously known as *Kale, boora* and *gavuru*. Usually it was the horn of a bull or a *ram* (*pottelu*) polished and covered at both ends with brass or silver or even gold. It was like a conch and gave thunderous noise when it was blown.[55]

The author of *Chandra Sekhara Satakam* tells us that people during his time, used to listen to *Veera Gathalu* (Ballads of heroes who died in the battle).[56] It is not unreasonable to believe that these Veera Gathalu which were so famous were none other than *Palanati Veera Katha* and *Katama Raju Katha*.[57]

There is a team of four people in this ballad singing—the main narrator and three assistants. One of the assistants helps the narrator in singing by catching the line half way and also provides refrain. Another member plays on *veeranam* which is also called *Pamba Jodu*—a pair of *Pambas*. A clear description of *Pamba Jodu* is given at *Pamba Katha* in previous pages. To his left side the main narrator has *shruti*, (*scale*) provided by a *titti* (percussion). The man who plays *Pamba* stands to the right side of the narrator. *Talam* (rhythm) also accompanies narration.[58] The method of narration is recitative. The narrator in between the narration dances a little. Narrations of war are certainly emotive. In Coastal area, particularly Guntur and Prakasam, *Kommulavaru* are called *'gudarulu'* because they erect a tent in which they perform and narrate their stories. In the tent generally the large paintings of *Gangamma* (caste-deity) of Gollas and Katama Raju, the hero of Yadavas are hung.[59] These hangings are called *'Tera Cheerelu'*. It is because of these painted hangings that Kommulavaru are called '*Tera Cheera Bhaktulu*'—the devotees of hung paintings. Apart from Katama Raju Katha, *Kommu Gollalu* also narrate some *Shakti* ballads.[60] These minstrels are seen in Guntur, Prakasam and in some parts of Nellore. They are called *'Bhattu Vallu'* (eulogists) in Rayalaseema area.[61]

Veera Mushtis

Veera Mushti (valorous-fisted) was a community which specialized in stick-fighting. They also narrated the story of

Kanyaka (kuladevata) of Komatis. According to a legend, *Veera Mushtis* were authorized to sing the story of *Kanyaka* and also the *gothrams* of Komatis. Thurston observes that Veera Mushtis were a professional class of acrobats and mendicants who attached themselves to *Devanga* and *Komati* communities from whom they made their living.[62]

Veera Mushtis were semi-nomadic people. According to a Saivite tradition, they should not build a house and live in it. They should live under trees in the outskirts of villages. They must not sleep on beds. They were also not supposed to use bamboo from the forest. Lastly they should not have permanent oven to cook food.[63] They should make oven of three stones every time they cook. An inscription of sixteenth century says about Veera Mushtis as:

> "... *Brahmmala mudiyam aneti savamanya*
> *agraharamandula Sri Someswara devuniki srisela*
> *simhavasanusthulaina Bikshavruti Ayyavari sishyulaina*
> *pushpagiri Veeramushti bhumaya komarundu chena*
> *Bsuvayya Dharavosi icchina dharmasasana kramam....*
> *Ayyavali mukyamina chalumula samastha*
> *pekamdra Sammatinimni sakala purantakula sammatini*
> *Brahmmala mudiyam gramamandu tammalu*
> *modalainavaru acheti veera mushti pannu*
> *mudiyyam somesvaradevuni deeparadhanaku*
> *sakala purantakulaku punyanganunnu*
> *Jumjunum gasenu narasamumnu motu palakanu*
> *pattede Veera mushtulaku punyamaa nunnu...srikrishna*
> *Jayanti punyakalamandu sri someswaradevara"*
> *samnidini.... Isthimi*"[64]

This inscriptional evidence reveals that some Saivite groups such as Ayyavali and Tammallavaru gave donations to *Veera Mushtis*. This was recorded as *Veera Mushti pannu* in inscriptions.

Also, a representative of theirs collected this *pannu* in each village. In the aforesaid inscription, Veer Mushti chena Basuvayya was collecting their donations from Brahmana's *Agraharam*. Sometimes they served as servants in Saivite temples. They had also a regional representative to collect their donations. This representative was called '*Ganachari*'.[65]

Veera Mushtis also narrated the story of '*Kanyaka*' the caste-deity of Komatis. According to a legend, Kanyaka was born to Kusuma Sreshthi and Kusumabai. Vishnuvardhana, king of Rajamahendravaram, as *Kanyakapuranam* has it, while on hunting expedition, came to Penugonda, happened to see *Vasavi kanya*.[66] He fell in love with her and asked *Komatis* for her hand. But his request was turned down. However, king insisted on his desire. Realizing that they could not withstand pressure, many *Komatis* and *Kanyaka* wanted to commit suicide by jumping into fire.[67] *Veera Mushtis* who were carrying the palanquin of the king delayed in reaching the place of wedding. This delay enabled some Komatis and *Vasavi Kanyaka* to commit suicide. While dying Kanyaka is said to have blessed *Veera Mushtis* who helped the community to save its honour and wanted *Veera Mushtis* to be narrators of her caste.[68]

Veera Mushtis still narrate *Vasavi Kanyaka* story and participate in the wedding and cremation ceremonies of *Komatis*. Veera *Mushtis* dress themselves as *Jangams*. They carry a *ganta* (a big brass plate), a *Sankham* (conch) and wear ankle bells while narrating the story of *Kanyaka*. Just like Jangamas, they also smear ash marks on their forehead, wear *ling kaya* (a symbol of Siva). The narrator tells the story with the help of *ganta*. They use *sankham* (conch) when they recite stories of valour. With *Veeranam* and *talam* accompanying, story is narrated.[69]

Tandana Tana Kathalu or Burra Katha

As we have already noted in the previous pages, *Jangam kathas* were precursors of Burra Katha. It has been argued that *Burra katha* is a modern, more sophisticated and complex form of

Jangam katha.[70] *Kridabhiramam*, tells us that women belonging to *panchama* castes, (*Bavaneelu* or *Madigavaru*) used to be possessed by spirit while singing before the idol of *Ekavira*. In one of the poems it refers to *Tandana Kaktha* as:

> "*Akalanka sthitigori kolchedaru brahmananda bhavambunan*
> *sakalanandamaika matalaguchun santosha chittambunan*
> *toka dummul yakatalamul javanikal tandanalammayyakun'*
> *eka virammaku mahurammaku nado hrimkara madyatmaku*"[71]

It also refers to various kinds of entertainment such as *Tandana Tana Kathalu, Yakshaganams, Tolubommalatalu*, which were performed in the temples of the fort of Warangal during the reign of Prataparudra II.[72] *Panditaradhya Charitra* also talks about *tanana tana kathalu*. It says:

> "*...Alarusu badiharulallu yamadarunu*
> *Lalinuchi Changubhala Yanuvaru*"[73]

The word *Bhala* is believed to be the root of '*Bhalanoyi Tammuda bhai balanoyi dadana*', the choruses of Burra Katha.[74]

The team consisted of three people—the main narrator and two assistants (*vanthas*) who assisted the main narrator on percussion instruments. They narrated the same old stories like *Palnati Yuddham* and *Bobbili Katha*. As the time passed by, they also took up struggles against the British as their themes. As a result, stories such as Alluri Sitarama Raju, Lakshmi Bhai of Jhansi and Rudrama Devi and so on, became part of Burra Katha narration. The author of *Chandra Sekhara Shatakam* also tells that one of the favourite pastimes of the people of his period was to hear the narration of *Thandana Tana kathalu.*[75]

DANCES

Kolatam

It was perhaps the most popular dance form in the entire country. It was variously known in Andhra as *kolatam, kolannalu.*

Both temple structures and literary texts bear testimony to this play. Temples at Bikkavolu,[76] Daksharamam and samarlakota (12th century), at Veerabadhra temple at Macherla,[77] Srisailam and Hampi (Vijayanagara) contain dance sculptures of Kolatam. Most of sculptures show women playing Kolatam.[78] Bukkaraya's court poet Nachana Somana (C.1344 A.D.) mentioned this play in his work *Uttaraharivamsam*. In this text Srikrishna goes on expedition against Hamsadidakulu, Srikrishna's army moves in batches as in Kolatam play. He says:

> "*Vadaku Pannagaraju Padagala meda sa*
> *rvam sahakanta peranamu supa*
> *nurruta lugedu nudayasta girulato*
> *nakasa lakshmi kolatamada*"[79]

Kridabhiramam (1420 A.D.) also talks about Kolatam.[80] Tarigoppula Mallanna (1570-1625 A.D.) described this play in his work, *Chandrabhanu Charitra*.[81] Surabhi Madhavaraya's work *Chandrika Parinayam* describes Kolatam of Gandharvas.[82] All of them mention kolatam particularly in connection with village festivities *(jataras). Kolatam* was a combination of pleasing rhythmic movements and a delectable song-text set to music. This play combines in itself music, song and dance.

Pietro della Valle, who observed this play, says that it was a festival which they celebrated for three days at the end of a certain feast in honour of *Gauri* wife of *Mahodaka* and it was celebrated by girls. He says that young girls trimly clad used to go round the streets in small batches, all of them carrying in each hand a little round painted stick, about a span long or a little more, which they struck together after a musical measure to the sound of drums and other instruments, and one of the skillfull of the company, sung one verse of a song, at the end of which they all replied seven or eight times in the number of their metre with the word cole, cole, cole. Evidently the refrain of the song was:

"kolu kole kolanna kole
kolu kole celi melu kore"

He further tells us that they went to the temple followed by other women and used to dance in circles in the temples till late in the night.[83]

'Kola' mean a stick. 'Ata' means a play or dance. Therefore, kolatam is a dance using sticks as its main rhythm. It was originally a ritual based dance, explicating a sequence in mythology through music and dance. However, over the period, a number of romantic and humorous songs were added to its repertoire. In the beginning this was played by women. However, later on men took over this play.[84]

Kolatam group consisted of any number of people between eight to forty. There was no bar on the number as long as the number was even. Besides, there used to be a leader of the group who was known as *pennudi* or *kolana pantulu* or *guruvu*. A pair of dancers was called *uddi*. One who initiated the striking of the stick was called *Ramudu* and the other one who received was called *Laxmanudu*. This division became important particularly when the group in course of dance, moved in two circles (*to uddi*) and all the receiving artists forming the outer circle (*veli uddi*). The leader was called *pennuddi*.[85] The performance contained several songs set to *kopus*. Each kopu differs from the other in the angles, in steps, movements while dancing. The tilting of the body and the whole gamut of movements suitable to that particular song and Kopus also vary from region to region. In Coastal Andhra, *uddi tirugudu kopu, vuyyala kopu, Krishna Garadi kopu, Kattera kopu, Jandhyala kopu, kuppigantu kopu* are popular kopus. In Rayalaseema, *talupu katti, sela katti, sivi kopu, tugudu kopu* etc. are among the prominent.[86]

Performance started with all dancers standing in a circle in the acting area or on the stage which was called '*garidi*'.[87] The leader and instrumentalists stood or sat at the centre of the circle. Usually harmonium, *maddela* (percussion) flute and sometimes clarinet accompanied *kolatam.*[88] It started with an invocation song to Ganesha.[89] As *pennuddi* sang refrain, dancers started moving slowly in a circle, repeating the line. He then gave a signal by saying '*kita tayyaku*' a sign for the change in the tempo of the song.[90] Each song was set in kopu and it also contained an *'ethugada'* (beginning) of a song, the leader either suggested it by a whistle or loudly announcing the signature of the *kopu*. To change the rhythm of beat into faster one, the leader again indicated it by changing the pace. Lastly, when he said '*Ita tayyaku tadhim*' or '*kita kita tayyaku tadhim*', it was an indication for the closing of the song.[91]

Panditaradhya Charitra describes various entertainments provided to the pilgrims keeping holy vigil on the night of *Mahasivaratri* day at Srisailam. Drama, dance, perhaps *kolatam*, music and singing were performed.[92] The various forms of dance and singing Kolatam were described by *Hamsavimsati* also.[93]

THEATRE FORMS

Yakshaganam

Yakshaganam can be described as an operatic ballet interspersed with song sung to varying rhythms for effective conveying of the mood of the episodic situation. It is a theatrical performing art form wherein music, dance, speech and make-up (including costume) are beautifully blended into one. This art form is also popular in Karnataka.[94] The earliest reference to it is to be found in *Panditaradhya Charitra*.[95] However, this was known as *Jakkula Pata* which was sung by *Jakkula*, a forest tribe. Later on this *Jakkula Pata* had been Sanskritized as *Yakshaganam*.[96] It was recitation of *desi* music by a *Yaksha* or *Yakshini* in its earlier state and after some stage evolved into a narration of episodes with the aid of more than one character and finally developed into an opera with different kinds of songs, dialogues and numerous characters. *Panditaradhya Charitra* of Palukurki Somanatha describes the various kinds of entertainments provided to pilgrims keeping holy vigil on the night of *Mahasivaratri* day at

Srisailam. He also wrote about *Yakshaganas* and traditional *desi* drama in the following words:

> *"Bahu Natakamulu*
> *Pramadha puratana patu charitramulu*
> *Gramamonda bahu Natakamu laduvaru*
> *Lalitanga rasa kalankara rekha lalavada bahurupa madedu varu*
> *Garanamul Meravanul gathulu gitramulu Naruduga Veddanga Madeduvaru"*[97]

Kridabhiramam also portraits a *Jakkula* lady's singing of the story of Kameswari's love.[98] E. Thurston described *Jakku* as a "dancing and theatrical caste".[99] According to the pieces of evidence, it seems that *yakshagana* began as a signing tradition. M. Nagabhushana Sarma holds that this development has taken place in three stages: (a) The *Sankeertana stage*, (b) the *narrative stage* (c) the *theatrical stage*.

The first stage of *yakshaganam* must have been closely related to the religious festivals. Because the first two references are in connection with temple festivals: at Srisailam temple and at draksharaama temple. Srinatha also mentioned it as a particular type of musical rendering.[100] *Kridabhiramam* also noted that this singing was done by *Jakkula Purandri*.[101] At this stage a singer merely participated in the worship of the deities through songs of various metres and rhythms. Tallapaka Annamayya, a singer-composer (15th century), also wrote that *yakshaganas* contained a variety of metres and rhythms to suit different occasions in his work *sankeertana Lakshanam*.[102] In its earlier stage of a development, *yakshaganam* was a musical rendering in different rhythms, sung in praise of different Gods and Goddesses. Singers disguised as *Yakshas* rendered their songs in the temple precincts during *Jatara* or *Tirunala* (festival). A story was added to devotional verses in its second stage of development. Only female singers disguised as *yakshinis* sang narratives. The first available text of this narrative is Obaya Mantri's Garvadachala Mahatmyam which contains songs and poems of a wide variety set in *jumpe, triputa, ata* and *eka talas*. It also had *desi* metres (*vrittas*) such as *dwipada, padyam, ela, sobhanam, dhavala* and *mangala harati*.[103]

Three prosodic texts confirm the literary qualities of *Yakshaganam*. *Lakshana deepika*, an anonymous text, attributed to sixteenth century mentioned that *Yakshaganam* contained *pada, daruvu, ela, dhavala, jakkula reku pada, chandamama suddi, ashtaka* etc. Chitrakavi Peddanna (c. 1550) described vividly how the above metres were constructed. In the same way Appakavi (c. 1650) also laid down norms for the construction of *Yakshaganam*.[104]

A woman disguised herself as a *Yakshini* narrated the story. This presentation involved descriptions of scenes, prose interludes, connecting one incident to the other, announcement of character, interaction and, of course, the dialogues of various characters, all rendered by one person. She probably stood on a raised platform so that she was heard and seen. Most of the time they were day performances. However, there were '*mashals*' to provide light if it was a night performance. This woman narrator moved backward and forward while singing and dancing.[105]

Panditaradhya charitra tells us about the costume and make-up of this woman narrator. According to it, she had ornaments around her head, her wrists and her neck. She also wore small bells to ankles; her face was made up of white colour. Also, she wore a garland of flowers. She sang and danced to the accompaniment of different instruments. She came out of the curtain, brought by two people and the curtain was dropped down when she appeared.[106] *Kridhabhiramam's* description of Jakkula woman-performer was almost on the similar lines.

Saubhari Charitra by Proluganti Chenna Sauri (15th century) was probably the earliest text of *Yakshaganam*. However, unfortunately, the original text is lost, its quotations were maintained by subsequent writers. It is significant to note that Chenna Sauri did not call his text *yakshaganam* but '*Jakkula Katha*', a story written for *Jakkus*.[107] The earliest available text is Kandukuri Rudra Kavi's *Sugreeva Vijayam*. Interestingly some scholars hold that Raghavacharya's *Vipranarayana Charitra* is the earliest *yakshaganam* text.

The third stage of development of Yakshaganam took place in Seventeenth century. Yakshagaman underwent a tremendous metamorphosis. It has acquired elite character from that of a singing tradition by a forest tribe. Also, it moved from being a narrative form in which one performer acted out the roles of several characters to various actors taking different roles and where locale was also given importance. Sometimes, stage directions were provided. Prose and dialogues were restricted.[108] Even now it is operatic, with less emphasis on movement and action and with grate reliance on song and dance. In the hands of kings and court poets, it leaned more toward literary flavour than to performatory ease.[109]

Tanjore Nayaka kings patronized this art form. The reign of Vijayanagara Nayaka (1633-1673 A.D.) is considered a golden age in the history of *Yakshaganams*. He was a great writer himself. He called Yakshaganams *Natakamulu (dramas*). He is said to have composed nearly twenty three Yakshaganams. However, only six of them are surviving now.[110] Thus it became a full-fledged dramatic performance under Tanjore kings.

The themes of *yakshaganas* of earlier centuries were drawn mainly from Ramayana, Mahabharata, Bhagavata and other Puranas. Later on, over the time, contemporary, historical, social and political themes also were taken up. Mythological heroes, Gods and demons peopled the stage.[111] Some *yakshaganas* have battle scenes, some deal with marriage and diplomatic missions. Almost all important battles in Mahabharata and Ramayana have been exploited in the *yakshagana* repertoire.[112]

Yakshagana theatre requires a thatched roof supported by four poles and covered on three side. In *yakshagana* performance, unlike in other art forms where the curtain goes up from below or moves into side, curtain comes down from above. They used to burn torches or *mashals* or caster oil lamps to get light.[113] *Mridangam* (percussion instrument), Harmonium and cymbals, usually accompany *yakashagana* performance. *Yakshagana's* towering headgears, high-pitched signing, wild drumming, and vigorous dancing offer the rare feast of dance-opera of the traditional type.[114]

The performance was usually held in a village square or a field. The performance would commence around nine at night and went on all night. Characters enter stage introducing themselves, although *Sutradhara* introduces the characters quite often. In medieval period, male alone played both male and female roles. *Vidhinatakam, Kuchipudi Bhagavatam* and *Yakshaganam* are mutually influenced in their composition, characterisation and presentation.[115]

Tolubommalata (The Shadow Puppet Theatre)

Tolu Bommalata, the shadow puppet play, is one of the earliest Telugu folk theatre forms. With multiple colours, the mythological and imaginary figures at once create a rare combination of nearness and distance through their translucence behind wide screen. The product is a series of aesthetically satisfying pictorial designs coming live through movement of song and word.

Uttaraharivasamu, a literary text of 14th century, written by Nachana Somanatha, mentions puppetry shows at two places. At one place, a woman was compared with a puppet; of falling chariot at another place. He made a comparison between a woman and a puppet in order to highlight the delicate side of the character keeping the technique of making of puppets flexible in mind.[116] Second time he mentioned puppetry while describing the war between Srikrishna and his people on one side and *Rakshasas* (demons) on the other. In this context, he says that falling chariots were like puppets which were thrown to the ground by the manipulator after using them. Yet another place he said that *Kumaravara* (best among sons) is said to have made her like a string puppet of the God of love (*Manmada*):

> "*Tudi modalikante dudikante modalu chala*
> *javaulaganu layinaratulaku januvu licchi*
> *poovilutu cheti jantrapu bhomma jese*
> *manineetilakambu gumaravarudu*"[117]

In the same way the chariots also fell as the puppets were thrown to the ground after use,

> "*Yantraku dadinchi Yavani dochnavralu*
> *Bommalagati radhapoogamulunu*"[118]

Some inscriptions also bear witness to the existence of *Tolubommalata*. Two inscriptions which belong to Kakatiya period talk about this art. A pillar inscriptions from Guduru in Janagama Taluq dated 1124 A.D. contains poems in Kannada language on three sides and Telugu on the other side. This inscription was laid down in commemoration of his grand father by Mallana of Virayal dynasty. The term Sutradhari, which appears at the end of Telugu poems, may be taken to mean, probably, a manipulator of puppets. It runs as,

> "*Sutradhari Kommejana baraha Sri Sri Sri*
> *adapagattu devaraku janu*"[119]

Panugallu inscription also contains the term 'Sutradhari' which probably means the manipulator of a puppet theatre. It says,

> "*Sutradhari brahmaoju berasina sutradharula*
> *kasya pallini banuganta dalavrutti pudapandlu*
> *bhema samudramu venuka pudamaruturu*"[120]

The material needed for the preparation of a puppet was the wet skin of a goat or deer. After skin was cleared and softened, it was made uniformly thin and translucent. Three parched skins were needed for making a big figure and two for a medium figure. Either big or medium puppet had three major parts—the head, the body and the limbs and each part was usually made of one goat or deer skin.[121]

To carve the figure out of translucent skin, first an outline was drawn. Most of the time an old puppet was used to draw the outline. The outline of the figure was drawn on the skin either with charcoal or pencil. However, when an artist was sure of the outline, he traced the outline with a sharp instrument which when traced left a groove on the skin. When the old figures were not available or when the artist wanted an altogether new figure, the figure was drawn imaginatively on the skin checking correct proportions and final sketch was made with a sharp chisel.[122]

Next was the design of the puppets. It mainly consisted jewellery and clothing. It actually revealed the finest aspect of workmanship of the artist. Usually this was done by performing different types of small designs on the skin with the aid of sharp chisel. Circles, triangles and crosses were usually shapes cut into the skin to indicate jewellery. For instance, if a necklace was to be shown around a figure's neck, the artist chose either a triangular or cross-like or circular chain.[123] Afterwards skin was punched with holes according to the designs already drawn. These punched holes mainly represented jewellery. This was done by cutting out holes of uniform size and design. Designs were alternated to present different types of ornamentation. For example, if one ornament such as a chain consisted of small, circular holes, another necklace would be triangular and so on.[124] When these puppets were properly coloured and were placed on the white screen against the background of lights falling on the figure, these holes looked as if finely made jewellery of different types and colours.[125]

The different parts were hinged together by means of a strong string. These strings were attached into holes perforated at different edges of the limbs for the purpose. But the head and body were attached by a strong bamboo stick which was fixed into loops at the central part of the figure from the head down to lower part of the trunk.[126] The sizes of the puppets ranged from one to six feet, depending upon the age and nature of characters like gods, demons and human beings. In the same way different kinds of animals, birds and reptiles were, also prepared. At times three to four puppets were prepared for a character like Rama as a boy, Rama in exile, Rama in the battle field, Rama during coronation.[127] Each troupe possessed 100 to 150 puppets to cater to the variety of themes which they presented. *'Ganiyam'* the puppet boxes were the most treasured and revered possession of the troupe.[128]

In the past, vegetable colours were used for colouring puppets. However, of late chemical dyes are being used for the same purpose. The dye colouring would start after two days of punching and perforation. The colours were mixed in water and were spread on the figure as per the design. A thick paste of colour mixed in water was applied with a piece of cloth rolled into lump of the colour mixture.[129] After a particular colour was applied, another piece of cloth was used to smoothen the colour more uniformly. This was done especially to draw the lines more sharply and the colours more aesthetically. They nemark:

Tallapaka *Vaggeya Karas* (fifteenth and sixteenth centuries) tell us that puppet shows were arranged even in cattle shed in their times. They remark:

"*Ata vari goodi taura*
atavari goodi anni chotla bomma
lata ladincha nadikunda vaitivi
gurutaramaga pedda kottamu lopala
tiramaina penu maya deragatti
aravi sugnanamulavi yaddamu jesi
paraga sugnana deepamulu muttinchi
tolu bommala dorakoni gadienchi
galicheta vani gadilinchi
tooleti rasamulu tommidi gadienchi
nalugu mukhamula naluvuna nadincha[130]

Puppeteers would erect a temporary theatre with a thatched roof in an open place. For the performance of a shadow puppet show, the stage with a white screen was a must. Because unlike in string puppet show, the puppets were operated behind the screen in the leather puppet performance. It means that the entire manipulation of puppets was behind a white curtain, usually 8 ft x 6 ft is tied tight to poles on all the four sides.[131] The top of the screen was tied so as to bend towards the audience at the top. This bending of about 20 to 25 degrees was to help the figure to stand perfectly and intact on the curtain. Then puppets were mounted on the screen by the *sutradharas* (manipulators) from behind so that the audience would never see puppet figures. They merely saw the shadows thrown on to the screen by the light from behind.[132] A black cloth measuring two feet wide pinned as border to the white screen served to cover the machinations of puppeteers behind the curtain. With a view to make puppets translucent, two powerful lamps were fixed behind the screen about one and half feet away from the screen and at a height of six feet. During seventeenth century time, a row of earthenware lights were erected behind the screen, the wicks therein lighted with castor oil. This old lighting system when thrown onto the dark coloured puppets, the translucency gave a marvellous silhouette of a multicoloured figure almost brought to life. The animation of a puppet figure largely depended on the way one used the sticks attached to the puppets hands. The puppeteers held the puppet on the screen with a stick attached vertically to the puppet figure itself and used the cross sticks particularly when the figure was engaged with another figure.[133]

Puppet theatre remained as one of the powerful folk performing arts. It served as a powerful instrument of entertaining and communicating traditional values as well as moral precepts at popular level. This art appears to have emerged with the purpose of propagating the great deeds of mythological heroes and gods, kings and ministers which had both ideological and political overtones. Although this art took up themes from mythology, to begin with, over the time, it also had historical themes for performance. Themes from Ramayana and Mahabharata became the chief source for tolubommalata in Andhra. Later on themes from *Bhagavatam* and historical episodes became part and parcel of *Tolubommalata* repertoire.[134]

S. Geeta has observed that in the olden days it was *kalimata* story that was popular. However, later this was replaced by Ramayana stories.[135] It is to be noted that two great epics constituted one of the overlaps of popular and learned cultures. P.V.P. Pathy also argues that themes of puppet theatre were mainly religious particularly episodes from Ramayana and Mahabharata. It has been argued that popular acceptance of the epics enabled puppet theatre to establish an acceptable communicative link with the popular audience.[136] However, as the epics cannot be performed in one day, puppeteers used to camp at a place and perform the whole story of Ramayana, spread over two to three days. At the end of performance, they would collect their remuneration in the form of voluntary contribution of grain, cattle and goats.[137]

As in all other folk performing arts, the text of a shadow puppet play was not a written one. It was basically a collected text from different sources and usually it was a hereditary text. S. Pratapa Reddy points out that poems of Gona Buddha Reddy were sung during the performance of Ramayana story.[138] M. Nagabhushana Sarma argues that although the text of Ramayana story was based on Ranganadha Ramayana, poems and songs from different version of Ramayana like *Molla Ramayana, Bhaskara Ramayana* and *Kuchikonda Ramayana* were drawn heavily so that the play—text became a perfect synthesis of *slokas*, metrical stanzas and songs (*daruvas*).[139] Sometimes, themes from historical events also became the subjects for the show.[140]

Usually the puppet show was a night-long performance, starting at 9 p.m. at night and ending at 5 a.m. Kakamani Murthy Kavi who wrote around 1568 A.D. indicate that the puppet performance used to be continued until dawn during his time. His work *Panchali Parinayamu* has referred to this in the following words:

"Appu diddinavani yatula veginadaka
bommalataganna bhogipagidi"[141]

(As the person who enjoyed the puppet show until the dawn).

In order to keep the play going several humorous interludes, often unconnected to the story were introduced. Comic characters like *Kethigadu, Bangarakka* and *Juttipoligadu* performed dance and sang humorous songs. These humorous figures occasionally participated in the actual incidents also as secondary characters.[142] They became servants in the King's courts, attendants to kings and confidants. Their actions and speeches in these roles, too, created a lot of humour as they would proceed against the proposed intentions (generally evil) of the major villainous characters. The fascinating manipulation of puppets, dramatic contrast of characters made this puppet show spectacular and one of the chief source of entertainment for rural as well as urban folks.[143] Besides, this was not only an item of entertainment but also a part of belief system. This in a way, too, contributed to the popularity of this art form. It has been argued that popularity of puppet shows rested on the belief that a leather puppet play brought plenty of rain.[144] When water was scarce, all villagers subscribed funds, sometimes, to pay to these nomads and enjoyed their play with reverence.[145] Similarly it was believed that puppet shows expelled evil spirits and brought rain during drought as well.[146] This belief persists in some parts of Andhra Pradesh even today.[147]

Dommari Ata

An itinerant tribe, known as *Dommaris*, took to acrobatics. They used to travel around, exhibiting their art. They would perform their skills at public squares, places where people would gather. Sometimes they would perform before a king or a village head.[148] They would beat the drum to draw the public attention to perform their skills. Bamboo poles, sticks, crowbars, swords, ropes of jute, tents and drums were the paraphernalia for their feats. They would pray to goddess earth before starting their show and also apply some earth on their forehead as a mark of respect.[149] They performed many feats such as rope dancing, gymnastic feats, tumbling and conjuring tricks; *Kridabhiramam*, (14th century text) mentions *dommari ata*, inter-alia.[150] Chenna *Basavapuranam*, also describes all these feats very clearly. Both men and women of this tribe were adept in acrobats.[151]

Palkurki Somanatha mentioned it as a cultural item among Sivaratri festival celebrations. He says:

> "*Anaranganalu divi nadedu madki,*
>
> *namaranga gadalapai nadeduvaru*"[152]

Srinadha's *Palanativeeracharitra* also had a reference to it.[153] Ayyalaraju Ramabhadra's *Ramabhudayam* (16th cent. A.D.) describes first rains as a dommari player's feasts. It says:

> "*Alare tolakaritari veriyatavaadu*"[154]

They used to receive a customary contribution from different castes every year. This was sometimes in cash and sometimes in kind. It was variously known as *Vartana* and *Dommari-pannu.*[155] R. Soma Reddy argues that Dommaris allotted villages among themselves for this purpose and each troupe was entitled to visit only those villages—exhibiting their art, collecting their customary allowance.[156] Persian Ambassador to Vijayanagara court, Abdur Razak, also testifies to the existence of acrobats entertaining the big gathering by their feats in *Mahanavami* festival. At the end of the show, the king presented them gold ornaments.[157]

Vipra Vinodamu

They were magicians who performed different tricks. This was also very popular during medieval Andhradesa. They were the followers of *Vaishnavism*. They used to perform their skills in the temple precincts. *Kridabhiramam* refers to some of the entertainments performed in the temples of the fort of Warangal during the time of Prataparuda II.[158] An epigraph Pedakommerla states that Vipravinodin's belonged to the Brahman caste and practiced *Yakshinividya* (magic or sorcery).[159] They would generally travel around the country with their wives and children. They would perform lot of tricks like creating ash in the open palms, bringing out frogs and parrots from nowhere, throwing up three stone or wooden balls in the air and catching them or rolling them over various parts of the body. They performed for Brahmanas and collected *vartana* only from Brahmans.[160] The customary contribution was known as *Vipravinodi Pannu*. It has been argued that later on some shudra castes also took up this profession and started performing before mixed audience. This professional class continued to exist even during the reign of Qutbshahi rulers.[161] S. Pratapa Reddy holds that a *Vipravinodi*, named Guntupalli maharaju, existed at the fag-end of Qutbshahi reign.

> "*Santatamaraginchuneda sajjanakotula poojaseyu sri*
> *mantudu guntupalli kulamantrisikhamani muttamantridou*
> *bantiya bantigaka kadupanda gulamula banotulellanool*
> *bantulu, dukkitedlayada bantulu, vipravinodigaradi*
> *bantulu dongavandru mulu bantulu summu*
> *dharatalambunun*"[162]

People believed that vipravinodinis could perform any trick through their mastery over *mantra* and *tantra*.[163]

Besides, the above mentioned entertainments, many games and cultural activities of rural people were referred to by poets of medieval Andhradesa. *Srikalahastimahatyam* mentions games like *dagudumutalata* (hide and seek) *kundenagudi, tannebilla* (*hopscotch*). It also mentioned some purely Telugu games such as *Chitlapotlakaya, Sirisinganavatti, Gudigudigunchalu* and *Vennelakuppalu*. All of these are expressed in a poem in the following:

> "*Chitla potla kaya, sirisinganavatti*
> *gudugudu gunchalu, kundenagudi*
> *dagali mruchchu latalu, grachcha kayalu*
> *vennela kumpallu, tannu billa*

turana tunkalu, giranaginjalu
pilla deepalanki, billagodu
chedugudavvala poti, bendu gattina bodhi."[164]

Girls seemed to have their own games. *Hamsavimsati* talks about some of these games like *bommarindlu* (dolls houses), *bommalapendli* (dolls marriages), *buvvapubantulu* (dolls dinners) *tadaata* (rope skipping), *gobbi* and *geeranaginjalu* etc.[165] *Basavapuranam* also lists some dances which were done in villages both by men and women. Dances such as *gondli, pernai, kesika* and *joka* are mentioned in this work.[166] *Gondli* is a sort of tribal dance.

Kridabhiramam mentioned other pastimes like sheep fight, cock fight and bull fight. These games occupied a prominent place in the entertainment of the people.[167] Sometimes these games led to rivalry. Cock fight between nayakuralu and Brahmanayudu in Palnativeeracharitra is too well-known to repeat it here gain. *Tolubammalata* (shadow puppet show), *Yakshini-vidya* have already been mentioned.

References

1. One finds that from 19th century various themes such as social, political and historical themes were also taken up, see R.V.S. Sundaram, *Andhrula Janapada Vignanam*, Hyderabad, 1992, p.103.
2. Ibid, p. 103.
3. Ibid., p. 118
4. M. Nagabhushana Sarma, *Folk Performing Arts of Andhra Pradesh*, Hyderabad, 1995, p.12.
5. Vallabharaya, *Kridabhiramam*, Hyderabad, 1960, Poem, 119.
6. *Inscriptions of Andhra Pradesh: Cuddapah District* (ed.) P.V.P. Sastry, Vol. 2, 1978, p. 227.
7. M. Nagabhushana Sarma, *Folk performing arts of Andhra Pradesh*, Hyderbad, 1995, p. 15.
8. Ibid, p. 16.
9. Ibid, p. 16.

10. Nidadavolu Venkata Rao (ed.) *Shataka Samputi*, Vol. 1, Ramalingeshwara Satakamu, p. 156. The original poem reads:

    " జంగాల పాలు దేవాంగుల చిత్తంబు. "

11. Poleramma was believed to be the Goddess of Cholera and Small-pox.
12. W.T. Elmore, *Dravidian Gods in Modern Hinduism,* New Delhi, (1913), Reprint, 1984, p.14.
13. M. Nagabhushana Sarma, Op.cit., p. 18. The Jamidika is an instrument which is used for scaling and as a percussion instrument. The main narrator uses Jamidika whenever there are changes either in the pace of the story or a transition from one mood to another.
14. Ch. Yadayya, *Janapada Vignamlo Bavaneelu – Oka Pariseelana,* (Telugu), Hyderabad, 1990, p.13.
15. B. Rama Raju, *Glimpses into Telugu Folklore*, Hydreabad, 1991 p. 84.
16. *Kridabhiramam*, 1960, poem, 130. The original text reads:

    " వీక్ష్యత్రైపర కడు నేరవాది యనగ
    ఏకవీరా మహాదేవి యెదుట నిల్చి
    పరశురాముని కథలెల్ల ప్రౌఢి పాడ
    చారుతర కీర్తి బవనీల చక్రవర్తి "

17. W.T. Elmore, *Dravidian Gods in Modern Hinduism*. p. 14.
18. Ch. Yadayya, op cit. p. 16.
19. W.T. Elmore, *Dravidian Gods*, (hereafter Dravidian Gods), p. 18, see also foot-note 3 of this chapter.
20. Srinatha Kasikhandamu, poem 7-231. The original poem reads:

    " శైవుడై యొకవేళ సర్వాంగకంబుల
    బూదియు రుద్రాక్షముల ధరించు
    బఠియించు శ్రీగీత పరమ భాగవతుడై
    యక్షరి నటియించు నొక్క నాడు
    గౌరగ మైలారుని గొనియాడు నొకవేళ
    నాసతప్పై బంపరు పుష్పుదాల్చు
    ప్రణుతించు ఏకవీరాదేవి నొకవేళ
    బవనీడయి, సమగ్ర భక్తి గరిమ "

21. Palavekari kadripati, sukasaptati, 2-415. The original poem reads:

" కలల్ వెవర చెప్పెరల మొదటం గన్పించి నెయ్యంబు, నా
టిల నీ పాలికి దెవ్వడింక, లవనీపేయంబు దానవ, గా
వతెన్ బాపన మొప్పితైన సరిమొ వారెల్ల సాలెవు, నీ
వతె గోచరించిరే దిన్నె కొల్తునంచు న్వార్జించుచున్ నంటటన్ "

22. B. Rama Raju, op. cit, Hyderabad, 1991, p. 84.
23. Ibid.
24. Ibid.
25. M. Nagabhushana Sharma, op. cit. p. 26. To begin with *Pambalavallu* narrated only *Ankamma* and *Yellamma* stories. However, as this was popular, leftist groups used this medium for political propaganda in modern times.
26. Nidadavolu Venkata Rao (ed.) *Shataka samputi*, Vol.1., *Ramalingeswara Satakam*, p. 156. The original line reads:

" కాపు విత్తంబు పంటకాని పాలు "

27. M. Nagabhushana Sarma, op. cit., p. 21.
28. Nidadavolu Venkata Rao, (ed.) op.cit. p. 156. The original text reads:

" గొల్ల విత్తంబు పిచ్చుకుంట పాలు "

29. C.V. Subbanna Satavadhani (ed.) *Hamsavimsati of Ayyala Raju Narayanamatya*, Andhra Pradesh Sahitya Academy, Hyderabad, 1977, p. 125.
30. M. Radha Krishna Murthy, *Andhra Natakaranga Charitra*, (Telugu), Madras, 1969, p. 46.
31. Mudigonda Virabhadra Kavi, *Palnati Veerabhagavatam*, Canto, 23, quoted by B.S.L. Hanumantha Rao, *Social Mobility in Medieval Andhra*, Hyderabad, 1995, p. 28.
32. Ibid.
33. Akkiraju Umakantam, *Palnati Veeracharitra*, Madras, 1911, p.53.
34. ibid., p. 153.
35. B.S.L. Hanumantha Rao, *Social Mobility in Medieval Andhra*, Hyderabad, 1995, p. 101.
36. These Malas are categorized as scheduled caste if they are Hindus by Government of India.

37. Akkirau Umakantam, *Palnati Veera Charitra*, Madras, 1911.
38. Pingali Lakshmikantam, *Palnati Veera Charitra*, Vijayawada, 1961.
39. M. Nagabhushana Sarma, op. cit. p. 35
40. Ibid, p. 35, R.V.S. Sundaram, et al., *Studies in Folkloristics*, Mysore, 1986, p. 60.
41. Sundaram, et al., *Studies in Folkloristics*, Mysore, 1986, p. 60.
42. Ibid.
43. Vallabharaya, *Kridabhiramam*, Hyderabad, 1960, poem, 119.
44. M. Nagabhushana Sarma, op. cit, Hyderabad, 1995, p. 35.
45. Ibid, p. 36.
46. R.V.S. Sundaram, op. cit. 1992, p.39.
47. Ibid, p. 36.
48. B. Rama Raju, *'Telugu-Performing Folk Art Forms'* in G. Naggayya (ed.) op. cit., p. 41.
49. *Hamsaavimsati*, 1977, p. 124.
50. R.V.S.Sundaram, et al., *Studies in Folkloristics*, 1986, p.61.
51. *Hamsavimsati*, 1977, p. 124.
52. M. Nagabhushana Sarma, op. cit. p. 37.
53. Ibid, p. 37.
54. M. Radhakrishna Murthy, *Andhra Natakaranga Charitra* (Telugu), Madras, 1969, p. 67.
55. M. Nagabhushana Sarma, op.cit. p. 37.
56. Please see, Nidadavolu Venkata Rao, (ed.), *Shataka Samputi*, pp. 157.
57. Ibid.
58. M. Nagabhushan Sarma, op. cit. p. 37.
59. Ibid, p. 38.
60. B. Rama Raju, op. cit. p. 41.
61. M. Nagabhushana Sarma, op. cit. p. 38.
62. Thurston Edgar, *Castes and Tribes of South India*, Madras, Vol. VII, p. 407.
63. K. Vidyavati, *Vijayanagara sasanalu: Bhasa Samskritika Sahityamsalu*, Hyderabad, 1994, p. 172. Since they were not supposed to live permanently at one place they were also not allowed to have a permanent kitchen at one place.

64. P.V.P. Sastry (ed.) *Inscriptions of Andhra Pradesh: Cuddapah district*, Vol. II, 1978, (Pedamudiyam), 224. The inscription reads as:

"…. బ్రాంహ్మల ముడియం అనేటి సమూన్స
అగ్రహారమందుల శ్రీ సోమేశ్వర దేవునికి శ్రీశల
సింహాసనస్థులైన భిక్షావృత్తి అయ్యవారి శిష్యులైన
పుష్పగిరి వీరముష్టి భూమయు కొమారుండు చెన
బసువయ్య ధారవోసి యిచ్చిన ధర్మశాసనక్రమం….
అయ్యావళి ముఖ్యులైన చాటుమూల సమస్త
పెకండ్ర సంమతినింన్ని సకల పురాంతకుల సంమతిని
బ్రాంహ్మల ముడియం గ్రామమందు తంమ్ముళ్లు
మొదలైన వారు అచ్చేటి వీరముష్టి పన్ను
ముడియ్యం సోమేశ్వర దేవుని దీపారాధనకు
సకల పురాంతకులకు పుణ్యంగా నుంన్ను
జుంజుంనుం గాశేను నారసముంను మోటు పలకాను
పద్దెపు వీరముష్టులకు పుణ్యంగా నున్ను….శ్రీకృష్ణ
జయంతి పుణ్యకాలమందు శ్రీ సోమేశ్వర దేవర
సంనిధిని …. యిస్తిమి".

65. Ibid, *Veeramushtis* were also called *purantakulu*.

66. *Sri Vasavai Kanyakapuranam*, 1951, Ch.32, stanzas, 12,13.

67. Ibid.

68. B.S.L. Hanumantha Rao held that *Vasavi* was Jain by faith and developed indifference to worldly pleasure from the beginning. When there was proposal, she disapproved it and committed *Sallekhana*. With Saivite wave, she was treated as an incarnation of *Parameswari* or *Durga*.

69. M. Nagabhushana Sarma, op. cit. p. 39.

70. Ibid.

71. Vallabharaya, *Kridabhiramam*, Hyderabad, 1960, poem 130. The original poem reads:

" అకలంక స్థితిగాఁ గాత్రిదరు బ్రహ్మానంద భావంబునన్
సకలానందముమైక మాతలగుచున్ సంతోష చిత్తంబునన్
లోక దుమ్మతే యూరెలాలమున జనకర తందాన లమ్మయమ్మన్
ఏకదేవమ్మకు మహారమ్మకు నడే హ్రీంకార మూర్త్యాత్మకు "

72. Ibid., p. 36-40, 96,97.

73. Palkurki Somanatha, *Sri Panditaradhya charitra*, (ed.) by Ch. Narayana Rao, Madras, 1974, p. 252-63.

" ... అలరుసు బసవారులల్ల యందరును
లలనుల్చి చూంగుభళా యనువారు "

74. K.H. Lakshmana Rao, *Influence of folk literature on Telugu film songs*, an M Phil dissertation submitted to Osmania University, p. 15.

75. Please see Nidadavolu Venkata Rao (ed.) Shataka Samputi. op. cit. p. 153.

76. A.P. Government Archaeological Series, No. 19, p.3.

77. Bittu Venkateswarulu, *Palnatisemalo Kolatam*, Hyderabad, 1988, p. 40.

78. Kameswara Rao, V. *Select Vijayanagara Temples of Rayalaseema*, Government of Andhra Pradesh, Hyderabad, 1976, p.63. In 1509 A.D., Saluva Timma, Minister of Veera Narasingaraya got a temple constructed at Tadipatri. In this temple sculpture, there are sculptures performing Kolatam. For further discussion, Please see, Tumati Donappa, *Janapadakala Sampada* (Telugu), Visakhapatnam, 1975, p.6.

79. Nachana Somana, *Uttaraharivamsam*, Madras, 1972, 4-216. The original poem reads:

" వడకు పన్నగరాజు పడగల మీద స
ర్వం సహాకాంత పేరణము సూప
నుత్సుత టూగెడు నుదయాస్త గిరులు
నాకాశలక్ష్మి కోలాట మూప "

80. Vallabharaya, *Kridabhiramam*, (Telugu) poem, 25.

81. Tarigoppula Mallanna, *Chandrabhanu Charitra*, Madras, 1922, 2-139. Chandrabhanu, Son of Srikrishna and Satyabhama, is the hero of this work. An ascetic, who was a friend of Chandrabhanu, while explaining *Kumudini* story says about Kolatam.
82. Surabhi Madhavaraya, *Chandrika Parinayam* (Telugu), Madras, 1904, 2-20.
83. Peitro della Valle, *Travels*, 11, p. 258-9.
84. Bittu Venkatesvarulu, op. cit. p. 48.
85. M. Nagabhushana Sarma, op.cit., p.73, For the etymological meaning of these words. Please see, Bittu Venkatesvarulu, op. cit. pp. 25-31; K. Muniratnam, *Kolatam: oka vinodakala* (Telugu) in G. Nagayya (ed.) op. cit. p. 158-159.
86. Petasri, *Chittoor Zilla kolatam patalu*, Tirupati, 1992, p. 45-120.
87. Bittu Venkatesvarulu, op.cit.p.25.
88. Ibid, p. 26.
89. Ibid, p. 29.
90. Ibid, p. 30; B. Rama Raju, op. cit. 1991, p. 47.
91. Ibid.
92. Palkurki Somanatha, *Sri Panditaradhya Charitra*, pp. 252-63.
93. Ayyalaraju Narayanamathya, *Hamsavimsati*, (ed.) by Subbanna Satavadhani, A.P. Sahitya Academy, 1977, poem: 122.
94. B. Ramaraju, *Telugu Performing Folk Art forms*, op. cit. p.49.
95. Palkurki Somanatha, *Sri Panditaradhya Charitra*, Madras, 1939, p. 256.
96. K.H. Lakshamana Rao, *Influence of folk literature on Telugu film songs*, an unpublished M. Phil. dissertation, Osmania University, 1979, p.12; see *Kridabhiramam*, poem. 138.
97. Palkurki Somanatha, *Sri Panditaradhya Charitra*, pp. 252-263. The original poem reads:

" బహు నాటకములు
ప్రమథ పురాతన పటు చరిత్రములు -
గ్రమమొంద బహు నాటకము లాడువారు
లలితాంగ రసకళాంకుర రేఖ - లలవడ బహురూప మాడెడువారు
గరణములతో మెరవణిల గతులు జిత్రములు - నరుదుగ
దెప్పంగ మాపెడువారు "

98. Vallabharaya, *Kridhabhiramam*, Hyderabad, 1990, pp. 45-48.
99. E. Thurston Edgar, *Castes and Tribes of South India*, Madras, 1909, p. 438.
100. Srinatha, *Basavapuranam*, 3-65. The original poem reads:

" కీర్తింతురెద్దాని కీర్తి గంధర్వులు గాంధర్వమున యక్షగానసరణి ·

101. Vallabharaya, Kridabhiramam, Poem, 136.
102. quoted by M. Nagabhushana Sarma in *Folk Performing Arts of Andhra Pradesh*, Hyderabad, 1995, p. 87.
103. Ibid, p. 87.
104. Quoted by M. Nagabhusahana Sarma, *Folk Performing Arts of Andhra Pradesh*, 1995, p. 87.
105. Ibid, p. 88, see also, G. Nagayya, *Pracheenadhara Kavvyallo Janapada drusya Kalarupalu* (Telugu) p.33.
106. Palkurki Somanatha, *Sri Panditaradhya charitra*, (ed.) by Ch. Narayana Rao, Madras, 1974, pp. 252-63.
107. K.H. Lakshmana Rao, *Influence of folk literature on Telugu film songs*, an unpublished M. Phil. dissertation, Osmania University, 1979, p. 13. S.V. Joga Rao also holds the same view please see his *Yakshaganam*, p.21.
108. B. Rama Raju, op. cit. 1991, p. 50.
109. K.H. Lakshamana Rao. op.cit. p.13.
110. M. Nagabhushana Sharma, op.cit,p.89. Also, G. Damodaranayudu, *Yakshaganam* (Telugu), in G. Nagayya (ed.), op. cit, 1991, p. 180.
111. B. Rama Raju, op. cit. p. 51.
112. Ibid. Also see, Balwant Gargi, *Folk Theatre of India*, Delhi, 1991, p. 145.
113. B. Rama Raju, *Glimpses into Telugu Folklore*, Hyderabad, 1991, p.89.
114. Ibid.
115. Ibid.
116. Nachana Somanatha, *Uttara Harivamsamu* (Telugu), Andhra Pradesh Sahitya Academy, Hyderabad, 1970 (Reprint) 1979, p. 197.

117. Ibid. The original poem reads:

" ముది మొదలకంటె ముదికంటె మొదలు చాల
జవ్వలగను లయునరయులకు జనువులిచ్చి
పూవిలుతు చేతి జంత్రపుబొమ్మ జేసె
మానినీ తిలకంబు సుకుమారవరుడు "

118. Ibid., p. 236. The original poem reads:

" యంత్రకు పాడించి యువని తోచినట్లు
బొమ్మల గతి రథపూగములను ."

119. P.P. Sastry, *Kakatiya Sasana Sahityamu* (Telugu), Andhra Saraswata Parishat, Hyderabad, 1981, pp. 100-101. The original inscription reads:

" సూత్రధారి కొమ్మజన బరపా (శ్రీ(శ్రీ(శ్రీ
అడపగట్టు దేవరకు జను "

120. S.V. Joga Rao, '*Bommalata* - *Yakshaganamu*' in *Saraswata Vyasamulu*, Vol.3, Andhra Pradesh Sahitya Academy, Hyderabad, 1969, p. 316. The original inscription reads:

" సూత్రధారి బ్రమ్మోజు పెరసిన సూత్రధారుల
కొన్న పట్టని బానుగంట దళవృత్తి పుడపండ్లు
బీడు సముద్రము వెనుక పుడుమరుయురు ."

121. K. Sarada, '*Bommalatalu*', (Telugu) in G. Nagayya (ed.) op. cit., 1991, p. 203.

122. Ibid.

123. Ibid.

124. Ibid.

125. B. Rama Raju, *Glimpses into Telugu Folklore*, Hyderabad, 1991, p.91.

126. G. Nagayya, op cit. p. 28.

127. K. Sarada, op. cit. p. 203.

128. B. Rama Raju, *Glimpses into Telugu Folklore*, Hyderabad, 1991, p.91.

129. M. Nagabhushana Sarma, op. cit. p. 110.

130. V. Ananda Murthy, *Tallapaka Kavula Padakavitalu: Bhasha Prayoga Viseshalu* (Telugu). Vol. 2, Hyderabad, 1976, p. 538. The original poem reads:

ఆటవారి గూడి తేరా
ఆట వారి గూడి అన్నిచోట్ల బొమ్మ
లాట లాడించు నదికుంపట్లైతలి.
గురుతరమగు పెద్ద కొట్వసు లోపల
తెరవైన పెనుమాయ దెరకట్టి
అరవి సుజ్ఞానములవి యుప్పము జేసి
పరగ సుజ్ఞాన దీపములు ముట్టించి
తోలుబొమ్మల దారకొని గదియించి
గొంతచేత వాని గదలించి
తూతెటి రసములు బొమ్మింది గదియించి
నాలుగు ముఖముల నలువున నాడించు

131. K. Sarada, op. cit. p. 204.

132. Ibid.

133. Ibid.

134. Ibid.

135. S. Geeta, *Tolubommalata* (Telugu) in *Abhinaya*, Andhra Pradesh Vrithikalakarulu Sangham, Hyderabad, 1990.

136. D. Ramanuja Rao, *Saraswata Navaneetamu* (Telugu), Andhra Saraswata Parishat, Hyderabad, 1955, p. 236; also see his another work, *Manakalasampada Sahityamu*, Hyderabad, 1984, p. 66.

137. P. Lakshamanayya, *Gnapakalu-vyapakalu* (Telugu) Machilipatnam, 1984, p. 40.

138. S. Pratapa Reddy, *Andhrula Sangheeka Charitra* (Telugu), Hyderabad, Reprint, p. 54.

139. M. Nagabhushana Sarma, op.cit, p.111.

140. M. V. Ramana Murthy, '*The art of puppetry is the folk treasure of India*' in *Natyakala*, Vol. 1, No. 7, Feb. 1964, p. 53.

141. G. Nagayya, *Dhakshinatya Sahitya Sameeksha*, (Telugu), Tirupati, 1976, p. 236. The original poem reads:

" అప్పు దిద్దిన వాని యటుల వేగనదాక
బొమ్మలాటగన్న భోగపరది "

142. K. Sarada, op. cit. p. 206.

143. Ibid.

144. People believed that if *Uttaragograhanam* story was enacted by puppeteers, it would bring rain.

145. P.V.P. Pathy, 'Moving pictures of the past' in *Silpi*, Vol. 1, No.2, Sept. 1946, p. 17.

146. R.V.S. Sundaram, *Andhrula Janapada Vignanam*, (Telugu), Hyderabad, 1983, p. 483.

147. S.V. Joga Rao, *Bommalata-Yakshaganam* (Telugu) in *Saraswata Vyasamulu*, Vol.3, Hyderabad, 1969, p. 231. He says that even now people in some villages of Kakinada, still believe that if the story of *Uttaragograhanam* is played, it will rain. Please also see M.Radhakrishna Murthy, 'Tolubommalatanu-Punaruddharinchali (Telugu), in *Natyakala*, Vol. 2, No.4, April, 1967, p.13.

148. G. Nagayya, op. cit. p. 21-23.

149. Ibid.

150. Vallabharaya, *Kridabhiramam*, Hyderabad, 1960, pp. 36-40, 96,97, poem 144. The original poem describes the feats of a dommari woman as:

వెనుకకు మొగ్గవ్రాలి కడువిన్ననువొప్పగ దాటి నీళ్ళలో
మునిగి తదంతరస్థమున ముంగర ముక్కున గ్రుచ్చుకొంచు లే
చెను రసనాగ్రపాళమున శీఘ్రము గ్రుచ్చెను నల్లపూసలే
రనుపమ లీల నిప్పుడుచు పాయము లొప్పిన మొల్ల నేర్చినన్ "

151. Papakavi, *Chenna Basavapuranam*, pp. 90-91.

152. Palukurki Somanatha, *Panditaradhya charitra*, Madras, 1939, p. 256. The original poem reads:

" అమరాంగనలు దివినాడెడు మాడ్కి
నమరంగ గడలపై నాడెడు వారు "

153. Srinatha, *Palnativeracharitra*, Madras, 1938, p. 388.

154. Ayyalaraju Rambhadra, *Ramabhudayam*, 6-18. The original poem reads:

" అలరి లోలకరిబటి పెటిమాటవాడు "

155. Annual Report of Epigraphy,1920, No. 363 and 370; *Nellore district inscriptions*, Vol. 11, Kandukur (41).

156. R. Soma Reddy, '*The Life of Dommaris as reflected in the literature and epigraphs of medieval Telugu country*' in *A.P.H.C.* 1984, p. 33.

157. H.M. Elliot, *'The History of India as told by its own Historians*, Vol.IV, pp. 118, 119.

158. Vallabharaya, *Kridabhiramam*, Hyderabad, 1960, pp. 36-40, 96,97.

159. *Inscriptions of Cuddapah district*, (ed) by N. Venkataramanaya, 1972, p. 652; *Amuktamalyada*, 4-112.

160. R. Narasimha Rao, *'Vipravinodinis': A new class of professional entertainers in the Vijayanagara Empire'* in *I.H.C.* 1966, p. 221.

161. *Annual Report of Epigraphy*, 1953-54, No. 52; S.I.I. Vol. XVI, Nos. 156 and 782; S.I.I. Vol. IX, No. 554 and 681.

162. S. Pratapa Reddy, *Andhrula Sanghika Charitra*, Hyderabad, 1949, p. 54, The original poem reads:

" సంతతమారగించునెప సజ్జన కోటుల పూజసేయు చ్రు
ముంయుడు సంటూపల్లి కులముద్రి శిఖామణి ముత్త మల్లితా
బంటియు బంటిగాక, కడుపంది సులాముల బంటు తెల్లనూత
బంటులు, ముక్కుబెజ్జయెప బంటులు, విప్రవినోదిగారడి
బంటులు దాంగరాండ్రు ముఖబంటులు సుమ్ము ధరాతలంబున "

163. However, this art, which was so popular once, now has become extinct.

164. Dhurjati, *Srikalahastimahatyam*, Hyderabad, 1961, poem, 3.33. The original poem reads:

"
చిట్లపొట్లకాయ, సిరిసింగాణవత్తి
సడుసడు సంబాళు, కుండెన పచి
దాగఱమ్రుచ్చులాటలు, గచ్చకాయలు
చిన్నెల కుంపులు, చన్ను చిళ్ళ,
చూరన చుంగాలు గీరన గింజలు
పిల్ల దీపాలంకి, చిల్లగోడు
చెడుసడవ్వల పోటి, చెండు గట్టిన బంతి'

165. Ayyalaraju Narayanamatya, *Hamsavimsati*, 5-155.

166. Palkurki Somanatha, *Basavapuranam*, (ed.) by G.V. Subramanyam, Hyderabad, 1969, p. 22.

167. V. Ananda Murthy (ed.) *Kridabhiramam*, Hyderabad, 1988, p.63.

6

POWER RELATIONS WITHIN THE STATE STRUCTURE

Generally the people at different times and in different places have had different understanding of the perception of state and the concept of power.[1] It is precisely these variations which produce identifiable patterns along which the paths of state-societal interactions can be traced. While glossing over, those differences, an attempt in this chapter is made to understand the structure of state and power. The people's subjection by the state would be treated as a valuable means for identifying the variety of activities which contribute to political processes at popular level in medieval Andhradesa.

To have a fuller understanding of the state in Medieval Andhra, an analysis of the nature, organisation, and the distribution of power has to be looked into. In a highly stratified society like India, relations of power at all levels have influenced state-societal relations. Since the over-all medieval Indian society was agrarian based, therefore, a clear linkage between the agrarian society and the administrative system has to be established if the state is to be understood in a right perspective.[2]

Scholarship until recently centred around the origin of Vijayanagara kingdom. Writing about the origin of Vijayanagara, Sewell held that the founders of Vijayanagara were tribal people and might have belonged to either Kurumba or Kadamba.[3]

N.Narasimhachar, B.A. Saletore, H. Heras and S. Krishnaswami Ayyangar have argued that the founders of Vijayanagar were Karnataka warriors. Others, the likes of Nilakantasastri and N. Venkataramanayya took the position that the founders were Telugus. However, a recent study established that the founders actually moved from Karnataka to Andhra.[4]

The question of feudal set up in relation to Vijayanagara was also attempted by some scholars. In fact, 'feudalism' is not a new historiographical convention. Having been limited to political plane, the concept has been a synonym for political fragmentation and the term has in fact been shuttled back and forth in Indian history to suit any period in which no `unitary empire' could be located on the political horizon.[5] Feudal polity is shown to be a stage which represents a structural change in the Indian social and economic order; it envisages the emergence of a hierarchical structure of society in place of the binary opposed entities of the state and the peasantry, and it is basically this hierarchical structure with its different tiers of intermediaries which explains the mechanism of exploitation and coercion of medieval state.[6]

Krishnaswami devoted two chapters to feudalism and feudatory relations in his work on Tamil country during Vijayanagara period.[7] Again, D.C. Sircar thinks that Vijayanagara fits correctly to description of feudal. This is because he thinks 'amaram' tenure as a military service tenure.[8] Another historian, N. Venkataramanayya opines Vijayanagara polity was not feudal especially because of absence of any idea of fealty and homage.[9]

Any attempt to characterize medieval state in Andhradesa, Vijayanagara and Golconda states, throw up some significant questions such as: (a) How polity was organized? (b) How power was distributed? (c) What were the relations of power and how did they effect the peoples' lives? For answering these questions the Vijayanagara provides us an appropriating starting point. Vijayanagara sovereignty seems to have confined only to the Karnataka country, South of Krishna—Tungabhadra and northern parts of Tamil country. It was only under Tuluva dynasty that the

Telugu area south of Krishna was incorporated in the kingdom.[10] It means that before the penetration of Vijayanagara rule, most of the Telugu areas were under different chieftains and local rulers. In Coastal areas of Andhra, Reddis of Kondavidu were ruling until early part of fifteenth century. Again, Reddi Kingdom of Rajahmundry continued to exist until it came under the sway of Kapileswara Gajapathi of Orissa in 1448.[11] Musunuru Nayakas ruled at Warangal until last quarters of fourteenth century. Recherla chiefs continued to rule eastern Telangana towards the end of fifteenth century.[12]

From the details it becames very clear that the political processes were not the same throughout Vijayanagara period. In fact, the two preceding centuries before Srikrishnadevaraya were historically significant. First Sangama rulers tried to consolidate their territorial acquisitions by creating administrative divisions called *raajyas* or provinces, under a superior government officer called *Pradhaani*.[13] To begin with *Pradhaani* happened to be a prince and later he was generally a military officer. The headquarters town of each *raajya* was called *caavadi* or *ucaavadi*. This term was also used as an alternative designation for *raajya*.[14] However, we don't come across this word in Telugu inscriptions. The *raajyas* incorporated in them the already existing local level ethno-social territories such as *naadu, seema* (in its restricted sense) *Parru* (in Tamil country) and *Kampana*.[15] However, we are not in a position to know exactly how many *raajyas* were there in Vijayanagara kingdom.

Hierarchy of local level territorial units, too, is not clear. *Seema* seems to have been a part of *raajya*. Many inscriptions speak of *seemas* as integral parts of *raajyas*.[16] Another term *valitham* (which was used in Kannada inscriptions) was also used as an alternative of *seema*.[17] N. Venkataramanayya felt that there is a great deal of confusion in inscriptions regarding the place of *seema* in the territorial divisions of Vijayanagara Empire.[18] The exact number of *seemas* in Vijayanagara cannot be ascertained with any precision. However, *seema*, either as an administrative unit or revenue unit was bigger than *naadu*. Because some inscriptions speak of *naadu* being a part of *seema*. *Magani* was also a unit which existed within *seemas*. But it is not clear how many villages were there in each *Magani*.[19] Whether *Magani* was bigger than *Naadu* is not clear either. They simply tell us that they were parts of *seema*. Another territorial unit that is frequently mentioned in inscriptions is *sthalam*. Even here inscriptions do not speak of the size of *sthalam*.[20] However, it seems that this territorial division was borrowed from Kakatiyas. During Kakatiya kingdom *sthalam* comprised anywhere from 18 to 60 villages.[21] In Vijayanagara Empire *sthalam* seems to be the lowest territorial division. *Sthalakaranams* were incharge of revenue accounts of *sthalams*.[22] In Telugu areas, *Chakibanda sthalam*,[23] *Pitapuram sthalam*,[24] *Eepikonda sthalam*[25] are mentioned in inscriptions.

Raajyas were important administrative and revenue units until early sixteenth century. However, *Raajyas* as the crucial, superior administrative units of the empire lost their original importance once *naayaka* or (*nayankara*) system matured under Krishnadevaraya. Therefore, *raajyas* under *Mahamandaleswaras* were gradually replaced by '*Nayankarams*' under *amaranaayakas* during the reign of Krishnadevaraya.[26]

Although *Raajyas* survived during sixteenth century, they did so only as a geographical nomenclature without any administrative significance. *Rayavachakamu*, a text of early 17th century tell us that at this later stage several towns including the headquarters of the earlier *raajyas* were fortified garrisons (*durga*) under the control of *amaranaayakas*. To extend his power in Tamil country, Krishnaraya had, apparently, to send Telugu army to reinforce, the Vijayanagara overlordship. Krishnaswami argues that this resulted in a 'momentous' change, namely the replacement of a system of *Mahamandaleswaras* (governors) by naayakas (military commanders) presumably to act under the kings orders with the assistance of *palaigars* (dependent warriors).[27]

There are divergent views on the origin of the institution of *Naayaka*. Venkataramanayya traced its origin to the Kakatiya times. Recent research on this topic, too, points to the emergence of *naayakas* during the reign of Rudramadevi and her successor.[28] It seems that Kakatiya rulers with a view to break the power of entrenched princely and chiefly lineages, started recruiting a large number of peasant-warriors who were designated as *naayakas* and *reddis*.[29] *Nayankara* a kind of revenue assignment over a relatively small number of villages must have been instituted as a means of rewarding these lower level subordinates. It figured as a type of authority over a given territory, generally a group of villages. However, it is unclear what duties were entailed; that is, whether Nayaka holder was expected to maintain troops and/or forward a portion of the revenues. It has been thus argued that *nayankara* actually originated earlier in Andhra country and was subsequently adopted and refined by Vijayanagara Emperors.[30]

The exact number of *naayakas* of Vijayanagara in Telugu country cannot be ascertained. This is because Telugu inscriptions available from 1400 to 1599 are only around 300. Even for later period i.e., 1600-1899, there are only about a hundred inscriptions.[31] As a result it becomes difficult to know precisely the powers of *naayakas*, their relations with the overlord, flow of taxes from *nayankarams* to the overlord, entailing military duties, whether all *naayakas* were the agents of the centre, or some naayakas were also local chiefs with local moorings.

Naayakas of Vijayanagara period are seen by most scholars as warriors possessing an office conferred by the central Vijayanagara state. The term *amaranayankara* signifies an office (*kara*) possessed by a military officer or chief (*nayaka*) in command (*amara*) of a body of troops.[32]

Karashima has estimated that there were more than three hundred *naayakas* spread over northern parts of Tamil country which comprised five *raajyas* and most of these *naayakas* belong to post 1485 period. Several of later *naayakas* are said to be in possession of their own territory bestowed on them by the king as (or for) their *nayakkattanam* (*nayakatana* in Kannada and *nayankaram* in Telugu).[33]

However, the exact number of *naayakas* of Telugu area cannot be ascertained. *Naayakas* had identified themselves *amaranayakas* of the reigning king. It also appears that they still used the *birudu* (epithet) *Mahamandalesvara.*[34] *Naayakas* continued to use these titles as late as 1578.[35] Usually *nayankara* tenure extended over a *seema*. Sometimes it extended as far as six *seemas.*[36] *Kaaryakarta* was another officer whom we come across in inscriptions. *Kaaryakartas* seem to have worked both under the king and *amaranayakas*. Kondamarusayya was a *kaaryakarta* of Srikrishnadevaraya.[37] Another *kaaryakarta* of Krishnadevaraya was Tirumalraajayya.[38] In the same way Yallapanayani was *kaaryakarta* of Mandraju Naagaraajayya, a *mandalesvara.*[39] Satani Varadappa was the *kaaryakarta* of another *mandalesvara*, matli kumara Anantaraajayya.[40] The exact nature of relationship between *Kaaryakarta* and king or between *Kaaryakartas* and *amaranaykas* is not known.

The argument that durga-dannayaka being himself an *amaranayaka* was compelled to stay in the king's court at Vijayanagara and ruled his province by proxy through an agent *kaaryakarta* is not tenable.[41] Because kings also had *kaaryakartas* working under them. If *kaaryakartas* were proxies who then were ruling provinces on behalf of *amaranaayakas*, we are at a loss to understand why Krishnadevraya had *kaaryakartas*. As kings always stationed at the capital, king's *kaaryakartas* could not be his proxies. It suggests that *kaaryakartas* had different functions.

It appears that *naayakas* had their own territory which was given to them by the king as *nayankaram*. *Naayakas* seem to have controlled the production within their naayankarams by encouraging the settlement of cultivators and artisans with tax concessions, by creation of commercial centres (namely *satha, angadi* and *peta*) and markets, by creating and maintaining irrigation facilities, etc. Timma Nayani had a *cheruvu* (tank) constructed in Darsi.[42] Velugoti Venkatapti naayudu, an *amaranaayaka*, had ten tanks constructed. Nearly ten inscriptions which were issued by him in connection with the construction of *cheruvus* (tanks) are available. They are: Juturi *grama cheruvu*,[43] Musunooru *cheruvu*,[44] Kaavali *grama cheruvu*,[45] *Alluru cheruvu*,[46] Kaangollu cheruvu,[47] Chennuru Cheruvu,[48] Nellori grama cheruvu,[49] Cherukuri cheruvu,[50] Vamavaram cheruvu[51] and Kanuparti cheruvu.[52] Apart from having tanks constructed, they also had canals dug to these tanks for irrigation purpose.[53] Canals were also repaired from time to time.[54] It seems that enterprising peasants who would take up either the construction of tanks, wells and channels or their repair were given some additional amount of land as *dasabandha manyam. Dasabandha manyams* were those lands on which ten per cent tax was levied and given to the enterprising peasants. This kind of system prevailed in Raayalaseema districts. *Dasabandha manyam* was arranged in Indukuru for repair works.[55]

Another dasabandha manyam was set up in a village pendlimari in the mulikinati *seema*, a *nayankaram*. This was given for embankment of the tank.[56] *Amaranayakas* also exempted certain taxes with a view to encourage trade and commence. An inscription from Mangalagiri says that many taxes were exempted in this temple town.[57] In the same way all goods which passed through *sakiliseema* were exempted from *maarga sunkam* (custom duties).[58] Cultivators, too, were encouraged with tax exemptions for promoting agriculture. Sambaturi inscription says that peasants were given tax relief for seven years for bringing virgin land under cultivation.[59] Many *naayakas* started as high officials (commander, governor etc.) and served as the kings agents.[60] Noboru Karashima has found some evidence from inscriptions for Nuniz statement that *naayakas* were obliged to stay at the capital and to leave the management of their respective territories (*nayanakarams*) to local agents. However, in Telugu inscriptions it is not clear whether or not *naayakas* were required to stay at the capital. But it seems that there was hierarchy among *naayakas*. Kaaryakartas, lower-level *naayakas*, were working under *amaranayakas*. In the same way, *mudala*, who was responsible for writing the orders of either kings or *naayakas*, was working under *kaaryakarta*, these *mudalas* also called themselves as *naayakas*. More often than not, *mudalas* stated in the inscriptions that they were working under a certain *kaaryakarta*. It seems that even they had authority to abolish tax under their jurisdiction.[61] It clearly shows the existence of sub-infeudation process among *naayakas*.

Elaborate systems of land tenure emerged during the mature period of Vijayanagara, that is by the late fifteenth and sixteenth centuries. The principles of these systems and bases upon which they operated were fundamentally different from those of Chola age.[62]

Three major tenures that existed during Vijayanagara can be classified into three. They are: *bhandaravadagramas, amaragramas* and *manya* (*agrahara* & *devasthana*). Burton Stein thinks that these categories pertain to only one aspect of land tenure, during the Vijayanagara period, namely, a classification of the disposition of the major portion of the proceeds of agricultural production on a village basis. He also argues that Vijayanagara inscriptions are concerned with new and public claims upon shares of village income. And the 'rights in land' always refer to shares of income, not 'dominion in land'.[63] However, Telugu inscriptions talk of dominion in land. Often land was donated or given to the donee with *asta-bhogam* eight-kinds of benefits or enjoyments of possession.[64] Besides, the rise of 'big-men', in the peasant organization, who managed agrarian activities, too, suggests that communal bonds of property rights were breaking up. This paved the way for more private rights leading to 'dominion in land' not merely rights in land.[65]

Asta-bhogam was presumably with the right to present, mortgage and sell.[66] There are instances of *naayakas* and other state dignitaries buying lands from brahmins for charitable or religious purpose.[67] In some cases even tax-free agraharas were sold by the descendants of the donee, although they were granted as hereditary property. However, the sale of land for non-religious purposes was under severe famine conditions. With the power of village assembly declining, and its replacement by village officials (*Reddi, Karanam* and *Talari*), private property in land became more pronounced than before.[68] However, the selling and buying appears to have confined only to religious or charitable purpose.

The other category of land was *bandaravada* or crown lands. A portion of income of these lands went to support Vijayanagara fortresses in various ports of the empire.[69] It has been argued that since *bhandaram* (treasure) connotes government, *bhandaravada* gramas meant the lands of the government.[70] N. Karashima has suggested that *bhandaravada* gramas have no separate existence from the *Nayankaramas* and therefore these cannot be distinguished from the territory assigned to *nayakas*. And *bhandaravada* is just a taxable land, like chola period, *vellanvagai*, and has to be contrasted only with *manya* or tax free land.[71] However, an inscription from Telugu country while registering the tax exemptions given to the barbers by Nandyala Timmarajayyadeva by the orders of Aliya Ramarajayya mentions that Ghandikota *seema* includes *amara gramas, umbalika gramas, agraharas* and *devasthanas*. It indicates the separate existence of *amaragramas* and *bhandaravada gramas* in the Ghandikota *seema*. It seems that as all these types of villages were in co-existence in the Gandikota *seema* which were independent and different from each other, specific reference has been made to them in the inscription. This inscription is from Katteragandla of Cuddapah issued in 1546 A.D. during the reign of Sadasivaraya.[72]

Amaram tenure of Vijayanagara was a military tenure. It was the control over land and its products possessed by those with military capability. B. Stein considers *amaranayakas* as highly local and quite independent warrior chiefs. Apart from them, there were great military commanders - *naayakas* who were also the most important political movers of fifteenth and sixteenth centuries; but they were few.[73] Stein further argues that *amaram* tenure consisted essentially of the power to distribute or redistribute the proceedings of agrarian production and to set and collect those charges in kind or in cash to be paid to personages with local authority. The term *amara* refers to war and some *amaranayakas* were great military commanders. He thinks that *amaram*, more broadly, denotes the rights and powers of local magnates. However, from Telugu inscriptions it is not known exactly what was the relationship of an *amaranayaka* with the king. Again, the flow of taxes from *nayankarams* to the centre cannot be ascertained either. The nature of land rights in Vijayanagara was complex and sometimes overlapping.

From the foregoing information it becomes clear that the agrarian society was increasingly stratified. The king stood at the top of this stratification. Below the king was *amaranayakas*. These *amaranayakas* also called themselves as *mahamandalesvaras*.[74] *Amaram, bhandaravada* and manya tenures existed in *nayankarams*. Sub-*nayaykas* like *kaaryakartas* were below *amaranaayakas*. Under *manya* category several service tenures like *Reddika manyalu*,[75] *Karanika manyalu*,[76] *Kavali Manyalu*[77] of *Reddi* and *Karanam* (village accountant) and *Talari* respectively existed. Apart from these, Washermen and barbers also had *manyas* for their services.[78] *Umbali* gramas were also included.

The other system often referred to in Vijayanagara period was *ayagara* system. It was Venkataramanayya who characterized this system for the first time.[79] It meant that those who performed services for the agricultural population of a village or a locality. Venkataramanayya asserted that the system was already there in full force during the time of the Kakatiya rule. *Ayagars* were thought to be twelve in number who were village officials or servants who performed most functions of village government that had earlier looked after by the village assemblies like *sabha*, *ur* etc. In fact, only three of the twelve were somewhat 'officials', namely *Reddi* (headman), *Karanam* (accountant) and *talari* (watchman). The remaining were just different artisans with the exception of the priest. Usually *ayagars* were twelve in number.[80] However, sometimes more than twelve ayagars were mentioned.[81] It cannot be said with any precision whether this system was confined only to villages. Because one inscription talks of twelve ayagars of Chakibanda *sthalam*.[82] *Sthalam* was a bigger territorial until which comprised anywhere between 18 to 60 villages under Kakatiyas.[83]

However, it is not known how many villages were there in a *sthalam* under Vijayanagara. But there is no doubt that *sthalam* comprised a number of villages. If we take all ayagars of all villages which were under chakibanda sthalam, then it would be more than twelve. But then this inscription records only twelve ayagars in connection with chakibanda *sthalam*. It suggests that *ayagara* system existed in its full force in bigger territorial units like sthalams also. In inscriptions it is not clear if all villages had twelve *ayagars*. In any case, one thing is clear that ayagars were involved in the establishment of villages and their office was hereditary.[84]

To the holders of each of these offices, (*Reddi, Karanam, Talari*) a portion of village income was allocated in the form of rights in particular plots of village land.[85] These plots were not liable for regular tax payments, hence they were regarded as *manya* or tax free, the holders of such rights might be subject to a fixed quit-rent payments.[86] The same form of payment went to other 'village servants' who possessed no governance or management functions 'within a village', but did provide services essential to the village community.[87] The priest and washer-man provided ritual services. However, for the most part, village servants provided goods and services of a more ordinary sort.[88] Among the latter would be the leather worker (madiga in Telugu areas) whose products included the leather bag used in lift irrigation devices (*mhote* or *kapila*) potter (*kummara*) blacksmith (*kammarai*), carpenter (*vadla*), barbar (*mangali*) etc. The villages thus allotted to these village servants were known as *umbali* (*kodage, srotriya* in Kannada and Tamil areas). B. Stein thinks that *mirasi* and *inam* rights and *umbali* rights were the same. They refer to rights of income from agricultural production which were exempt from the customary dues on agricultural income in lieu of direct payments for services. In cases where there were direct payments for services, payments in kind were usually designated as, *danyadaya* those in money as *suvarnadaya*[89] or *kasu Kadamai*.[90]

B. Stein argues that what is distinctive is not the existence of *ayagara* system but the special allotment of income shares from land and specified cash payments were for the first time generally provided to those holding these offices. The shift to this more formal, tenure mode of payment underscores the transformation, according to Stein, from the anonymous, organic agrarian relationships of the Cola period to the more stratified and complex relationships later.[91] However, for Telugu areas apart from the existence of *manyas* to village servants, nothing can be ascertained at present.

These service tenures apart, another distinctive category of Vijayanagara land tenures was *dasbandham*. This may be called 'rural developmental entrepreneurship'. In Karnataka area, it was called *kattu-kodage* rights. These were special, private rights to a share of the new productivity created by an investment in irrigation improvement in existing agricultural villages.

Among the most active rural entrepreneurs were *amaranaayakas* and lower-level *naayakas*. These powerful men, perhaps, were seeking the maximum, protected return to their descendants on resources they commanded in many parts of the macro region; a kind of insurance against the vagaries of political fortune.[92] In agrarian tracks where productivity could be increased by a relatively modest new construction or improvement, irrigation facilities, there was scope for agrarian entrepreneurship or developmental activity.[93]

This developmental investment was undertaken by individuals of means and local prominence in return for which they secured income rights to a portion of the enhanced productivity as personal, heritable, and transferable property.[94] This is the meaning of *dasabandham*. Under these arrangements, it was usually stipulated that a share of increased product from the construction of a tank or channel was to go to the cultivators of the village in which the construction was carried out and a smaller share was to be granted to the person who financed or otherwise executed the construction.[95]

When we consider the question how resources flowed from *nayankarams* to the centre, the emerging picture is not a happy one. Nilakanta Sastri opined that "the chief sources of revenue were taxes on crown lands, annual tributes from feudatories and provincial governors paid at the time of *Mahanavami* festival, port and customs dues from the commerce passing through the numerous ports of the empire, which were collected in cash and kind.[96] The land was carefully surveyed and assessed according to its quality, the rates differing between wet and dry lands and in accordance with the crops and the yield. The proportion of produce claimed as revenue varied from the traditional sixth to as much as half the gross yield. Taxes on professions and houses, fees for licences of various kinds, transit and market dues and judicial fines were other sources from which the state got its money. Most of these taxes were framed out to the highest bidder both in areas directly administered from the centre and in the provinces, and the impression produced is that of high and even oppressive taxation.[97]

Burton Stein on the other hand thinks that Vijayanagara king could not have commanded the resources of the entire country under its rule. Basing on the political situation prevailing in the reigns of Krishnadevaraya and Achyutadevaraya (1509-42), he stressed that it was very difficult for the king to command even the resources of the rich Kaveri delta or that of southern Karnataka due to recalcitrant subordinates. Trade, too, could not have yielded much. However, he thinks that there was a lot of monetization and taxes in money.[98]

Karashima made an attempt to systematically analyse the revenue terms in Tamil inscriptions.[99] However, such an analysis for Telugu areas is difficult because of the scanty nature of sources available. We can only know from the inscriptions that *naayakas* were the direct revenue authority in their respective *nayankarams*.[100] It seems that *Karanam* (accountant) and *sunkadhikari*[101] (Tax-collector) were involved in assessment and collection of revenue. *Karanam* maintained a revenue record of the village. This record was called '*Vahi*'.[102] But how much revenue was remitted by *naayakas* to the central kings treasury is not known.

But one thing is certain that the large officialdom of the state pocketed portion of revenue disproportionate to the duties they rendered. Both the temptation of power and the resources that they enjoyed by dint of being the part of the administrative hierarchy did result in the extension of the state's dominion. This develcpment led to the colonisation of various remote areas which were inhabited by different tribal and pastoral groups. They included hunter-gatherers like Chenchu, Boya, Yerukala, and pastoralists like Golla and Kuruba.[103] These new power relations gave rise to the institutions of *kavaligars* and *polygars*. According to *Kaifiyats Kavaligars* were appointed to safeguard the villages, pilgrims and trade routes in the hilly and forested zones. We have noted in the previous pages that *kaavali* manyas existed in the villages.[104] During Vijayanagara period, along the pathway from Markapuram to Srisailam, the villages, Yacavaram, Rayavaram, Kurivipalle and Goguladinna were established.[105] Gujjala Parampa Naidu, a Boya was appointed as a *Kavaligar* of Adoni, Gutti, and Kurnool areas. Villages established in the hilly and forested lowland country were organised into *palems*. These *Palems* were given to forest people, pastoralists, dominant peasants with hereditary rights.[106] To begin with Boyas were drawn to temple service and later on they rose to the position of *mahamandalesvaras*.[107] *Rayavachakam* speaks of *Boya Nayankarulu*.[108] Tarigoppula Mallanna in his *Chandrabhanu Charitra* mentions *Yerukapalegadu*.[109] Yeruka, another tribe, also rose to political power.

Recent studies have established that Vijayanagara period saw some remarkable development in industries, commerce, and urbanization. During thirteenth century the southern peninsula began to undergo an urbanization driven by the development of larger temples and chiefly fortifications. During Vijayanagara period many places emerged as important urban centres in medieval Andhra as well. Important among them were Bezawada, Vijayanagaram, Penugonda, Nellore, Chadaluvada, Addonki, Rollamadugu, Bukka Patnam, Animela, Udayagiri, Kanigiri, Kandukuru and Kakandi. Mangalagiri in the present Guntur district became an important pilgrimage centre.[110] Kakandi was also a great pilgrimage centre.[111]

In the same way, Daksharamam, Pitapuram, came into prominence.[112] In Cuddapah region, Animela, Pulivendala, Siddavatam,[113] Chidipirala[114] and Porumamilla[115] rose as commercial and urban centres. Tirupati temple's prominence in this period is well-known, attracting enormous number of pilgrims.[116]

With their large priestly and non-priestly staffs and their ever-increasing throngs of pilgrims, temple centres fostered elaborate urban facilities and attracted permanent commercial and artisan populations. By the sixteenth century, the forces tending towards greater urbanization were crowned by the cumulative impact of Vijayanagara rule. Agents of Rayas were urban magnates; their fortified headquarters, were garrisons that underpinned dispersed Vijayanagara authority, and large bodies of soldiers and numerous chiefly courts made towns centres of wealth and consumption.[117] Such political centres either were temple centres at the outset or they became that as a result of the largesse of chiefs. In these numerous new towns of Vijayanagara period a major redefinition of 'lower orders' occurred, this having to do with the division of right and left castes.[118] This development resulted in very important changes which were central to the medieval Andhra Society at Popular level.

It has been argued that in myth and in social process, the left division of castes in the Vijayanagara domains suffered the historical disadvantage of being marginal to the dominant rural-centred society in which they lived. The core of the left division in most places consisted of highly skilled artisan trading groups and regional merchant groups at popular level. To this core was added a substantial section of untouchable producers of commodities such as the widely-traded leather commodities of Tamil and Telugu scavengers and leather workers (*Chakkilars* and *Madigas*). Most important cultivating groups like Tamil *Vellalars*, Karnatak *Vakkaligas* and Telugu *Reddis* were either affiliated with the right division or were regarded with Brahmanas and some transregional merchants and bankers (such as Telugu *Komatis*) as neutral or unaligned.[119] To the core of the right division were added other agrarian groups such as most herdsmen, grain traders and transporters, those providing goods and services for village people, such as potters, barbers, washermen, non-brahman priests and untouchable field labourers (Telugu, *Malas*, Tamil *Paraiyans* and *Karnataka* Holeyas).[120]

However, this two-fold division i.e., right-hand and left-hand does not figure in Telugu Vijayanagara inscriptions. Instead, we come across 'eighteen castes' in inscriptions including fifth caste.[121] Major artisan groups figure as *Panchanamvaru* in medieval inscriptions and literature.[122] The word means five occupational groups. They are essentially artisans or craftsmen each specialising in one craft. They are: 1) *Kamsale* (gold-smith) 2) *Kancari* (metal smith), 3) *Kammari* (black-smith) 4) kase (sculptor) and *vadrangi* (carpenter). From about the 8th century A.D. the socio-religious atmosphere in the land turned favourable for the ascendancy of the *panchanam* castes.[123] There was vigorous temple-building activity throughout Andhradesa. Medieval temple was a big employer. For building temples and for chiselling gods and goddesses, the architect and sculptor (*kase*) were in great demand; the jeweller was required to decorate the images attractively with ornaments; the services of the smith were indispensable for making brass vessels, plates, lamp stands, bells and cast vehicles such as *Nandi* and *Garuda* and the carpenter had to carve the wooden push carts to carry the vehicles with images in processions.[124] The *Kamsale* was further required to record the donations to the Gods either on copper plates or stones. Besides, the steady expansion of agriculture through the multiplication of *Devabhogas* increased the demand for agricultural implements. Thus the services of *Panchanam* castes were demanded on a large scale.

They were given *manya* lands in recognition of their service. These villages which were given to *Panchanamvaru* are categorised as *Kanachi* villages.[125] Supplying arms to the army was called *amaram-adangi*. Most often *Panchanamavaru* worked under the leadership of their local caste leader. It seems that these caste leaders sometimes got *amaram* tenure for their service. An inscription from Nellore says that Kammara Jangam Vadla Prasannam, who was either caste leader or elder of *Panchanam* guild, was given Boyamadugu village in Udayagiri durgam as an *amaram*, during Tirumaladevaraya's reign.[126] With the improvement in their economic position, they naturally looked for enhanced social status.[127] They started tracing their descent from a sage *Visvakarma* with a view to improve their social status. An inscription of fifteenth century mentions *Panchanamvaru* as the descendants of *Visvàkarma*.[128] Although later inscriptions record them as belonging to fourth caste,[129] their status certainly seems to have improved as a result of their increased economic power.

In the same way the *komatis* of Andhra region became economically powerful as a result of the development of industries, commerce, and urbanization. By Vijayanagara period we see *Komatis* working as '*Pattanaswamis*' (officers) of the towns. Gangisetti was called *Penukonda Puravaradhisvara* (Lord of Penukonda). He was the officer of Penukonda.[130] Papi Setti, son of Vallabhasetti, was the officer of mangalagiri.[131] Varadasetti was *Pattanaswami* of Nosam (in Cuddapah district).[132] *Komatis*, too, wanted to improve their social status. In fact, this process started from eleventh century when they started using *gotra* names. A Draksharama inscription describes Eriyapota, son of Vennaya as *Sresthi, vanija* of Vaisya caste.[133] The next step in the process was to claim *Rsi gotras*. Again, another record of Draksarama describes a certain Vaisya as 'Yah Kasyapo Vaisyakulabdhi candrah' (Vaisya of Kasyapa gotra).[134] A fifteenth century inscription from Anantapur District contains the *Prasasti* of a *Vaisya Vamsa* which mentioned sage *Agastya* as its *Purohita* (priest).[135] Gangisetti, Pattanaswami of Penugona, issued an inscription wherein he claimed that he was from Punagasila gotra and belonged to Vaisya caste.[136]

Vaisyavamsa Sudhakaram, a Sanskrit poem of the Vijayanagara period gives an account of the dispute among the *komatis* which came for settlement before Devaraya II (1426-1446). Some of the Komati families claimed that they were

Sajati vaisyas who alone had the right to call themselves as *Vaisyas* or *urujas* or third varna. The others were *Vijati vaisyas* who were only *komatis*. In support of their claims, they cited a certain *kanci sasana*. Then an eminent scholar by name Mallinatha was asked to study the case and recommend a settlement. After carefully examining the case, Mallinatha recommended the abolition of distinction between *Sajati* and *Vijati Vaisyas* and grant equal rights to all to trade with 18 towns and 108 temples.[137] This case represents an instance of families who gained higher social status through increased economic prosperity denying the same position to families of lesser fortune, as *satsudras* looked down upon other *sudras*.

As the weaving industry was also developed during Vijayanagara period. *Sale* (weaver) caste also improved its economic position. Varieties of textiles were produced to cater to the needs of both luxury class and general population.[138] Once their economic position improved, they strived for higher social status, they traced their gotra to *Markendeya*.[139] Over the period there were two sects. Both claimed descent from two sons of Markendeya. *Jendravaru* claimed their origin to *Panchamaharisi* and *Padmasale* to *Bhavanarisi Bhadravati*, who were the two sons of Markendeya. Out of these two, Padmasala seems to have become powerful economically. As a result they claimed higher status than Jendravaru, another sect. A dispute arose between these two sects on the question of status. So both of them approached Purshottamaraya for settlement. Finally, verdict was in favour of Padmasale, i.e., Padmasale was higher than Jendravaru. Happy, as Padmasale were, they gave nearly twenty thousand *varhas* as present to Purushottamaraya.[140]

Thus the pace of urbanization during fifteenth and sixteenth centuries altered the balance between the right and left coalitions of castes. Leading groups of the right division, whose core interests were agrarian, had become deeply implicated in town life and in the more generalized exchange systems of the age.[141] At the same time, the left division of castes, the core of whose interests were commodity production for extended exchange, and whose locus of operations were the new towns, were in a better position to demand quality of status and social privileges with those of right division. As a result royal adjudications were sought and gained by the leading groups of left castes and skilled artisans.[142]

With the growth of complex land system and attendant tenure arrangements, with the assertive emergence of non-agricultural producer and with large-scale movements of people, society everywhere was bound to face tensions and conflicts. Such problems were either ignored or glossed over in the previous works on Vijayanagara.[143] Often disputes broke out on the question of holding religious processions and displaying emblems. One such incident was recorded in the inscriptions. In a village, Ontimetta, *Panchanamvaru* of that village were prevented by *Balijas*, a dominant peasant caste, which also acquired some political power, from getting onto the chariot in the religious procession. Therefore, they approached their local lord for adjudication, then Matte Ananta Rajayya, *Mahamandalesvara* after consulting *Jiyyam* and taking the past custom into account, allowed *Panchanamvaru* to get onto the chariot with their tools.[144]

Studies by Karashima and Subbarayalu for Tamil region have revealed socio-economic confrontation between the direct producers on the one hand and landlords and the ruling class on the other. Stein's account of right-hand and left-hand castes is most comprehensive. He further states that formal political and administrative structure generated as much fission as fusion.[145] And he would stress that the Hindu temple and Hindu sects created a kind of integration that provided a significant measure of identification with some meaningful whole for most people of the macro-region in Vijayanagara times.[146] However, it has been argued that this may be true of such big temple centres as Tirupati, Srirangam, Kanchipuram and Srisailam etc. which attracted pilgrims from all over the macro region. At the same time sectarian rivalries cannot be ignored.[147]

It was amidst this socio-politic scenario that Golconda state[148] was established. Golconda state had a more organized form of administrative structure. The state was not divided into provinces in its early phase. Only from 1636 A.D. onwards as more and more territories were added, the need for a proper administrative set up arose. During Abul Hasan Qutb Shah period, kingdom was divided into *sarkars* or districts and *Paraganas* or groups of villages.[149] *Tarafs* or provinces of Bahamani times came to be known as *simt. Tarafs* were also called as *qaryats*. Several *tarafs* formed a *paragara* which was rarely of a uniform size and varied from place to place. *Mauza* was a village and many villages were combined to form a *Taraf.*[150]

Qutb Shahis appropriated a large share of peasant's production through land tax which was nearly one-half of total surplus produce.[151] In some parts of Golconda *Muqasadars* or great nobles were given revenue assignments on specific land or '*Muqasa*'. While in other parts, specially in Coastal Andhra '*Sar-asamata*' or district governors had the authority of tax collection. In each case tax farming through an elaborate series of leases and sub-leases was the usual approach to revenue collection. The testimony of Thevenot assumes significance in this matter. He says that the nobles have gratifications from the king, of lands and villages whereof he allows them use, where they commit extra-ordinary extractions by the Bramanas who are their farmers.[152]

Sar-samatu or district governors of Coastal Andhra also indulged in rapacious tax-farming. Before securing his appointment each governor had to agree to pay to the central treasury a fixed sum each year. Once established, the governor was free to try to recoup his expenses and make a profit on tax collections. Only the authority of the central treasury, exercised through the revenue superintendents in each district or *amildars* offered any restraint on governor's actions. However, *amildars* were more concerned with the punctual payment than the welfare of the peasantry.[153] Contemporary travellers while deploring the severities of land-tax collections exclaim the obvious prosperity of the countryside. Tavernier comments that "the Kingdom of Golconda, generally speaking, is a rich country, abounding in corn, rice, cattle, sheep, fowls and other commodities necessary to life.[154]

The fertility of deltas in Andhra, tank irrigation in Telangana partly explains this abundance. Again, the availability of diamonds and consequent trade in diamonds also brought lot of profits.[155] The direct involvement of Golconda in the rich Coromandal trade as active administrators and as traders brought lot of resources to the kingdom. This factor lent a relatively greater potential to central power of the Golconda regime. These resources helped Golconda to strengthen its central authority.[156]

Central and local governments have been treated as separate entities particularly in medieval polities of Southern India, though both form parts of one whole. This has been viewed as incorrect characterisation which is useful only so far as to recognize the continuity of political formations from kings to village headmen and it is here that some of the forms of local and central authorities become evident.[157] Golconda was centralized in the sense that the local authorities had no clearly defined powers that could not be disturbed arbitrarily by the centre, which was more elaborately organized than the local structure, although local lords depended on hereditary officials like *Reddi* and *Karnam* for revenue collection.

Evidently Muslim rulers of Golconda made large accommodation to the sub-stratum of Telugu territorial chiefs of their realm.[158] Sultans of Golconda offered military services to their Telugu subjects and patronage for their cultural and other institutions. They also left territorial chiefs in undiminished, if not enhanced, authority in their local domains. Stein thinks that in this sense neither regime had much choice, since each was based upon an elite of Muslim warriors that was Deccani, not foreign, in culture and affinity and whose numbers were never so great as to overwhelm local, ancient, Hindu Lordships.[159] However, notwithstanding these limitations upon the ambitions of these Muslim regimes, theirs was more powerful centralised structure than Vijayanagara.[160] This is because, neither Golconda nor Bijapur brooked any notion of shared sovereignty, claims of *Dayada*, however substantial the degree of local power held by *Reddi*, *Velama* or *Maratha chiefs*, whereas this was the core of Vijayanagara sovereignty from first to last. Also prebendal rights conferred by Muslim regimes were less easily transformed into hereditary chiefly rights. This factor coupled with huge resources from Coromandal trade strengthened central authority of Golconda beyond any available to Vijayanagara.[161]

Temporal power, in early as well as in later theoretical writings, was required to guarantee protection. This protection does not simply mean the physical protection of subjects. Protection related to the ideal social order as defined by the guardians of the sacred domain. Curiously, the ideal social order was defined, but *dharma*, nevertheless, was not uniform and although the king was required to preserve social order, he was at the same time enjoined to allow the disparate *dharmas* of regions, guilds and associations and of social groups to continue.[162]

Vijayanagara kings claimed themselves as protectors of *Varnashramadharma*.[163] The Vijayanagara campaign against Muslim principalities was carried out between 1365 and 1370 by Kumara Kampana, son of Bukka I, and was as much a propaganda as military success because it was memorialised in numerous inscriptions over the southern peninsula proclaiming a new dharmic kingship and an end to Muslim oppression. Thus the first generation of Vijayanagara rulers established their moral or dharmic claims to kingship by their publicised protection of Hindu shrines from the desecration of Muslims.[164] However, these *dharmic* credentials have been lost when Devaraya II recruited Muslim soldiers into his armies, conferred high posts and rewards upon them, constructed a mosque in Vijayanagara.[165] This became inevitable because of the pressing problems of the time. To cope with the large and mobile cavalry forces of the Sultans, Vijayanagara rulers had to have similar force. The *Sangama* Founders of Vijayanagara knew the new conditions better than most, having been victims of Muslim expansion against Kakatiya and having later taken service under their Muslim conquerors. The lesson of improved war capability was dearly learned until the fifteenth century when Vijayanagara rulers began incorporating Muslim and later European fighters into their forces. Whatever the lost dharmic credentials of this decision, it was more than compensated by an enhanced ability to hold off Muslim predations and later to allow counter-incursions into sultanate territories.[166]

The state sought to achieve legitimacy through what is called royalization of cult centres.[167] At one level this involved Sanskritization of the village pastoral and forest goddesses. While the folk gods were made the incarnation of *Siva* and *Vishnu*, the great gods of brahmanical pantheon, the Goddesses were universalized as their consorts, and as the manifestations of the great Goddess *Shakti* or *Durga*. We have noted in the previous pages that *Posamma*, the Goddess of Small-pox was treated as the daughter of *Siva*. *Renuka*, a brahmana woman and *Ellamma*, a madiga woman were integrated. The syncretism of the folk and brahmanical belief systems was the most vital of the ritual processes that integrated the 'lower orders', forest people on the one hand and the state on the other. The folk traditions, mythologies and rituals (which existed side by side with the Brahmanical pattern) show the metamorphoses of the forest deities, through the village deities into the state deities.[168]

Kings, queens, *amaranayakas* and lower-level *naayakas* became the patrons of these deities. An inscription dated 1394 A.D. refers to Bukka as *Bhadra-Kali-Ghata-Vidheya*, indicating that Bukka, was also a worshipper of *Kali*.[169] King Harihara got the *mukhamandapa* in Mallikarjuna temple at Srisailam constructed in 1404 A.D.[170] Kings usually bestowed a lot of gifts on Sivaratri day.[171] Krishnaraya, donated a village Malukanna to Mallesvara temple at Koka for his welfare.[172] While Harihara constructed estern tower (*gopura*) of Srisailam temple Krishnadevaraya got *mandapa* (outer-hall) constructed to the same temple.[173] This exchange of honours between royal powers and *mathadipatis* (the leader of a sectarian centre) strengthened their alliance.

This process is no where clearer than in the celebration of *mahanavami* festival, an annual royal ceremony of fifteenth and sixteenth century. This occurred every year about 15 September to 15 October. Since Vijayanagara times the nine day festival (*navaratri*) followed by a tenth and final day—*dasara*—has been important in many parts of the macro region. It was celebrated in honour of goddess *Durga*.[174] This festival was also celebrated by nayaka successors of Vijayanagara. This *Mahanavami* is described in vivid detail by Portuguese sojourners of sixteenth century, Paes and Niniz. This is also mentioned by the Italian Nicolo Conti and Abdur Razzak, the Persian ambassador.[175]

Paes gave the most elaborate description of the festival. Throughout the nine days, festivities are centred in the 'Citadel' area - of Vijayanagara, before the palace and on two, large, permanent structures: one of which is called 'The House of Victory' by Paes (Longhurst called it Throne Platform,[176] *mahanavami dibba* according to the modern residents of Hampi) and the other 'The kings Audience Hall'.

In the festival what was seen was a combination of great *durbar* with its offerings of homage and wealth to the king and the return gifts from the King—exchange of honours, reconsecration of king's arms—his soldiers, horses, elephants—in which hundreds or thousands of animals were slaughtered; *darshana* and *puja* of the king's tutelary—the goddess. B. Stein thinks that *mahanavami* was a combination of *Asvamedha* with its celebration and consecration of kingly military prowess as symbolized in the horse of the king.[177]

However, it is doubtful if *asvamedha* ceremonies had any real meaning during medieval South India, although a Pallava king is said to have performed *asvamedha*.[178] No Vijayanagara dynasty seems to have performed *asvamedha* either. It is suggested here that this festival might have made sense from the point of view of propitiation of a goddess. We have already pointed out that it was believed by people of Medieval Andhra that disease, epidemic and drought were thought to be result of wrath of a goddess. People, therefore, propitiated the Goddesses to get rid of sickness, epidemic and drought. In this sense, village Goddesses were worshipped for the general welfare of the people in *Jatras* where many animals were killed.

The same belief pattern seems to have been held by both lower and higher orders, including Brahmanas. This explains why local Goddesses have to be Sanskritised as manifetations of *Durga* or *Shakti*. Paes, who described the *mahanavami* festival, so vividly, also recorded another incident which took place during his sojourn. He says, "A tank in the empire burst twice and thrice. The king asked his Brahmans to consult their idol for the reason as to why it burst so often and the Brahmans said that the idol was displeased and desired that they should make a sacrifice and should give the blood of men and horses and buffaloes. And as soon as the king heard this he forthwith commanded that at the gate of *Pagoda* the heads of sixty men should be cut off and of certain horses and buffaloes which was done at once. According to his account they were prisoners and deserved death.[179]

This incident reveals some basic beliefs of Medieval South India. Propitiation was done not only to get cure from illness but also to the general welfare of the people. This belief was shared down from the man in the street to the King. Welfare of the people depended on the happiness of a Goddesses. If king went to the extent of killing 60 men, besides, horses and buffaloes, in order to keep a tank (which was often burst) by the extension of same logic, he would do anything for the welfare of the Kingdom.

In this context it is significant to note that the idol that was worshipped during *mahanavami* was not either *Vishnu* or *Shiva* who were more popular during this time. But it was Durga who was considered *Shakti*.[180] As Paes observed on the first day twenty four buffaloes and one hundred and fifty sheep were slaughtered. Again another day, a large number of buffaloes and sheep were killed. Nearly 250 buffaloes and 4,500 sheep were killed on the closing day.[181] The slaughter of a large number of animals might not have been only for the consecration of king's arms. It appears that this slaughter of animals might have been for the propitiation of Durga perhaps for the general welfare of the kingdom and its people. This is not to say that Vijayanagara kings did not patronise other sects such as *Vaishnavism* and *Saivism*. We have noted in the previous pages how Saivite and Vaishnavite cult centres received royal patronage. But then the mode of worship of these gods was different. Propitiation was never done for greater Gods who were considered benevolent. Propitiation was done only to *Shakti* or manifestations of *Shakti* who were believed to be both benevolent and malevolent.

The local leaders (*Mandalesvaras* and *Naayakas*) also tried to derive legitimation through ritualized action, i.e., religious donations. A number of references are available from inscriptions. Ahobilesvarudu, a *naayaka* of Sadasivaraya, donated a village, Sambatoor renamed as Sribashyapuram, to Kesvaperumallu, the local deity.[182] Again, during the reign of Achuytaraya Gollamadinendu, had built a tank in Udayagiri temple.[183] An *amaranayaka* got a local temple renovated in Chundi town.[184] Chinatimraju Nandayya, *mandalesvara* of Udayagiri gave Komarapudi village as *devabhoga*.[185] Siddiraju Timmarajayya, donated lands to the presiding deity of Mangalagiri temple.[186] Srirangaraju, *mahamandalesvara* of Sadasivaraya, donated Pulu Patturu village to Raghunath temple.[187] Thus *amaranayakas* and lower level *naayakas*, too, emulated the example of their overlords. These *agrahara* or *devabhoga* assignments become understandable from the perspective of the interdependence between temporal power and sacred authority. It has been argued that while spiritually, absolutely, the priest is superior, he is at the same time, from a temporal or material point of view, subject and dependent.[188] Heesterman, also, argues that the greater the king's power, the more he needs the brahman.[189] Assignments of *devabhoga* or *agrahara* were not administrative but a socio-religious necessity for the temporal power.

Priestly validation of power continued beyond 'Hindu' dynasties. Qutb Shahi rulers sought to achieve legitimation through offering military service to Hindus and by extending patronage for the cultural and religious institutions of their Hindu subjects.

Madanna, a Telugu Brahman from Hanumakonda was made *Mir Jumla* or Chief Minister. Akkanna, Madanna's brother served as Commander-in-chief of the army. Venkanna and Kancherla Goppanna and many other Hindus served in the Golconda kingdom. Malik Ibrahim patronised many poets like Addanki Gangadhara, Kandukuri Rudrakavi and Ponneganti Telganarya in his court. Malik Ibrahim took a lot of interest in Telugu language and literature. He even took a Hindu woman, named *Bhagirati*, as his wife.[190] Amin Khan, a noble of Ibrahim, patronised Ponneganti Telaganarya. Malik Ibrahim's successor patronised Sarangu Tammayya, a Vaishnava poet and Karanam of Golconda.

Religious policy of Qutb Shahis was that of toleration. They seem to have realized the necessity of getting the support of Hindu religious authorities. Rudrakavi was given the village of Chintalapalem as agraharam.[191] An epigraph, from Masayapeta village (Nellore district) records the grant of a village as agrahara to several Brahmins by Lalkhan, a mulsim official, to promote the liberality of Quli Qutb Shah.[192] In these conditions of reciprocity, Malik Ibrahim's name was Sanskritized as *Malkibharamu* or *Ibharamu*. This was how Qutb Shahis power was validated by the priestly class of medieval Andhra.

Burton Stein is critical of the concept of feudal state to Vijayanagara, although he characterises Vijayanagara as highly militaristic. He still thinks that Vijayanagara was a segmentary state.[193] However, he now conceives it as a system of political economy pointing towards the patrimonial regimes that became familiar in late seventeenth and eighteenth centuries. He thinks that Vijayanagara state exhibited protopatrimonialism. Vijayanagara state was transitional in two ways to later patrimonial regimes of Tipu Sultan or Peshwa Baji Rao. First, during the nearly three centuries of Vijayanagara rule fundamental changes in agrarian and commercial production and organization provided the material base for the patrimonial systems that were to develop in seventeenth and eighteenth centuries. Secondly the deeply martial character of the society in which it pointed from medieval order, in which states income was partly realised through plunder, to one based upon a more rational mobilization of landed wealth along with some collections from the expanding trade. Vijayanagara kings could not have direct command of local resources which is a necessity for a full patrimonial order since they remained only as ritual figures.[194]

Golconda polity was more centralized, according to Stein, than Vijayanagara. Because no notion of shared sovereignty was brooked in Golconda, however substantial the degree of local power held by *Reddis* or *Velmas*, whereas this was the core of Vijayanagara sovereignty from first to last. Again, prebendal rights conferred by Golconda were less easily transformed into hereditary chiefly rights. Another factor also helped Golconda's central authority. That was the direct involvement of rulers and nobles in Coromandal trade. This brought lots of resources for strengthening their central authority beyond any available to Vijayanagara rulers.[195]

Karashima preferred to characterise sixteenth century Vijayanagara political economy as a feudal system. However, this feudal system is not identical with western Europe's as the state had control over *naayakas*. Vijayanagara feudalism is, therefore, a 'state feudalism'.[196] From our study it appears that Vijayanagara polity was equally centralised, if not more centralised as Golconda, and Bijapur. State had effective control over *naayakas* at least upto the battle of Talikota. *Naayakas* started asserting more and more independence defying central authority only after this battle. However, since we are not in a position to know how much revenue was remitted by *naayakas* to the centre, or what exactly were their political or military organization, we cannot ascertain the degree of central control over *naayakas*.

References

1. No element of social structure can be a better example of the interaction among various factors such as economy, polity, society and culture than the state. But the forms and ways of such an interaction are always determined by the character of a given civilization and the levels of its development. Generally state is viewed as a stabilized form of socio-politico phenomena by

anthropologists and they distinguish such types of state as industrial and pre-industrial; see Fried Morton, H., *The Evolution of Political Society,* New York, 1967; Service Elman. R., *Origins of the State and Civilization*, New York, 1975; H.J.M. Claessan & P. Skalink, '*The Early State: A Structural Approach*' in the early state, Hague, 1978, pp. 533-96; Perry Anderson opines that pre-capitalist modes of production cannot be defined except via their political, legal and ideological superstructures, since these are what determine the extra-economic coercion that specifies them.

2. One view characterizes polity of pre-modern India as traditional. This view emphasizes more on Kingship and rituals associated with Kingship, for discussion on this line see, R.J. Moore (ed.), *Tradition and Politics in Asia* (Delhi, 1979); J.F. Richards (ed), *Kingship and Authority in South Asia* (South Asian Studies, University of Wisconsin, No. 3, 1978); Another view see pre-modern polity as Oriental *Despotism* which characterizes changeless polity and society; see K.A. Wittfogel, *Oriental Despotism: A Comparative Study of Total Power*, Yale University press, 1970; opposed to this view of traditional polity is the assumption which envisages possibilities of change. But the views on change or on mechanisms of change are not identical.
3. Robert Sewell, *A Forgotten Empire* (Vijayanagar), London 1900, p.33.
4. P. Sree Rama Sarma, '*Saluva Dynasty of Vijayanagar*', an unpublished Ph.D. thesis, Osmania University, Hyderabad, 1972, p.38.
5. Brajadulal Chattopadhyaya, *The Making of Early Medieval India*, O.U.P. 1997, p. 189
6. Ibid, p. 190.
7. A. Krishnaswami, *The Tamil Country under Vijayanagar*, Annamalai University, 1964, pp.100-2.
8. D.C.Sircar, *Landlordism and Tenancy in Ancient and Medieval India as Revealed by Epigraphical records*, University of Lucknow, Lucknow, 1969.
9. N. Venkataramanayya, *Studies in the History of Third Dynasty of Vijayanagara*, Madras, 1935, pp.171-2.
10. B. Stein, *Vijayanagara*, The New Cambridge History of India, Delhi, 1994, p.42.

11. Ibid., p. 29.
12. P.R. Rao, *History and Culture of Andhra Pradesh*, Delhi, Reprint, 1995, p.91.
13. N. Venkataramanayya, *Studies in the History of Third Dynasty of Vijayanagara*, p. 103
14. Y. Subbarayalu, 'Socio-political Formation of South India: Vijayanagara Period' in K.K.N. Kurup (ed.) *New Dimensions in South Indian History*, Calicut, 1996, p. 68.
15. Ibid., p. 68.
16. *Inscriptions of Andhra Pradesh: Cuddapah district*, (ed.) by P.V.P. Sastry Vol. II, 65, (Hereafter I.A.P.C.) Nellore District inscriptions, (ed.) by A. Butterworth & Venugopal Chetty, Vol. 1, Ongole 31, (Hereafter N.D.1.), A.R. No. 276, of 1967;
17. N.D.I. Vol. 1, Nellore, 54.
18. N. Venkataramanayya, op. cit, p. 146.
19. S.I.I., Vol. 4, No. 278.
20. *Sthalam* was a territorial division.
21. S.I.I. V. 10. No. 521. ARE No. 307 of 1934-35.
22. I.A.P.C. Vol. III, No. 1672.
23. A.R. No. 19 of 1967.
24. S.I.I. IV, No. 1344.
25. S.I.I. IV, No. 686.
26. Y. Subbarayalu, op. cit. p.69.
27. A. Krishnaswami, *The Tamil Country under Vijayanagara*, Annamalai, 1964, pp. 193-95.
28. Cynthia Talbot, *Political Intermediaries in Kakatiya Andhra*, 1175-1325, in *IESHR*, Vol. 31, No.3, 1994, pp. 261-289.
29. Ibid, p. 262.
30. Ibid, p. 278.
31. Vidyavati, *Vijayanagara Sasanalu*, (Telugu), Hyderabad, 1994, p.20.
32. Krishna Swami, op. cit, p. 179-80, D.C. Sircar, *Indian Epigraphical Glossary*, Delhi, 1966, p. 214.
33. Noboru Karashima, *Towards a New Formation: South Indian Society Under Vijayanagara Rule*, O.U.P. 1992.

34. A.R. No. 9 of 1967.
35. Ibid.
36. N.D.I. I, Atmakur
37. N.D.I.1., Atmakur, 6.
38. A.R. No. 614 of 1938-39.
39. N. Venataramanayya, *Cuddapah Inscriptions*, Madras, 1972, p. 449.
40. I.A.P.C. III, 165.
41. Venkataramanayya had interpreted that *durga-dannayakas* were provincial governors—who were mostly Brahman commanders—ruling *bhandaravada* or crown territory in their respective provinces and there were *amaranaayakas* holding territories surrounding fort-towns in the same provinces. See Venkataramanayya, *Studies in the History of Third Dynasty of Vijayanagara*, Madras, pp. 170-171. Mahalingam and Krishnaswami more or less hold the same opinion.
42. N.D.I.1. Darsi, 1586.
43. N.D.I.1 Kaavali, 49.
44. N.D.I.-I, 46.
45. N.D.I.-I, Kaavali, 50.
46. N.D.I.-I, Nellore, I.
47. N.D.I.-I, Nellore, 4.
48. N.D.I.-I, Nellore, 7.
49. N.D.I.-I, Nellore 6,
50. N.D.I.-I, Nellore, 9
51. N.D.I.-I, Nellore 11.
52. N.D.I.-I, Nellore 26.
53. N.D.I.-I, Darsi, 9.
54. I.A.P.C. II, 29.
55. I.A.P.C. 11, 19.
56. I.A.P.C. 11, 34.
57. S.I.I. IV, 709.
58. I.A.P.C. 11, 200.
59. I.A.P.C. III, 114.
60. Noboru Karashima, op. cit. p. 110.

61. N. Venkataramanayya, *Cuddapah inscriptions*, Madras, 1972, p. 193-4; Mandraju Nagarajayya, a *mudala* of Ramaraju, abolished tax on barbers in Vemuluru village.
62. Burton Stein, op. cit., p. 415.
63. Ibid, p. 420-21.
64. S.I.I. IV, 800.
65. Y. Subbarayalu, op. cit, p. 75, Rights in land merely referred to shares in agricultural produce and dominion referred to the right to sell, mortgage the land by donees.
66. E.I. Vol. III, p. 126, Ibid, Vol. XVI, p. 257
67. S.I.I. Vol. IX, 436, 458, 580, 582, 587, 590.
68. S.I.I. Vol. IX, 580, 587, 588.
69. B. Stein, op. cit. p. 420.
70. M. Krishna Kumari, 'were the Bhandaravada Gramas taxable lands' in *APHC*, Tenali, 1994, p.51.
71. N. Karashima, op. cit, p. 205-208. He reaches this conclusion after his contextual analysis of Tamil inscriptions.
72. I.A.P.C. Vol. II, No. 183.
73. B. Stein, op. cit, p. 423.
74. A.R. No. 9 of 1967; S.I.I. Vol. XVI, No. 139, 144, 156 163; I.A.P.C. Vol. II, No. 209.
75. I.A.P.C. III, 115.
76. I.A.P.C. II, 104, A.R.No. 241 of 1968.
77. Inscriptions of Cuddapah, p. 607.
78. I.A.P.C.-III, 122.
79. N. Venkataramanayya, op. cit, pp. 160-8.
80. I.A.P.C. III, 31.
81. N. Venkataramanayya, *Cuddapah Inscriptions*, Madras, 1972, p.2-3
82. I.A.P.C. III, 31.
83. S.I.I. 10, 521, ARE No. 307 of 1934-35.
84. N. Venkataramanayya, *Cuddapah Inscriptions*, op. cit. p. 576.
85. Venkataramanayya, *Studies in the Third Dynasty*, p. 163 (*Manya* holders paid quit-rent called *jodi* on their holdings).

86. Ibid, p. 163.
87. B. Stein op. cit., p. 424.
88. Ibid., p. 424.
89. S.I.I. XVI, No. 103.
90. N. Venkataramanayya, *Studies in the Third Dynasty*, p. 199.
91. B. Stein, op. cit. p. 424-425.
92. B. Stein, op. cit. p. 426.
93. Ibid, p. 426.
94. Ibid, p. 426.
95. M. Rama Rao (ed.) *Inscriptions of Andhradesa*, Tirupati, 1969, No. 891, Chittoor district, I.A.P.C. 11,19, I.A.P.C. 11, 34, I.A.P.C. 11, 106, N.D.I-I, p. 264.
96. Nilakanta Sastri, *A History of South India from Pre-historic Times to the Fall of Vijayanagara*, O.U.P. 1966, p. 306,7.
97. Ibid, p. 307.
98. B. Stein, *Vijayanagara*, The New Cambridge History of India, Orient Longman, 1990, p. 65.
99. Noboru Karashima, *Towards a new Formation: South Indian Society under Vijayanagar Rule*, O.U.P. 1992.
100. N. Venkataramanayya, *Cuddapah Inscriptions*, p. 351, 455.
101. S.I.I., X, No. 528.
102. SII, IV, No. 698.
103. M.L.K. Murthy, 'Environment, Royal Policy and Social Formation in the Eastern Ghats South India A.D. 1000-1500' in *I.H.C.* Warangal, Feb. 1993, p.19.
104. N. Venkataramanayya, *Cuddapah Inscriptions*, p. 607.
105. Markapuram Kaifiyat, *Mackenzie Manuscripts*, Vol. 149, No. 1169.
106. M.L.K. Murthy, op.cit. p.19.
107. S.S.I., Vol.4, No.765, Vol.5, No.156, Vol. 10, Nos. 318, 327, *Epigraphica Indica*, Vol.3, V.50.
108. *Rayavachakam* (ed.) by Jayanti Ramayya Pantulu, A.P. Sahitya Academy, Hyderabad, 1982, Lines 10-15, p.79.
109. *Chandrabhanu Charitra* of T. Mallanna (ed.) by D. Chinnikrishna Sarma, Vijayawada, 1973, 2-2.

110. S.I.I., IV, No. 709.
111. S.I.I., IV, No. 702.
112. S.I.I., IV, No. 1344.
113. I.A.P.C. II, No. 183, 244.
114. I.A.P.C., II, No. 137.
115. I.A.P.C., II, No. 200.
116. T.K.T. Viraraghavacharya, *History of Tirupati*, Tirupati, 1954, V.2, p. 565-6.
117. B. Stein, *Vijayanagara*, The New Cambridge History of India, Orient Longman, Reprint, 1994, p. 107.
118. Ibid, p. 107.
119. Ibid, p. 107.
120. Ibid, p. 107.
121. S.I.I. X, No. 98, 489, 495, 507, 533; *Hyderabad Archaeological series*, Vol. XIII, 53, 54, Vol. XIX, 6,9,13; I.A.P.C. 11, 120. Also see B.S.L. Hanumantha Rao, *Social Mobility in Medieval Andhra*, Hyderabad 1995, chapt.4.
122. S.I.I., Vol. V, No. 158, Vol. VI, Nos. 200, 1179.
123. B.S.L. Hanumantha Rao, op. cit, 1995, p. 174.
124. Ibid, p. 174.
125. I.A.P.C. 11, 230.
126. N.D.I. III, Udayagiri, 2.
127. B.S.L. Hanumantha Rao, op. cit, 1995, p. 174.
128. S.I.I., IV, No. 219.
129. ARE No. 332 of 1936-37, these three inscriptions are from Ayyangarivaripalem, Pondugala, Palnad Taluk, Guntur (Dist).
130. I.A.P.C., 111, 117.
131. S.I.I., IV, No. 709.
132. N. Venkataramanayya, *Cuddapah inscriptions*, op. cit. p. 442.
133. ARE No. 190, of 1896.
134. ARE No. 357 of 1893.
135. ARE No. 11 of 1918.
136. S.I.I., IV No. 660, 696.

137. New Indian Antiquary, 11, p. 442.
138. N. Venkataramanayya, *Cuddapah inscriptions*, op.cit. p. 835, Varieties were *puli vanne, popalli vanne, garuda vanne, lakshminarayananchu, gavakshulanchu, sannaniovolu puttalu.*
139. *Markendeya* was considered to be a great rishi (sage).
140. N. Venkataramanayya, *Cuddapah Inscriptions*, p. 835.
141. B. Stein, *Vijayanagara*, op. cit. p. 108.
142. Ibid, p. 108.
143. Y. Subbarayalu, op. cit, 1996, p. 82.
144. N. Venkataramanayya, *Cuddapah Inscriptions*, p. 179.
145. B. Stein, *Peasant State and Society*, p. 451.
146. Ibid, p. 451.
147. Y. Subbarayalu, op. cit, 1996, p. 82.
148. A *Tarfardar* or Governor of Bahamani kingdom, Quli Qutb-ul-Mulk in-charge of Tilang established Qutb Shahi dynasty in 1518 A.D. with the capital at Golconda. After the death of Shihauddin Mahmud Bahamani in 1518 A.D., many Tarafdars declared independence.
149. H.K. Sherwani, *History of Qutb Shahi Dynasty*, Delhi, 1974, p. 654.
150. Ibid., 510-13.
151. J.R. Richards, *Mughal Administration in Golconda*, p. 22-29.
152. S.N. Sen, *Indian Travels of Thevenot and Careri*, Delhi, 1949, p.143.
153. J.F. Richards, op. cit. pp. 22-24.
154. Tavernier, Jean Baptiste, *Travels in India*, Vol. I, Delhi, 1977, p.121.
155. *Travels of Thevenot*, p. 98.
156. B. Stein, *Vijayanagara*, op. cit. p. 144.
157. Burton Stein, '*State Formation and Economy Reconsidered, in MAS*, Vol. XIX, (3), 1985, p. 388.
158. B. Stein, *Vijayanagara*, op. cit. p. 143.
159. Ibid, p. 143.
160. Ibid, p. 144.
161. He arrived at this conclusion because he viewed Vijayanagara polity as segmentary state, B.Stein, *Vijayanagara,* op. cit., p.144.
162. B. Chattopadhyaya, *The Making of Early Medieval India*, O.U.P. 1997, p. 198.

163. S.I.I. X.400, Here they claimed as the preservers of four varnas, Bukka was praised as *Brahmana's protector, inscriptions of Cuddapah* (ed) by N. Venkataramanayya, p. 407.
164. B. Stein, Vijayanagara, op. cit. p. 29.
165. Ibid., p. 29.
166. Ibid., p. 141.
167. H. Kulke, *'Royal Temple policy and structure of Medieval Hindu kingdoms'* in A. Eschmann, H. Kulke and G.C. Tripathi (eds.) *The Cult of Jagganath and the Regional Tradition of Orissa*, Delhi, 1986, pp. 125-137.
168. M.L.K. Murthy, op. cit, p. 15.
169. E.C. XII, p. 72.
170. MER, 1915, NO. 11.
171. S.I.I., Vol. IX, No. 407, 521, MER, 1937-38, No. 197, Ibid, 1915, No. 40.
172. S.I.I., Vol. IX, No. 481.
173. Srisailam Kaifiyat, *Mackenzie Manuscripts*, 127, No. 964, S.I.I., XVI, Nos. 86, 87 E.I. Vol. 3, p.291.
174. S.I.I. IX, No. 540, TTD,1, Vol. No.1. IV, No. 142.
175. Sewell, *Forgotten Empire*, Paes, Chronicle Pp. 253-64, and Nuniz's Chronicle, pp. 357-60. Conti's and Razzak's accounts are found in R.H. Major, *India in the fifteenth century: A Collection of Narratives of Voyages to India*, London, 1857.
176. A.H. Longhurst, *Hampi Ruins: Described and Illustrated*, Madras, 1917, pp. 57-70.
177. B. Stein, *Peasant State and Society*, p. 387.
178. Romila Thapar, *A History of India*, Vol.1, Penguin Books, 1966, p. 169.
179. Domingos Paes, *Narrative*, Tr. by Robert Sewell in *Forgotten Empire*, p. 245.
180. S.I.I., Vol. IX, No. 540, TTD1, Vol. IV No. 142.
181. Paes Chronicle in Sewell's '*A Forgotten Empire*', op. cit. p. 268.
182. I.A.P.C. III, No. 269.
183. N.D.I. III, Udayagiri.
184. N.D.I. - I, Kandukur, 14.

185. N.D.I. - II, Nellore 34.
186. S.I.I., IV, No. 709.
187. I.A.P.C. II, Pulapatturu.
188. L. Dumont, 'The Concept of Kingship in Ancient India' in *Religion Politics and History in India*, Mouton Publishers, 1970, p. 65.
189. J.C. Heesterman, 'The Conundrum of Kings' authority' in J.F. Richards (ed.) *Kingship and Authority in South Asia*, pp. 1-27.
190. H.K. Sherwani, 'Cultural and Administrative set up under Ibrahim Qutbshah' in Islamic Culture, Vol. XXXI, No.2, 1957, p.130.
191. B.V. Krishna Rao, 'Telugu Literature under Qutub Shahis' in the *Triveni Quarterly*, Vol. XIV, No.2, April-June, 1942.
192. N.D.I. No.2, p. 667.
193. B. Stein, *Vijayanagara*. op. cit. 1994, p. 145.
194. B. Stein, *Vijayanagara and the Transition to Patrimonial System* in Dallapiccola, A.L. et al. eds. *Vijayanagara city and Empire: New Currents of Research*, 1985.
195. B. Stein, *Vijayanagara*, op. cit. 1994, p. 144.
196. N. Karashima, op. cit. 1992, p.8.

CONCLUSION

The study of popular culture and state in Medieval Andhra desa is carried out with an idea which is deliberately and openly more empirical, looking back to portray the actual picture of various relationships which existed among various social groups from fourteenth to seventeenth centuries. These relationships were carried out to perpetuate the tendencies of dominance and subjection not only through myths, rituals, customs, traditions and religious practices but also through the naked power of political elements. Moving from social structures to collective attitudes and representations involved, the whole problem of the complex mediators between the real human life at popular level and the images which people constructed, these constructions defined and redefined the positions of people in society and their roles. This becomes clear from the foregoing aspects that the dialectical relationships between the objective conditions of human life and the ways in which people narrated and lived in them. This was how the whole process of mystification of the real existence could ultimately lead to an essential hierarchization of social groups and prevented them from coming together to overthrow the dominance imposed on them by cultural, political, social and other symbols.

We have adopted a working hypothesis which asserts that there is a crude but indispensable co-relation between the gestures of religious practices and religious beliefs. It was through this basis that the communication was opened with popular culture. No doubt this whole process took place in stages over a long historical period, which we have studied. More profoundly, what one feels was essential in working the dynamics of popular culture and there was an attempt by the socially dominant to try and arrive at an understanding of these synonymous masses who were unable to afford the subsistence if not luxury and any other expression except immerse deeper and deeper into the process of subordination and servitude in Medieval Andhra desa. Sanskritization of popular religious practices and cultural forms also proves this point.

The study of popular culture in medieval Andhra doubtlessly reflects that the collective unconscious operated at mentalities rather than domain of clear thought and clearly formulated expressions. In fact, in this aspect, the information offered by our sources has been most profitable. One of our evaluation has been that the existence of popular culture was always surrounded by a whole system of masks, devices, taboos and even magical practices. Therefore, the image of people that one sees, generally, was peculiarly distorted one the meaning of which we have tried to decipher by decoding what was religiously demanded as real. Because at different terminals of human experience were always sensitive indicators like *Karma, Svarga* or *Vaikuntam*, myths, participation in *Jatara*, and other ceremonies which never allowed the people at popular level to gauge and assess their positions.

But such practices retained a specific and exemplary value within the then complex-social system in which the socially dominant and politically powerful elements had no other means to sustain their nexus. The study of popular culture has also helped us to explain how the ancient systems were preserved by practising at popular level. For example, the phenomenon of death was always of equal significance. Therefore, the sensitivity of death marked advances and retreats. On one side, it was a painful sorrow because of frequent epidemics which took a heavy toll of human life, particularly of those who were undernourished and unprotected against such occurrences. On the other hand, the cattle wealth and human life was also offered voluntarily to prevent natural calamities.

This was not only true of panicky convulsions of periods of epidemic but also in a more defused way of these times when collective sensibility was obsessed with death. This clearly shows how such problems came to pre-occupy people at popular level. The demographic factors also did not explain everything in the realm of popular behaviour, we need to underline the astonishing obstinacy of rituals, the deeply rooted gestures reproduced even when they were not understood as in superstitious and innumerable magical rituals which found the sole popular response to death and disease.

All these heterogeneous forces whose interaction produced a great variety of local situations seem to have always emerged very fruitful to medieval Andhra state during the period of our study. Though the sacred and temporal authorities had their own roles, yet that did not prevent a constant communication between the state and religious institutions which was directed to evolve their hegemonic structures. It was through religious institutions that the relations of power were structured and political influences were radiated to subordinate those who practised, performed and constituted popular culture. The possibility of the continuance of such a coherent hegemony turned out to be states illusion because over a period of time, all those forces which produced such exploitative structures converged at a point where it became essential for the dominant to abandon their roles. In this, a significant contribution was made by the external elements such as Turks or Muslims who established their political authorities in Medieval Andhra. But they also began to take popular masses for royal rides and sponsored the institutions of *khanqas, Dargahs* and temples to preserve the age-old unholy alliance between religion and power to keep popular culture subordinate.

We have not tried to make any considerable advance in the process of conceptualization of popular culture. But we have tried to venture into exotic territory of popular culture by bringing together various essential pieces of evidence and unveiled those sharp edges the study of whose nature will contribute very significantly to the reconstruction of cultural history in Medieval Andhra.

Bibliography

Primary Sources

(a) Medieval Literature

Amuktamalayada of Srikrishnadevaraya (ed.) by Venkataraya Sastry & Brothers, Madras, 1964. This work was written by famous Vijayanagara Ruler Srikrishnadevaraya (1509-30). This work covers various aspects of his time. It also throws light on general conditions of the period.

Basavapuranam of Palkurki Somanatha (ed.) by Subramanyam G.V., A.P. Sahitya Academy, Hyderabad, 1969. Somanatha was a Saivite poet of thirteenth century. This work describes various rituals followed by Saivites of his times.

Bhimesvara Puranam of Srinatha, Vavilla Ramaswamy & Sons, Madras 1967. Srinatha was a court poet of Reddi Kingdom of Medieval Andhra (1426-40). This text talks about the sanctity of Draksharamam as a pilgrimage centre. He discusses various festivals, rituals connected with the worship of Bhimesvara, (local deity).

Chandrabhanu Charitra of Tarigoppula Mallanna (ed.) by Chinnikrishna Sarma, D. Vijayawada, 1973. Mallana lived during sixteenth century.

Hamsavimsati of Ayyalaraju Narayanamatya (ed.) by Subbanna Satavadhani, C.V. A.P. Sahitya Academy, Hyderabad, 1977. This text basically hovers around fornication and gives primacy to morals in the society. In between the poet describes various social, economic, and cultural conditions of his time. He lived around early part of eighteenth century.

Harivilasam of Srinatha, Venakteswara, R & Co. Madras, 1939.

Kalapurnodayamu of Pingali Surana, A.P. Sahitya Academy, Hyderabad, 1980. The poet lived during 1540-70 A.D.

Kasikhandam of Srinatha, (ed.) by Ramaswami Sastrulu. V. Madras, 1969. This work describes the importance of Kasi as a pilgrimage centre. Poet describes contemporary religious beliefs, rituals. etc.

Keyurabhahucharitra of Manchana, A.P. Sahitya Academy, Hyderabad, 1966.

Kridabhiramam of Srinatha (ed.) by Ananda Murthy, V. Manimanjari, Hyderabad. 1988. Srinatha pointed out many social evils of his society. He also described many social activities, like Jataras, gambling and everyday life of common people.

Manucharitra of Peddana, (ed) by Muralikrishna, K. Vijayawada, 1986. He lived from 1475-1540 A.D. This work is an important source of contemporary period.

Palnativeera Charitra of Srinadha (ed.) by Pingali Lakshmikantam & A. Surya Rao, Vishalandhra Publications, Vijayawada, 1961. This is a historical poem. It describes the events which took place during late twelfth century. However, its importance lies in the fact that it became a popular historical ballad in subsequent centuries.

Panditaradhya Charitra of Palkurki Somanadha (ed.) by Ch. Narayana Rao, Telugu University, Hyderabad, 1992. The poet was a Saivite. As such, he wrote this work eulogizing Saivism. Contemporary conditions were also reflected upon.

Pandurangamahatyam of Tenali Ramakrishna (ed.) by T. Ananta Krishna Sarma & G. Rama Subba Sarma, A.P. Sahitya Academy, Hyderabad, 1984. Poet lived during sixteenth century. This work describes many rituals, customs and beliefs of the contemporary period.

Paramayogivilasam of Tallapaka Triuvengalanatha, A.P. Sahitya Academy, Hyderabad, 1967.

Ranganadharamayanam of Gona Buddha Reddy, Madras, 1961.

Sarangadharacharitra of Chemakura Venkatakavi, (ed.) by D.Pichaiah Sastry, A.P. Sahitya Academy, Hyderabad, 1967. This work belongs to early seventeenth century.

Simhasanadwatrimsika of Koravi Goparaju (ed.) by G. Ramakrishna Sarma, A.P. Sahitya Academy, Hyderabad, 1968.

Sivaratrimahatyam of Srinadha, Hyderabad, 1968. This work talks about the importance of Sivaratri, Srisailam's importance as a pilgrimage centre and various rituals customs etc. performed on this day are mentioned.

Sri Kalahasti Mahatyam of Dhurjati (ed.) by Ch. Papaiah Sastri, Hyderabad, 1961. He was a court poet of Srikrishnadevaraya. Srikalahasti's importance as a pilgrimage centre was described in this work.

Srungara Sakuntalam of Pillalamarri Pinavirabhadra, (ed.) by N. Krishna Kumari, Hyderabad, 1969. This work was written around, 1480, A.D.

Sukasaptati of Palavekari Kadiripati, (ed.) by B.Rama Raju, A.P. Sahitya Academy, Hyderabad, 1979.

Vaijayantivilasam of Sarangu Thammaiah, Hyderabad, 1975.

Valmikicharitra of Raghunadhanayaka (ed.) by B. Rama Raju, A.P. Sahitya Academy, Hyderabad, 1968.

Vasucharitra of Ramaraju Bhushana, (ed.) by K. Suprasanna Charya, Hyderabad, 1980.

Yayati Charitra of Ponneganti Telanganarya, Madras, 1970.

(b) Inscriptional

Annual Report of South Indian Epigraphy.

Archaeological Reports.

Archaeological Survey Reports.

Copper Plate Inscriptions of Andhra Pradesh, A.P. Government Museum, Vols. 1 & 2 (ed.) by N. Ramesan, 1962, 1970.

Corpus of Telingana Inscriptions, Vol. 1 to 3 (ed.) by P. Srinivasachari, 1940, 1958 & IV by Somasekhara Sarma, 1973.

Cuddapah Inscriptions (ed.) by N. Venkataramanayya, 1972.

Epigraphica Andhrica, Vols. 1 to V

Epigraphica Carnatica.

Inscriptions of Andhra Pradesh: Cuddapah District (ed.) P.V.P. Sastry, Vols. 1 & 2, 1977, 1978.

Inscriptions of Andhra Pradesh: Karimnagar District (ed.). P.V.P. Sastry, 1974.

Inscriptions of Andhra Pradesh: Warangal District (ed.) N. Venkataramanayya, 1974.

Nellore District Inscriptions, 3 Vols. (ed.) A. Butterworth & Venugopal Chetty, 1905.

South Indian Inscriptions.

Tirumala Tirupati Devasthanam Inscriptions.

Vijayanagara Inscriptions. Vol. 1 & 2, Directorate of Archaeology and Museums, Government of Karnataka, Mysore 1985.

Vijayanagara: Progress of Research 1983-84, Directorate of Archaeology & Museums, Mysore, 1985.

(c) Governmental Records

Selections from the records of the Madras Government No. VII. 1854, Reports on the swing festival and the ceremony of walking through fire.

(d) Village Kaifiyats

Guntur District, (ed.) V.V. Krishna Satry, A.P. State Archives, Hyderabad, 1990.

Krishna District (ed.) Rajendra Prasad, A.P. State Archives, Hyderabad, 1990.

Srikakulam District (ed.) Rajendra Prasad, A.P. State Archives, Hyderabad, 1990.

West Godavari District, (ed.) Rajendra Prasad, A.P. State Archives, Hyderabad, 1990.

(e) Foreign Travellers Accounts

Brabosa, Durate, *The Book of Durate Barbosa - An Account of the countries bordering on the Indian ocean and their inhabitants*, 2 Vols. London, 1918.

Della Valle, Pietro, *The Travels of Pietro Della Valle in India*, 2 Vols. London, 1892.

Nuniz, Fernao, *Chronicle of Fernao Nuniz* in A Forgotten Empire, by Robert Sewell, Delhi, 1985.

Paes, Domingos, *Narrative of Domingos Paes*, in A Forgotten Empire, by Robert Sewell, Delhi, 1985.

Samuel Purchas, *Purchas his pilgrims*, 2 Vols. Glasgow, 1905.

Tavernier, Jean Baptiste, *Travels in India*, Vols. 1 & 2, Delhi, 1977.

Secondary Sources

(a) Books

Ahmad, Imtiaz — *Rituals and Religion among Muslims in India*, Delhi, 1981.

Aiyangar, S. Krishnaswami — *Some Contributions of South India to Indian Culture*, Delhi, 1981.

– – (ed.) — *Sources of Vijayanagara History*, Delhi, 1986.

Alavi, Rafi, Ahmad — *Studies in the History of Medieval Deccan*, Delhi, 1971.

Appadurai, Arjun — *Worship and Conflict under Colonial Rule: A South Indian Case*, Delhi, 1977.

Archer, S. Margaret — *Culture and Agency: The Place of Culture in Social Theory*, New York, 1988.

Artz B. Frederick — *The Mind of the Middle Ages A.D. 1200-1500*, London, 1980.

Baartmans, Frans — *Apah, The Sacred Waters: An Analysis of a Primordial Symbol in Hindu Myths*, Delhi, 1990.

Banerjee, Suresh Chandra — *Folklore in Buddhist and Jaina Literatures*, Delhi, 1987.

Barz, Richard — *The Bhakti Sect of Vallabhacary*, Haryana, 1976.

Banton, Michael — *Anthropological Approaches to the Study of Religion*, New York, 1985.

Barth, J. — *History of Religions in India*, London 1882.

Bayly, Susan — *Saints, Goddesses and Kings: Muslims and Christians in South Indian Society, 1700-1900*, Cambridge University Press, 1992.

Bhandarkar, R.G. — *Vaisnavism, Saivism and Other Minor Religious Sects*, Poona, 1938.

Bhatt, Gurunja — *Studies in Tulava History and Culture*, Manipal, 1975.

Bhattacharya, Narendra N. — *The Indian Mother Goddess*, Delhi, 1977.

Bigsby, C.W.E. (ed.) — *Approaches to Popular Culture*, London, 1976.

Burke, Peter — *Popular Culture in Early Modern Europe*, London, 1978.

Bilgrami, S.A.A. — *Landmarks of the Deccan*, Hyderabad, 1927.

Carmody, John et al. — *Interpreting the Religious Experience: A World View*, New Jersey, 1987.

Carpenter, J. Estlin — *Theism in Medieval India*, Delhi, 1977.

Chaudhari, C. Nirad — *Hinduism: A Religion To Live By*, Delhi, 1977.

Chaudhury, Tapan Ray and Habib, Irfan (eds.) — *Cambridge Economic History of India*, Hyderabad, 1982.

Chitnis, K.N. — *Socio-Economic Aspects of Medieval India*, Poona, 1979.

Chopra, P.N. et al. *History of South India*, Vols. 1 & 2, Delhi, 1979.

Cole Brooke, H.T. *Essays on the Religion and Philosophy of Hindus*, Delhi, 1972.

Conolly, Peter *Perspectives on Indian Religion*, Delhi, 1986.

Crooke, W. *The Popular Religion and Folklore of Northern India*, Vol. 1 & 2, Delhi, Reprint, 1978.

Damge Sadashiv, Ambadas *Encyclopaedia of Puranic Beliefs and Practices*. Delhi, 1989.

Daniel, Gold *The Lord as Guru: Hindi Sants in North Indian Tradition*, New York, 1987.

Donald & Johnson (ed.), *God and Gods in Hinduism*, Delhi, Reprint, 1976.

Durga, S.A.K. *The Opera in South India*, Delhi, 1979.

Eaton Richard, Maxwell *Sufis of Bijapur, 1300-1700*, Princeton, 1978.

Elmore, W.T. *Dravidian Gods in Modern Hinduism*, Delhi, 1984.

Eisenstadt, S.N. et al. *Patrons, Clients and Friends: Interpersonal relations and the structure of Trust in Society*, Cambridge, 1984.

Elliot & Dowson *The History of India as Told by its Own Historians*, Allahabad, Reprints, 1964,69.

Engineer, Ashgar Ali *The Origin and Development of Islam: An Essay on its Socio-Economic Growth*, Reprint, 1978.

Engles, Max *On Religion*, Moscow, Reprint, 1975.

Filliozat, Vasundhara (ed.) *The Vijayanagara Empire as seen by Domingos Paes and Fernao Nuniz*, Two Sixteenth Century Portuguese Chroniclers, National Book Trust Publications, Delhi, 1977.

Frykenberg, R.E. *Land Control and Social Structures in India*, Delhi, 1979.

Fukazawa, *The Medieval Deccan: Peasants and State Systems*, Delhi, 1990.

Gardiner, Juliet, *What is History Today...?*, London, 1988.

Ghurye, G.S. *Gods and Men*, Bombay, Reprint, 1983.

Ginzburg, Carlo *The Night Battles: Witchcraft and Agrarian Cults in Sixteenth and Seventeenth Centuries*, tr. by John & Anne Tedeschi, London, 1965.

— — *The Cheese and The Worms: The Cosmos of a Sixteenth Century Miller*, tr. by John & Anne Tedeschi, London, 1980.

Gombrich, F. *Oxford University Papers on India*, Part I, Delhi, 1986.

Gurevich, A.J. *Categories of Medieval Culture*, England, a Reprint, 1985.

Hall, R. John. et al. *Culture: Sociological Perspectives*, New Jersey, 1993.

Hawley, John et al. *The Divine Consort: Radha and the Goddess of India*, Delhi, 1984.

Hanumantha Rao, B.S.L. *Religion in Andhra*, Guntur, 1993.

Hazara, R.C. *Studies in the Puranic Records on Hindu Rites and Customs*, Delhi, Reprint, 1975.

Heitzman, James — *Gifts of Power: Lordship in an Early Indian State*, O.U.P. Delhi, 1997.

Heras, Henry — *South India under the Vijayanagara Empire*, Vols. 1 & II, Delhi, 1980.

Hiltebeitel, Alf (eds.) — *Criminal Gods and Demon Devotees: Essays on Guardians of Popular Hinduism*, Delhi, 1989.

Hopkins, E.W. — *The Religions of India*. Boston, 1985.

Hubert, Henri et al. — *Sacrifice: It's Nature and Function*, Chicago, 1964.

Hussain, Yusuf — *Glimpses of Medieval Indian Culture*, Bombay, 1973.

Jagadis Ayyar, P.V. — *South Indian Shrines*, Madras, 1920.

Jorgenson, G. Joseph — *The Sun Dance Religion: Power for the Powerless*, Reprint, Delhi, 1974.

Jyotsna, Kamat K. — *Social Life in Medieval Karnataka*, Delhi, 1980.

Kameswara Rao — *Select Vijayanagara Temples of Rayalaseema*, Hyderabad, 1976.

Kapllan, S. (ed.) — *Understanding Popular Culture*, Berlin, 1984.

Karashima, Noboru — *South Indian History and Society: Studies from Inscriptions A.D. 850-1800*, Delhi, 1984.

-- — *Towards a New Formation: South Indian Society Under Vijayanagara Rule*, Delhi, 1992.

Kersenboom-Story, C. Saskia — *Nityasumangali*, Delhi, 1987.

Kinsley, David — *Hindu Goddesses: Visions of the Divine Feminine in the Religious Tradition*, Delhi, 1987.

Klein, Augusta — *Legends and Myths of Spiritual India*, Delhi, Reprint, 1984.

Kolenda, Pauline — *Caste, Cult and Hierarchy: Essays on the Culture of India*, Meerut, 1983.

Kosambi, D. — *Myth and Reality*, Bombay, Reprint, 1983.

Krishnaswami Aiyangar, S. — *Some Contributions of South India to Indian Culture*, Calcuta, 1923.

Kumari, M. Krishna. — *The Rule of the Chalukyas—Cholas in Andhradesa*, Delhi, 1985.

Ladurie, Emmanuel Le Roy — *Montaillou: Cathors and Catholics in a French Village, 1294-1324*, Penguin Books, Reprint 1980.

Leeming, David — *Mythology*, New York, Reprint, 1979.

Leonard, Karen. Isaksen — *Social History of an Indian Caste: The Kayasthas of Hyderabad*, Delhi, 1978.

Lewis, I.M. — *Religion in Context: Cults and Charisma*, London, 1986.

Longhurst, A.H. — *Hampi Ruins: Described and Illustrated*, Madras, 1917.

Lorenzen, N. David (ed.) — *Bhakti Religion in North India: Community, Identity and Political Action*, Delhi, 1996.

Mahalingam, T.V. — *Administration and Social Life Under Vijayanagar*, Madras, 1969.

– – — *Economic Life in the Vijayanagar Empire*, Madras, 1951.

– – — *South Indian Polity*, Madras, 1967.

Marriot, Mckim (ed.) — *Village India: Studies in the Little Community*, Chicago, 1955.

Mcrobbie, Angela, — *Post-Modernism and Popular Culture*, London, 1994.

Mitchell, A.G. — *Hindu Gods and Goddesses*, London, 1958.

Michell, George — *The Hindu Temples*, Delhi, 1977.

Moreland, W.H. — *Relations of Golconda in the Early Seventeenth Century A.D. 1608-22*, London, 1931.

— — *India at the Death of Akbar*, Delhi, 1974.

Muchembend, R. — *Popular Culture and Elite Culture in France, 1450-1700*, Baton Rouge, 1985.

Mukhia, Harbans — *Historians and Historiography During the Reign of Akbar, Delhi*, 1976.

Nandi, R.N. — *Religious Institutions and Cults in the Deccan*, Delhi, 1973.

Nilakanta Sastri, K.A. — *A History of South India from Pre-historic times to the fall of Vijayanagar*, Madras, Reprint, 1991.

Nilakanta Sastri, K.A. & Venkataramanayya, N. — *Further Sources of Vijayanagara History*, 2 Vols. Madras, 1946.

Ojha, P.N. — *Aspects of Medieval Indian Society and Culture*, Delhi, 1978.

Oddie, A. Geoffrey — *Popular Religion, Elites and Reform: Hook-Swinging and its Prohibition in Colonial India, 1800-1894*, Delhi, 1995.

O'Flaherty, Wendy Daniger — *The Origins of Evil in Hindu Mythology*, Delhi, 1976.

Oteau — *Travels and Travellers in India (1400-1700)*, London, 1909.

Patil, N.B. — *The Folklore in Mahabharata*, Delhi, 1983.

Preston, J. James — *Cult of the Goddess: Social and Religious Change in a Hindu Temple*, Delhi, 1980.

Radharkishna Sarma, M. — *Temples of Telangana*, Hyderabad, 1972.

Raj, Sheela — *Medievalism to Modernism: Socio-Economic and Culture History of Hyderabad*, 1869-1911, Bombay, 1987.

Rama Raju, B. — *Folklore of Andhra Pradesh*, Delhi, 1978.

Rama Rao, M. — *The Temples of Srisailam*, Hyderabad, 1967.

– – — *Buddhism in Andhradesa*, Hyderabad, 1956.

– – — *Saivite Deities of Andhradesa*, Tirupati, 1966.

– – — *Select Andhra Temples*, Hyderabad, 1969.

Ramaswamy, Vijaya and Rao, Velcheru Narayana — *Textiles and Weavers in Medieval South India*, O.U.P., Delhi, 1985.

Shulman, David and Subrahmanyam, Sanjay — *Symbols of Substance: Court and State in Nayaka Period Tamilnadu*, O.U.P. Delhi, 1992.

Reay, B. (ed.) — *Popular Culture in Seventeenth Century*, England, London, 1985.

Reddy Soma, R. — *Hindu and Muslim Religious Institutions of Andhradesa, 1300-1600 AD*, Madras, 1984.

Richards, J.F. — *Mughal Administration in Golconda*, O.U.P. 1975.

Rizvi, Saiyid Athar Abbas — *A History of Sufism in India*, Vol.1. Delhi, 1978.

Saletore, B.A. — *Social and Political Life in Vijayanagara Empire*, 2 Vols. Madras, 1934.

Samuel, Raphael — *People's History and Socialist Theory,* London, 1981.

Sarojini Devi, K. — *Religion in Vijayanagara Empire*, Delhi, 1990.

Sastri Krishna, H. — *South Indian Images of Gods and Goddesses*, Delhi, 1986.

Satyanarayana, K. — *A Study of the History and Culture of the Andhras*, Vol.2, Delhi, 1982.

Sen, S.P. (ed.) — *Sources of History of India*, Vol. 1, Calcutta, 1978.

Sequeira, Issac — *Popular Culture: East and West*, Delhi, 1991.

Sewell, R. — *A Forgotten Empire*, London, 1900, Reprint, Delhi, 1985.

Sharma, Krishna — *Bhakti and Bhakti Movement: A New Perspective*, Delhi, 1987.

Sherwani, H.K. — *History of Qutb Shahi Dynasty*, Delhi, 1974.

Sherwani, H.K. & P.M. Joshi (eds.) — *History of Medieval Deccan (1295-1720)*, Vols. 1 & 2, Hyderabad, 1974.

Shiach, Morag — *Discourse on Popular Culture: Class, Gender and History in Cultural Analysis, 1730 to the present*, O.U.P., 1989.

Sider, M. Gerald — *Culture and Class in Anthropology and History*, Cambridge, 1988.

Somerville, Augustus — *Crime and Religious Beliefs in India*, Delhi, 1984.

Stein, Burton — *Peasant, State and Society in Medieval South India*, Delhi, 1980.

Stein, Burton — *Vijayanagara*, The New Cambridge History of India, 1.2, Orient Longman, 1994.

– – — *All the King's Men*, papers on Medieval South Indian History, Madras, 1989.

– – — *Essays on South India*, Delhi, 1976.

– – — *South Indian Temple: An Analytical Reconsideration*, Delhi, 1978.

Sundaram, K. — *Studies in Economic and Social Conditions of Medieval Andhra, A.D. 1000-1600*, Waltair, 1968.

Suryakumari, A. — *The Temple in Andhradesa*, Delhi, 1988.

Thiruvenkatachari, S. (ed.) — *Madhuravijayam of Gangadevi*, Annamalai Nagar, 1957.

Thurston, E. — *Castes and Tribes of Southern India*, Madras, 1909.

Valentine, A. Charles — *Culture and Poverty*, London, 1968.

Varadarajan — *India in the 17th Century—Memoirs of Francois Martin (1670-94)*, Delhi, 1981.

Varghese, Anila — *Religious Traditions at Vijayanagara as revealed through its Monuments*, Delhi, 1995.

Veer, Peter Van Der — *Gods on Earth*, Delhi, 1989.

Vitsaxis, G. Vasillis — *Hindu Epics, Myths and Legends in Popular Illustration*, Bombay, 1977.

Venkataramanayya, N. — *Vijayanagara - Origins of the City and Empire*, Madras, 1933.

– – — *Studies in the History of the Third Dynasty of Vijayangara*, Madras, 1935.

Vovelle, Michael — *Ideologies and Mentalities*, (tr.) by Eamon O'Flaherty, Polity Press, 1990.

Waites, B. et al. — *Popular Culture: Past and Present*, Beckenham, 1982.

Weber, Max — *The Religion of India*, London, 1958.

Wheeler, J. Talboys (ed.) — *Early Travels in India (16th and 17th centuries)*, Delhi, 1976.

Whitehead, Henry — *The Village Gods of South India*, O.U.P. 1916.

Williams, Raymond — *Culture*, London, 1981.

– – — *Problems in Materialism and Culture*, London, 1980, Reprint, 1989.

Yazadani, G. — *Early History of the Deccan*, Vols. 1 & 2, Delhi, 1960.

Zore — *Qutb Shahi Sultans and Andhra Sanskriti*, Hyderabad, 1962.

(b) Articles

Ahmad, Qeyamuddin — 'Some norms of Social and Economic Behaviour - A Late 17th century Indian point of view' in *I.H.R.*, Vol. VIII, No. 1 & 2, 1981 & 82.

Akkidas, John — 'Agrarian Conditions in Golconda (1687-1724)' in *A.P.H.C.*, Guntur, 1986.

Ansari, Muhammad, Azhar — 'The Economic Condition of Golconda in the 17th century', in *I.H.C.*, Allahabad, 1965.

Bailey, Peter — 'Conspiracies of meaning: Music Hall and the Knowingness of Popular Culture' in *P&P* No. 144, Aug. 1994.

Bayly, Susan — 'Hindu Kingship and the Origin of Community: Religion, State and Society in Kerala 1750-1850', in *M.A.S.*, Vol. 18, No.1, 1984.

Beik, William — 'The Dilemma of Popular History' in *P&P*, No. 141, Nov. 1993.

Brigden, Susan — 'Religion and Social Obligation in early 16th century London' in *P&P*, No. 103, May 1984.

Bruce, Rosenberg — 'Was there a popular culture in the Middle Ages?' in *J.O.P.C.*, No. 14, 1980.

Burguiere, Andra — 'The Fate of the History of Mentalities in the Annales' in *CSSH*, Vo. 24, 1982.

Burke, Peter — 'From Pioneers to Settlers: Recent Studies of the History of Popular Culture', in *CSSH*, Vol. 25, 1983.

– – — The Invention of Leisure in Early Modern Europe in *P&P*, No. 146, Feb. 1995.

Champakalakshmi, R. — 'Peasant State and Society in Medieval South India: A Review Article' in *IESHR*, Vol. XVIII, No. 3 & 4, 1981.

– – — 'The Sovereignty of the Divine: The Vaishnava Pantheon and Temporal Power in South' in H.V. Sreenivasa Murthy, et. al (ed.) *Essays on Indian History and Culture*, Delhi, 1990.

– – — 'The Bhakti Movement and Religious Persecution in Tamilnadu' in *IHC*, Calicut, 1976.

Clark, Stuart — 'Inversion, Misrule and the meaning of witchcraft' in *P&P*, No. 87, May 1980.

Clark, Stuart — 'French Historians and Early Modern Popular Culture' in *P&P*, No. 100, Aug, 1983.

— — 'Popular Culture and Politics in the English Revolution: A Review Article' in *CSSH*, Vol.30, 1988.

Coss, P.R. — 'Aspects of Cultural diffusion in Medieval England: The Early Romances, Local Society and Robinhood' in *P&P*, No. 108, Aug, 1985.

Edwards, John — 'Religious Faith and Doubt in Late Medieval Spain Circa 1450-1500' in *P&P*, No. 120, Aug. 1988.

Fox, Adam — 'Ballads, Libels and Popular Ridicule in Jacobian England' in *P&P*, No. 145, Nov. 1994.

Ghauri, Iftikhar Ahmad — 'Local Governments Under the Sultanates of Bijapur and Golconda-Hydarabad' in *IC*, Vol. 51, 1977.

Gold, Ann Grodzins — 'Spirit Possession Perceived and Performed in Rural Rajasthan' in *CIS*, Vol. 22, No. 1, 1988.

Goswamy, Niranjan — 'Vatuka-Bhairava and the Kapalika Cult' in *IHC*, Chandigarh, 1973.

Hansen, Kathryn — 'Sultana the dacoit and Harischandra: Two Popular dramas of Nautanki Tradition of North India' in *MAS*, Vol. 17, No.1, 1983.

Hanumantha Rao, B.S.L. — 'History of Religious Movements in Medieval Andhra' in *JIH*, 1936.

Ingram, Martin — 'Ridings, Rough Music and the Reform of Popular Culture' in early modern England' in *P&P*, No. 105, Nov. 1984.

Jaiswal, Suvira — 'Evolution of the Narasimha Legend and its Possible Sources' in *IHC*, Chandigarh, 1973.

James, Mervyn — 'Ritual, Drama and Social Body in Late Medieval English Town, in *P&P*, No. 98, Feb. 1983.

Jash, Pranabanada — 'The Kapilikas—An Obscure Saiva Sub-sect', in *IHC*, 1973.

Jinnah, Mohammad Ali — 'Corporate Life in Medieval Guntur: Guntur Region,' in *A.P.H.C.*, Guntur, 1986.

Josie, Campbell — 'Popular Culture in the Middle Ages: Introduction' in *JOPC*, No. 14, 1969.

Kamath, Jyotsna K. — 'Sports and Pastimes in Vijayanagara Times' in *ITIHAS*, No. 11 (2), 1974.

Kameswara Rao, K.S. — 'Some Factors of Social Mobility: A Case Study of the Artisan Community of Medieval Andhra' in *APHC*, 1988.

Kapadia, Karin — 'Dancing the Goddess: Possession and Class in Tamil South India' in *MAS*, Vol. 30, Part-2, 1996.

Kanaka Durga, P.S. — 'Nagara in Medieval Andhra (1000-1323 A.D.) in *APHC*, Kakinada, 1984.

Kondos, Vivinne — 'Images of the Fierce Goddesses and Portrayals of Hindu Women, in *CIS*, Vol. 20, No.2, 1986.

Krishnamurthy, M. — 'Vijayanagara Interest in Irrigation Facilities in Cuddapah District, A.P.' in *ITIHAS*, Vol. IX & X, No. 1-4, 1981-82.

Majumdar, Bimanbehari — 'Image of Feudal Society in the Vaishnava Literature of the Sixteenth Century, *I.H.C.*, Ranchi, 1964.

Mangamma — 'Diamond Industry of Andhra in the Bygone days' in *APHC*, Kaavali, 1977.

Martin, Denis-Constant — 'Popular Culture, Identity and Politics in the context of the Trinidad Carnival: I is another, all of we is one' in *SIH*, Vol. 12, No.2, 1996.

Mohan Chandra, P. — 'Popular Culture and Socio-Religious Reform: Narayanaguru and the Ezhavas of Travancore', in *SIH*, Vol. 3, No.1, 1987.

Murthy, M.L.K. — 'Presidential address: Social and Economic History as Reflected in the Folk Traditions and Myths in Andhra Pradesh', in *APHC*, Anakapalle, 1988.

Murthy, Suryanarayana R. — 'The Bhat Brahmins of Andhradesa' in *APHC*, Guntur, 1986.

Murthy, T.S.N. — 'Corporate Life in Medieval Andhra Village' in *ITIHAS*, 1978.

Nagabhushanam, A. — 'Temple in Medieval Deccan', *ITIHAS*, Vol. XI, No. 1& 2, 1983.

-- — 'Agricultural Guilds in Medieval Deccan' in *A.P.H.C.* Vijayawada, 1978.

Nagabhushanam, K.S. — 'Life in Vijayanagara Empire as Reflected in Amuktamalyada'. in *APHC*, Vijayawada, 1978.

Nandi, R.N. 'Social Life in the Agraharas of the Deccan' in *IHC*, Aligarh, 1966.

-- 'Pot Worship and Pot-Goddess of the Deccan', *IHC*, Patiala, 1967.

-- 'Origin of Virasaiva Movement' in *IHR*, Vol. II, No.1, 1975.

-- 'Client, Ritual and Conflict in early Brahmanical order,' in *IHR*, Vol. VI, No. 1 & 2, 1979 & 80.

Naqvi, Saidq 'Cultural Synthesis in Qutb Shahi Kingdom,' in *APHC*, Kurnool, 1985.

Oddie, A.G. 'Hook-Swinging and Popular Religion in South India during 19th century,' in *IESHR*, Vol. XXIII, No.1, 1986.

Ownby, David 'The Heaven and Earth Society as Popular Religion,' in *JOAS*, Vol. 54, No.4, 1995.

Parthasarathy, R. 'Administration under Qutb Shahis: An Overview,' in *ITIHAS*, No. 104, 1981-82.

Perlin Frank 'State Formation Reconsidered,' in *MAS*, Vo. 19, part-3, 1985.

Ralph, W. Nicholas 'The Goddess Sitala and epidemic Small-pox in Bengal', *JAS*, Vol. XLI, No.1, 1981.

Ramalakshmi, P. 'The Mariah Practice and the East India Company,' in *APHC*, Guntur, 1986.

Ramaswamy, Vijaya 'Some enquiries into the condition of weavers in Medieval South India', in *IHR*, Vol. VI, No. 1 & 2, 1979.

Ramaswamy, Vijaya — 'Weaver Folk Traditions as a Source of History,' in *IESHR*, Vol. XIX, No.1, 1982.

-- — 'Artisans in Vijayanagar Society,' in IESHR, Vol. XXII, No. 4, 1985.

-- — 'Anklets on the Feet': Women saints in medieval Indian Society,' in *IHR*, Vol. XVII, No. 1 & 2, 1990 & 91.

Rao, Narasimha R. — *'Viprovinodis: A New class of Professional entertainers in Vijayanagara* Empire', in *IHC*, 1969.

Reddy, Soma R. — 'The Life of Dommaras as reflected in the Literature and Epigraphs of Medieval Telugu country', in *APHC*, Kakinada, 1984.

-- — 'Taxation and Hindu Temples in the Telugu Districts under the Vijayanagara Empire', in *IHC*, Hyderabad, 1978.

Regani, Sarojini — 'The Shataka Literature—Source material for a study of the History of Andhra Pradesh', *ITIHAS*, Vol. XVI, No.1, 1990.

Richards, J.F. — 'The 17th century crisis in South Asia' in *MAS*, Vol. 24, 1990.

Sarkar, Jadunath — 'Haidarabad and Golconda in 1750 as seen through French eyes', in *IC*, Vol. 10, 1936.

Satish, Chandra — 'Writings on Social History of Medieval India: Trends and Prospectus' in *IHR*, No.2, 1997.

Sharma, R.S. — 'The Segementary State and Indian Experience', in *IHR*, Vol. XVI, No. 1-2, 1989, 1990.

Sherwani, K.K. — 'Deccan: The Region of Co-existence and Integration' in *MIAM*, Vol.4, 1977.

Sitapathy, P. — 'The History of Srisailam: Sri Mallikarjuna Swamy Temple,' in *ITIHAS*, Vol. VIII, No. 2, 1980.

Skaria, Ajay — 'Witchcraft and Gratuitous violence in Colonial Western India' in *P&P*, No. 155, May 1997.

Smout, T.C. — 'Born Again at Cambuslang: New Evidence on Popular Religion and Literacy in 18th century Scotland', in *P&P*, No.97, Nov. 1982.

Stein, Burton — 'Vijayanagar, C. 1350-1564' in Tapan Rayachadhuri and Irfan Habib (eds.), *The Cambridge Economic History of India*, Vol.1, (Indian ed. Orient Longman), Hyderabad, 1984.

— — 'Reapproaching Vijayanagar' in R.E. Frykenberg and P. Kolenda (eds.) *Studies of South India: An Anthology of Recent Research and Scholarship*, Madras, 1985.

— — 'State Formation and Economy Reconsidered' in *MAS*, Vol. 19, Part-3, 1985.

Strauss, Geralnd — 'The Dilemma of Popular History', in *P&P*, No. 132, Aug. 1991.

Subrahmanyam, Sanjay and Shulman, David — 'Aspects of State Formation in South India and Southeast Asia, 1500-1650' in *IESHR*, Vol.23, No.4, 1986.

Subrahmanyam, Sanjay Shulman, David — 'The Men who would be King? The Politics of Expansion in early 17th century Northern Tamilnadu' in *MAS*, Vol. 24, Part-2, 1990.

Sugget, Richard — 'Festivals and Social Structure in early Modern Wales', in *P&P*, No. 152, Aug. 1996.

Talbot, Cynthia — 'Temples, Donors and Gifts: Patterns of Patronage in 13th century South India', in *JOAS*, Vol.50, No.2, 1991.

– – — 'Political Intermediaries in Kakatiya Andhra 1175-1325', in *IESHR*, Vol.31, No.3, 1994.

Thapar, Romila — 'Religion and Social Order', in *CIS*, Vol. 21, No.1, 1987.

– – — Epic and History: Tradition, Dissent and Politics in India,' in *P&P*, No. 125, No. 1989.

Thompson, E.P. — 'Folklore Anthropology and Social History', in *I.H.R.*, Vol. III, No.2, 1997.

Torre, Angelo — 'Politics Cloaked in Worship: State, Church and Local Power in Piedmont, 1570-1770,' in *P&P*, No. 134, 1981.

Zelechow, Bernard — 'The Opera: The Meeting of Popular and Elite Culture in the 19th Century', in *JOPC*, Vol. 25, No.2, 1991.

Zika, Charles — 'Hosts, Processions and Pilgrimages: Controlling the sacred in 15th century Germany,' in *P&P*, No. 118, Feb. 1988.

Books (Telugu) and Folk Literature

Balaswamy, Bukka — *Mahaboobnagar Zilla Janapadakathalu*, Hyderabad, 1978.

Balaramamurthy, Yetukuru — *Bharatiya Sanskriti*, Hyderabad, 1993.

Krishna Reddy, — *Gramina Sanskriti*, Ananatapur, 1987.

Mohan, G.S. — *Janapada Vignana Vyasavali*, Anantapur, 1981.

Nagayya, G. — *Dakshinatya Janapada Drsya Kalarupalu*, Tirupati, 1991.

Petasri, — *Chittoor Zilla Kolatam Patalu*, Tirupati, 1992.

Premalata, Ravi et. al. — *Janapada Vignana Pariseelanam: Vyasa Samkalanam*, Hyderabad, 1990.

Radhakrishnamurthy, M. — *Teluguvari Janapada Kalarupalu*, Telugu University, Hyderabad, 1992.

Ramacharyulu, — *Janapada Nrtyakala: Gorava Sampradayam*, Hyderabad, 1993.

Ramaraju, B. — *Telugu Janpada Sahityamu*, Hyderabad, 1978.

Reddy, Pratap S. — *Andhrula Sanghika Charitra*, Hyderabad, 1949.

Reddy, Rami Subba A. — *Kadapa Zilla Janapada Geya Gathalu: Nirmanam, Samajam, Samskriti*, Cuddapah, 1991.

Venkateswarlu, B. — *Palnatiseemalo Kolatam*, Hyderabad, 1988.

Journals and Periodicals

Anthropology Today
Contributions to Indian Sociology
History of Religions
Indian Economic and Social History Review
Indian Historical Review
Islamic Culture
ITIHAS, Journal of the Andhra Pradesh Achieves.
Indian Historical Quarterly
Journal of Andhra History and Culture
Journal of Comparative Studies in Society and History
Journal of Current Anthropology
Journal of Economic and Social History of the Orient
Journal of the Indian History
Journal of Modern Asian Studies
Journal of Past and Present
Journal of Peasant Studies
Journal of *Popular Culture*
Proceedings of *Andhra Pradesh History Congress*
Proceedings of *Indian History Congress*
Social Scientist
Studies in History

(c) Unpublished Dissertations and Theseis

Janardhana Rao, P. *Ideology and Popular Culture: A Case Study of Telugu Tolubommalata*, an M.Phil. Dissertation, submitted to the University of Hyderabad, 1995.

Lakshama Rao, K.H. *Influence of Folk Literature on Telugu Film Songs*, an M.Phil. Dissertation, submitted to the Osmania University, 1979.

Mastan Rao, *Prakasam Zilla Janapadulu*, an M.Phil. Dissertation submitted to the University of Hyderabad, 1989.

Pulikonda, Subbachary *Janapada Vignanamlo Asritasahityam*, a Ph.D. Thesis, submitted to the Osmania University, 1992.

INDEX

M

N

O

P

❑❑❑